ISBN: 979-8-90057-231-4 - Ebook

ISBN: 979-8-90057-232-1 - Paperback

ISBN: 979-8-90057-233-8 - Hardcover

Disclaimer: This book is intended for informational and educational purposes only. The concepts, frameworks, and examples presented are designed to help leaders think more clearly about customer value, strategic planning, and integrated business decision-making, but they are not a substitute for professional advice tailored to specific organizational, financial, legal, or operational circumstances. Every organization operates within unique market conditions, regulatory environments, and competitive dynamics, and outcomes will vary based on execution, context, and external factors beyond the author's control. Readers should use their own judgment and, where appropriate, consult qualified professionals before making strategic, financial, or operational decisions based on the ideas discussed in this book.

At last—a framework that brings finance, supply chain, and commercial teams together around a single, powerful language: value. Dov has led transformations that have delivered remarkable business outcomes across industries, drawing on extensive hands-on IBP experience. CEOs who want to create true enterprise alignment must read this book and personally lead their IBP journey.

—Sanjiv Sidhu, o9 Chairman and Co-Founder

A powerful evolution of planning—Value-Centric IBP bridges the missing link between operational excellence and a true obsession with customer and business value.

—Greg Smith, Medtronic EVP of Enterprise Operations

A cross-functional and common threading of value orientation is critical in unlocking the next wave of business performance. Dov's framework for a value-driven paradigm for integrated business planning comes at an important time as organizations explore new operating models, decision and governance rights, and state-of-the-art AI and agentic technology enablers. Now more than ever, there is a need to anchor on the first principles of taking a value and outcomes driven approach to business transformation.

—Razat Gaurav, Kinaxis CEO

I've seen too many supply chain transformation projects fail because they never asked the right question: What problem are we actually solving for customers? This book explains how to structure your entire planning process around that premise.

—Matt Elenjickal, FourKites **Founder and CEO**

VALUE CENTRIC

THE PROVEN FRAMEWORK FOR HOW MODERN COMPANIES TRANSFORM AND WIN

DOV SHENKMAN

M&A MELAMUD & ALTER PUBLISHING

To **Judith, Alex,** and **Jonathan**—my compass, my courage, and my joy. Thank you for every step of this journey.

Progress is impossible without change.

—George Bernard Shaw

CONTENTS

Part 1: The Foundation of Value

Part 2: The Engine of Value

A Simple Test with Big Implications

Before we begin, take a moment to answer a few questions honestly, without buzzwords or best-case scenarios:

Do you know the **real value** your customers gain from your products or services?

Do you understand how that value compares to what your **competitors** offer? What's your **value gap**?

Can you predict the risks to that value, or better yet, the **opportunities to expand it**?

Do you know the **capabilities** you'll need to strengthen and grow that value over time?

Do you know which **customer segments** realize the most value, and how much you're capturing in return?

Do you know how **loyal** those customers really are, and what drives their loyalty?

Is your organization **aligned around a common definition of value**, not just revenue or margin?

Do you have a **strategy** to maximize both **customer value and business value**, and is it truly integrated into your **day-to-day planning and execution**?

Is your company culture **obsessed with value**, for both the customer and the enterprise?

And finally: Are you using **emerging technologies and AI** not just to automate, but to **amplify value creation**, uncover insights, and plan proactively?

If you answered **"yes" to all** of these questions, congratulations. You're either running an exceptional company or on the fast track to building one. In fact, you might be better suited to *write* this book than read it.

But if, like most leaders, your answers included a few **"no"s** or **"not sure"s**, then this book is your guide. It offers a practical framework to help you **build, measure, and lead through value** and transform your business in the process.

Why This Book Exists

We're living in a world of constant disruption where customers have more power, more choice, and higher expectations than ever before. Yet many organizations still operate with outdated assumptions, chasing efficiency instead of relevance, scale instead of meaning, and price instead of value. Survival isn't about being bigger. It's about being more agile, more aligned, and relentlessly value-centric.

This book offers a different path. It's a guide to re-centering your strategy around the creation, delivery, and capture of value for your customers and for your business. It's a practical journey through frameworks, questions, and tools that will help you lead with clarity, act with purpose, and compete not just harder, but smarter. While large enterprises will find it essential, the same principles are just as relevant and transformative for small and mid-sized organizations as well as startups.

This book introduces a refined approach: **Value-Centric Integrated Business Planning (IBP)**. More than a process, it's a mindset, one that places customer and business value at the heart of every planning step, from long-range strategy to tactical execution.

- **Customer value** is why they buy: the perceived benefits, experiences, and outcomes that make a product or service worthwhile.

- **Business value** is why you want them to buy: the profit, growth, and sustainability your company gains from the transaction.

- And just like in life, **value is the attraction**. It's what draws them together and keeps them together.

Value-Centric IBP is what makes this relationship optimal, aligning the two sides so that both customer and company consistently win.

Like any relationship, this balance doesn't just happen. It takes deliberate attention. In many ways, Value-Centric IBP is like couples therapy for business:

- It ensures both sides are heard.

- It identifies where expectations aren't being met.

- It builds a process for trust, loyalty, and growth.

When it works, the outcome isn't just transactional. It's transformational. It creates a mutually beneficial, long-lasting relationship.

In business terms, that's loyalty, advocacy, and profitable growth.

In human terms, it's called love.

And when business becomes a relationship rather than a transaction, everything changes. This is the value revolution we begin exploring in Chapter 1.

The Value Revolution

*The customer's perception of value is the
only reality that matters. Everything
else is just internal conversation.*
—Jack Welch

The Wrong Race

About 10 years ago, I was sitting in a boardroom with the executive team of a Fortune 500 company, watching them debate their latest strategic initiative. They had spent millions on digital transformation, hired top consulting firms, and implemented best-in-class systems. Yet their market share was declining, customer satisfaction scores were flat, and their most innovative competitors seemed to anticipate market needs they didn't even see coming.

The CEO turned to me with a question that would frame everything that followed: "We're executing our strategy flawlessly. Our operations are efficient. Our technology is state-of-the-art. So why are we losing?"

The answer wasn't in their strategy documents or operational metrics. It was in a simple truth they had lost sight of: They had become obsessed with internal excellence while forgetting that business success is ultimately determined by one external judge: the customer.

They weren't losing because they were executing poorly. They were losing because they were executing the wrong things excellently. The corporate equivalent of winning the wrong race. Their entire planning system was optimized around internal capabilities, competitive efficiency benchmarking, and financial targets, with customer value treated as an afterthought rather than the foundation.

That conversation sparked a journey that would transform my understanding of what separates thriving organizations from those that merely survive. The companies that consistently outperform don't just deliver customer value. They organize everything around creating, delivering, and capturing value in ways that make them indispensable to the customers they serve.

The Great Disconnect

Most businesses today suffer from what I call "the great disconnect," a fundamental misalignment between what companies think drives success and what actually drives success in the marketplace.

Walk into any corporate planning session, and you'll hear conversations about market share, operational efficiency, competitive positioning, and financial targets. You'll see detailed spreadsheets tracking hundreds of internal metrics. You'll witness passionate debates about resource allocation, technology investments, and organizational restructuring.

What you'll rarely hear is deep, systematic discussion about what customers truly value, how that value perception is changing, or how every business decision impacts the customer's experience and outcomes. Customer value, if discussed at all, is often relegated to marketing messaging or post-hoc justification for decisions already made.

This disconnect isn't just unfortunate. It's dangerous. In today's hyperconnected, choice-abundant marketplace, customers have more power than ever before. They can switch providers with a few clicks, share their experiences instantly with thousands of people, and access alternatives that didn't exist months ago.

Companies that don't put customer value at the center of their strategy and operations are essentially playing a game they don't understand by rules that no longer apply.

Why Traditional Planning Falls Short

Traditional business planning was designed for a different era, one characterized by predictable markets, limited customer information, and competitive advantages based on scale, location, or proprietary assets. The planning processes that served companies well for decades are now actively undermining their ability to compete.

Internal Focus over Customer Insight

Most planning processes begin with internal assessments: How did we perform to our budget or forecast? Did we improve our forecast accuracy? How well did we execute our production schedule? What's our margin performance against the plan?

While these questions matter, starting with internal perspective creates a dangerous bias toward incremental improvements rather than breakthrough value creation.

Efficiency over Value Creation

Traditional IBP is about coordination and efficiency, making sure demand, supply, and finance are aligned. It focuses on operational excellence: accurate demand forecasting, supply chain optimization, inventory management, and cost control. The monthly planning cycles revolve around volume targets, capacity utilization, margin protection, and meeting financial commitments. Success is measured through operational KPIs like forecast accuracy, on-time delivery, cost per unit, and inventory turns.

But this approach treats customer satisfaction and company profitability as separate optimization problems. You forecast demand, optimize costs, improve efficiency but miss the fundamental insight driving market leaders: The most profitable businesses operate in "mutual value zones" where delighting customers systematically generates superior business economics.

Functional Silos over Integrated Value Delivery

Traditional planning treats different business functions as separate optimization problems. Sales plans for revenue growth. Operations plans for efficiency. Product development plans for feature delivery. Finance plans for cost management.

But customers don't experience your business as separate functions. They experience it as a unified value delivery system. Work is performed in functions, but value is delivered through processes.

When planning happens in silos, value creation happens by accident rather than by design.

This disconnect becomes more dangerous as organizations scale. A startup might coordinate informally across functions, but a global enterprise needs systematic integration. Scaling organizations often optimize each function brilliantly while destroying the integrated customer experience that created their initial success.

Short-Term Metrics over Long-Term Value Building

Quarterly planning cycles and annual budgets create pressure to optimize for immediate, measurable results rather than sustainable value creation. This leads to decisions that hit short-term numbers while eroding long-term customer relationships and market position.

From Portfolio Management to Capability Building

Traditional IBP focuses primarily on optimizing the product and service portfolio. It ensures the right products are in the right place at the right time, at the right cost.

Value-Centric IBP builds on this foundation but goes further. It asks: What capabilities must we develop to create and sustain differentiated value in the market? And how can we optimize business value in the process? This means planning not just for what we sell, but for what we can uniquely do, capabilities that:

- Deliver value customers can't get elsewhere

- Strengthen competitive position over time

- Create barriers that make it difficult for others to match your advantage

In Value-Centric IBP, these value-creating and value-differentiating capabilities become part of the planning process itself, funded, prioritized, and measured alongside products, volumes, and margins.

The Value-Centric Alternative

This book presents a fundamentally different approach to business planning, one that puts customer value and the associated value to the company at the center of every strategic and operational decision. Value-Centric Integrated Business Planning isn't just about being more customer focused. It's about recognizing that customer value creation is the engine that drives all sustainable business success and organizing everything around optimizing that engine.

Customer and Business Value as the Strategic Foundation

Instead of starting with internal capabilities or competitive analysis, Value-Centric IBP begins with a deep understanding of what customers truly value, not just what they say they want, but what they're actually trying to accomplish and how they define success. This customer value understanding and the corresponding business value become the foundation for all strategic decisions.

The intersection of these dimensions creates four distinct customer types, each requiring fundamentally different competencies and capabilities. Understanding these quadrants is essential because competency development requires significant time and investment. You cannot build world-class expertise for all customer types simultaneously. Organizations must make strategic choices about where to develop value moats, where to achieve differentiation, where to add value efficiently, and where to eliminate waste.

Integrated Planning Around Value Delivery

Rather than optimizing functions independently, Value-Centric IBP aligns all business functions around delivering superior customer value efficiently and profitably. Sales, operations, product development, finance, and every other function plan and execute as part of a unified value delivery system.

Long-Term Value Creation over Short-Term Optimization

Value-Centric IBP balances short-term performance with long-term value building, recognizing that sustainable competitive advantage comes from creating customer relationships and market positions that compound over time.

Outcome Focus over Output Obsession

Success is measured not by what the company produces, but by what customers achieve. Features, services, and capabilities are evaluated based on their contribution to customer value realization rather than their internal elegance or competitive novelty.

What You'll Learn

The different chapters of this book have been written, rewritten, and refined over the past 30 years. They reflect a tapestry of experiences and lessons gathered throughout my career in both industry and consulting.

Each page carries the imprint of countless hours of brainstorming, spirited debates, and collaborative conversations with the many remarkable people I have met along this journey of discovery. They are too numerous to name, yet each one left an indelible mark, and for that, I am deeply grateful.

This book provides both the conceptual framework and practical tools to transform your business around customer value creation. It is not meant to be received as if it were the Ten Commandments handed down from Mount Sinai. Think of it less as scripture and more as a script, one you can edit, remix, or even poke fun at. I hope you'll challenge, debate, improve, and above all, find your own "value-centric voice."

The real value isn't in following my words to the letter, but in finding the letters that spell out your own identity. If along the way I managed to touch you, to spark a thought, a smile, or even a groan at a bad joke, then the journey has already begun.

I should add that if these ideas resonate, I welcome the opportunity to continue the conversation and learn how your organization is approaching its own value-centric journey.

Similar to value itself, which is individual and contextual, the Value-Centric IBP journey needs to be customized to each company's unique circumstances: their competitive position, financial situation, organizational culture, market dynamics, and countless other factors that shape how value creation can be optimized. While the principles and the framework are universal, the application and tools must be tailored to your specific context.

In this book you'll discover:

How to Understand What Customers Truly Value: Moving beyond surveys and focus groups to develop deep, systematic understanding of customer jobs, pains, and gains across multiple value dimensions.

How to Build Competitive Advantage Through Value Focus: Creating sustainable differentiation by delivering value in ways that competitors can't easily replicate while building economic moats around your most valuable customer relationships.

How to Design Integrated Planning Processes: Aligning strategy, operations, and finance around customer value delivery rather than internal optimization, creating planning rhythms that connect customer insights to resource allocation decisions.

How to Measure and Manage Value Creation: Developing metrics and management systems that track both customer value realization and business value capture, ensuring your organization stays aligned around what matters most.

How to Build Value-Driven Culture: Embedding customer value thinking into organizational DNA through hiring, training, decision-making frameworks, and cultural norms that prioritize long-term value creation over short-term metrics gaming.

How to Leverage AI and Technology for Value Creation: Using artificial intelligence, machine learning, and advanced analytics to discover customer insights faster, predict value opportunities more accurately, and deliver personalized value at scale while optimizing resource allocation and operational efficiency.

Who This Book Is For

This book is written for leaders of large enterprises, small and medium-sized businesses, and startups who recognize that customer value must be more than a marketing slogan. It must be the organizing principle for their entire business.

Whether you're:

- A CEO or executive team member seeking to transform your organization's strategic approach

- A strategy or planning professional looking for frameworks to connect customer insights to business decisions

- A product or marketing leader wanting to align your function with broader value creation

- An operations or finance leader seeking to optimize for customer value rather than just internal efficiency

- An entrepreneur, startup, or business owner building a company that customers can't imagine living without

You'll find practical frameworks, proven methodologies, and real-world examples that you can apply immediately to your specific context.

You'll also notice that some sections in chapters go deeper than most CEOs will want to go, and that's intentional. Senior leaders need the strategic logic, the choices that matter, and the few levers that change outcomes; implementation teams need the mechanics that make those choices real in the messy constraints of data, cadence, roles, systems, and rollout. Wherever the book shifts into that "how-to" depth, you'll see clear callouts: a **This Section's Executive Takeaway** that distills what you need to know to lead and decide and a **For Implementation Teams** lens that provides the practical guidance required to build, deploy, and sustain Value-Centric IBP in practice. The intention of these callouts is simple: to make your reading experience more seamless, so you can go deep where it serves you and stay high-level where it doesn't.

How This Book Is Organized

This book is structured as a practical journey from understanding the fundamentals of customer and business value to implementing comprehensive value-centric planning systems. It is divided into two parts:

Part 1: The Foundation of Value: What Customers Value, Why It Matters, and How to Measure (Chapters 2 to 9) builds the intellectual and strategic groundwork required for meaningful action. It clarifies what customer value really is, how it differs across segments, how it can be measured, and how it aligns or conflicts with business value. These chapters establish the mental models, metrics, and capability thinking needed to make customer-centricity real rather than rhetorical. For readers eager to act, this foundation may feel deliberate by design: Without it, value-centric planning becomes well-intentioned motion without traction.

Part 2: The Engine of Value: Operationalizing Value Through Integrated Business Planning (Chapters 10 to 15) is where that foundation is put to work. It shows how organizations translate value insight into coordinated strategy, planning, execution, culture, technology, and ecosystem leadership. This is the operating system for turning customer value into sustained competitive advantage, where disciplined preparation becomes decisive action.

Just as Part 2 builds off of the foundation established in Part 1, each chapter builds on the previous one while providing standalone frameworks you can implement immediately. Whether you read straight through or focus on specific challenges, you'll find practical tools, real-world examples, and applications that apply to your unique context.

And, as you know, this is a business book. You probably won't find yourself staying up until 2 a.m. to discover if the butler did it. Instead, read it slowly, pause often, and let the ideas and concepts do the work.

The Choice Is Yours

The shift to value-centric business planning isn't just about adopting new tools or processes. It's about fundamentally changing how you think about business strategy and success. It requires moving from inside-out thinking to outside-in thinking, from functional optimization to system optimization, from short-term metrics to long-term value creation. This transformation isn't easy, but it's essential.

The companies that master value-centric planning will be the ones that thrive in an increasingly complex and competitive marketplace. They'll build stronger customer relationships, more sustainable competitive advantages, and more resilient business models.

The companies that don't make this shift will find themselves trapped in a downward spiral of price competition, feature proliferation, and customer indifference, working harder and harder to achieve results that become more and more elusive.

You can continue optimizing around internal metrics while hoping customers will appreciate your efforts. Or you can transform your business around what customers actually value and build a company that customers can't imagine living without. The frameworks, tools, and methodologies in this book will show you how. The only question is whether you're ready to begin the journey.

The value revolution is already underway. Companies like Amazon, Apple, Netflix, and countless others have demonstrated the power of organizing around customer value. The question isn't whether value-centric approaches work. It's whether your organization will adopt them before your competitors do.

Let's begin by establishing the foundation, starting with the customer. After all, the customer is the business.

PART 1
The Foundation of Value

What Customers Value,
Why It Matters,
and How to Measure It

CHAPTER 2

The Customer Is the Business

The purpose of business is to create
and keep a customer.
—Peter Drucker

The Simple Truth Everyone Forgets

It's a simple idea. Almost too simple and may seem obvious. After all, who else buys the stuff? But it's surprising how many companies, even successful ones, get it backwards. The starting point of any business is not the product, not the quarterly profit, and definitely not the org chart.

It's the customer!

Profit is not the goal. It's a result. Profit without value is like applause without music: awkward and short-lived.

The real goal is to deliver differentiated value to the customer. Do that right, and the rest follows. This is a course reset for businesses that started thinking of profit as the destination instead of the outcome. For leaders who spent more time optimizing spreadsheets than listening to customers. For companies that forgot why they existed in the first place.

Most businesses declare their mission with great fanfare: "We will be #1 in our category" or "We will unlock shareholder value."

Ambitious, yes.

Inspiring? Not really.

Mission statements often sound like they were written by a committee that skipped lunch: ambitious, but oddly detached from reality.

Your reason for existing shouldn't start with what you want. It should start with what the customer needs.

Case in point: As I write this book, I remind myself that it's not about me. It's about you, the reader. Ultimately, you will define whether this book succeeds or not.

The Gap Between Knowing and Doing

However, knowing that the customer is the business and actually organizing your planning processes around customer value are two different challenges. Most organizations struggle to translate customer insights into coordinated action across functions like product development, demand planning, supply chain, and financial planning.

Marketing might understand customer needs perfectly while supply chain optimizes for cost efficiency without considering customer impact. Sales might build strong relationships while operations prioritizes internal metrics over customer experience.

This is where Value-Centric Integrated Business Planning becomes essential: transforming customer understanding into systematic planning processes that align every function around customer value creation.

You Are What Your Customer Hires You to Do

A business is not defined by the company's name, statutes, or articles of incorporation. It is defined by the value the customer realizes when they buy a product or a service. You are what your customers hire you to do.

You can manufacture shoes, but your customer may be buying style. You can build software, but they're paying for simplicity. You can sell insurance, but what they really want is peace of mind.

The Hardware Store That Sells More Than Drills

Take the hardware store example. The store thinks it sells power drills. But here's what I'm actually thinking: I don't want a drill. I want a hole. Actually, I want to hang a family photo. And if we go one layer deeper, what I really want is to walk past that photo and smile every time I see it.

Nobody wakes up in the morning thinking, "I really need a drill." I wake up thinking, "I'd better get that photo on the wall before my wife notices it's been leaning against the couch for six months!"

The drill is just a means to that end.

This hardware store example illustrates a crucial concept we'll explore throughout this book: Customers "hire" your product or service to do a specific job. Understanding these jobs-to-be-done becomes the foundation for all planning decisions, from product development priorities to inventory allocation to customer service design.

When a customer hires your solution, they're trying to make progress in their life or business. Your planning processes must ensure that every function contributes to that progress rather than optimizing for internal convenience. If your business gets stuck thinking only about what it offers, you'll miss the bigger opportunity: to solve the real problem your customer is trying to fix. That mindset unlocks better product design, better messaging, and better loyalty.

More importantly, it provides the North Star that aligns all your planning processes around creating genuine customer value.

The Outside-In Reality

The purpose of a business starts on the outside from the customer and works its way in because a business only exists for one reason: because someone is willing to pay for what it offers. That's it. No customer, no business. Not even a clever one.

Peter Drucker put it simply: "It is the customer who determines what a business is ... because it is the customer who pays."

Startups get this instinctively. They must start with value. It's their only oxygen supply. Unlike established corporations, which can coast for years on momentum until they eventually drift into obsolescence, startups have no cushion. All they've got is coffee, conviction, and hopefully a working product. Their only lifeline is finding that gap in unfulfilled customer value and seizing it.

Big companies, on the other hand, sometimes lose focus. They lean too heavily on cost cutting as the path to improvement.

Don't misunderstand me: Efficiency and discipline are essential for long-term success, and I will emphasize that later in this book. But when cost cutting becomes the main strategy, it turns into a dangerous illusion. It's like saving money on a parachute. Sure, you can cut the cost, but you won't enjoy the ride down.

The Evidence: Stakeholder Value
Drives Financial Returns

Strategy has traditionally been seen as a competition-focused discipline, a zero-sum game where winners take market share and optimize profit. But in today's stakeholder economy, that view is no longer sufficient. Strategy must now be viewed as the art and science of allocating resources to create value not only for shareholders, but also for the broader ecosystem: customers, employees, suppliers, and communities.

In July 2024, Bain & Company published a comprehensive study analyzing 4,228 companies across eight industries over a 10-year period. They assessed which companies excelled at delivering stakeholder value—measured through customer satisfaction, employee engagement, supplier relationships, and community impact—and which delivered the strongest financial returns. The results were compelling: Companies that outperformed on both dimensions of value creation, both stakeholder and financial, consistently generated the highest shareholder returns. These firms didn't just balance interests. They aligned them, turning stakeholder trust into sustainable growth.

The Bain study revealed that while technology delivered the highest average shareholder returns across industries, that's only part of the story. In every industry, the top 10% of companies outperformed the average returns of tech firms. What this points to: Being in a "hot" or high-growth industry doesn't guarantee superior performance. What truly matters is how well a company aligns its capabilities and value model to stakeholder needs within its chosen context.

The Bain analysis empirically reinforces that stakeholder value, particularly customer satisfaction and loyalty, directly correlates with long-term financial performance. High-performing firms who consistently invest in understanding and delivering superior customer value benefited from repeat business, higher pricing power, and brand advocacy, all of which translated into revenue growth and margin improvement.

The study helps resolve the old debate: shareholder versus stakeholder. The answer is both, and the best strategies are those that align their ambitions. In a world where stakeholder metrics are measurable and actionable, competitive advantage goes to the companies that build stakeholder trust into the core of their planning, execution, and performance measurement.

This research validates what we'll explore throughout this book: Customer-centric planning isn't just the right thing to do morally. It's the most effective strategy for sustainable competitive advantage and financial performance.

The Planning Challenge: From Understanding to Action

Not all customers are the same, and not all customers provide equal value to your business. Some customers may love what you do but provide limited business returns, while others may generate significant revenue but perceive limited value in your offering. Some customers expand their relationships over time while others remain static despite high satisfaction.

Understanding these dynamics and planning accordingly requires sophisticated approaches that balance customer value creation with business value capture. Traditional business planning often optimizes for internal metrics: forecast accuracy, cost efficiency, operational coordination. While these remain important, they're no longer sufficient. Modern planning must optimize for customer outcomes while maintaining operational excellence. This requires planning processes that can segment customers by value potential, predict behavior changes, and coordinate responses across all functions.

The challenge becomes even more complex in today's digital environment. Customer expectations have been shaped by digital leaders like Amazon and Apple. Customers expect personalized, responsive, and proactive experiences that require sophisticated technology capabilities and real-time coordination across multiple systems and functions.

However, technology alone isn't enough. It must be guided by genuine customer insight and coordinated planning that ensures all organizational activities contribute to customer value creation.

How Leading Companies Put Customers at the Center

The Bain findings aren't just academic. The companies that achieve stakeholder-financial alignment share a common approach: They orchestrate every aspect of their business, from strategy to operations to planning, around delivering exceptional customer value. Each of these successful companies didn't just understand their customers. They built planning processes that consistently delivered on customer value promises through coordinated action across all functions.

Let me walk you through five standout examples.

Amazon: "Make It Frictionless"

Few companies illustrate the power of customer-centric planning better than Amazon.

Early on, Amazon recognized a simple but profound customer truth: People don't love shopping. They love being finished with shopping. Every extra click, unknown shipping cost, or painful return was friction that eroded value in the eyes of the buyer.

Acting on this insight, Amazon orchestrated the launch of one-click ordering that collapsed the purchase journey to seconds. Prime layered in fast, "free" delivery that rewired customer expectations across retail. Finally, a no-questions-asked returns policy turned post-purchase anxiety into confidence. Each initiative required tight coordination across technology, supply chain, finance, and customer service, an early example of cross-functional, value-centric orchestration.

Amazon's planning processes coordinate technology development, supply chain investments, inventory positioning, and customer service capabilities around delivering frictionless experiences. Their monthly planning cycles don't just forecast demand. They predict friction points and coordinate solutions across multiple functions before customers experience problems.

From the customer's perspective, these changes built an unshakable promise: "I trust Amazon to save me time, every time." That promise translated into extraordinary loyalty. Net Promoter Scores climbed into the sixties, elite territory in retail, while Prime membership surpassed 200 million worldwide.

The financial payoff mirrored the stakeholder win. During Prime's first decade, Amazon sustained revenue compound annual growth above 20%, turned once-skeptical Wall Street into believers, and ultimately secured a position in the upper-right quadrant of Bain's Stakeholder × Financial Value matrix: high stakeholder value and high financial return.

In short, Amazon didn't just remove clicks. It removed doubt, delay, and disappointment. That relentless focus on value as experienced by the customer turns insight into integrated action and, ultimately, superior performance.

Apple: "It Just Works"

Apple's ascent is rooted in a foundational insight: Most people crave powerful technology but loathe feeling incompetent while using it. Instead of chasing spec sheets, Apple directed its integrated planning processes toward simplicity, elegance, and seamless cross-device integration, from the original iPod-iTunes combo to today's iPhone-Watch-Mac ecosystem. Hardware, software, silicon, and retail teams plan in concert, anchored on a shared definition of customer value: "It just works."

Each product cycle aligns supply readiness with a tightly choreographed launch experience, ensuring that the promise of simplicity is never broken by stockouts, quality issues, or inconsistent customer experiences across touchpoints. Apple's planning synchronizes hardware development, software engineering, supply chain operations, and retail experiences around their customer value promise. Their integrated business planning ensures that manufacturing capacity, component sourcing, software development, and retail preparation all align to deliver seamless customer experiences at launch.

Customers respond viscerally. Using an Apple device makes them feel smart, empowered, and just a little proud, an emotional payoff few competitors match. Loyalty rates hover near 90%, and Apple's NPS sits above +60 in multiple categories.

Financially, that stakeholder love converts into premium pricing power and margins north of 40% on flagship devices. Unsurprisingly, Apple occupies the upper-right quadrant: high stakeholder delight, high financial return, proof that intuitive user experience is not an expense, but an investment.

IKEA: "Design for Real Life"

IKEA began with a clear mission: Deliver stylish, functional furniture people can actually afford—today.

Traditional furniture retail pushed high prices, long lead times, and intimidating showrooms. IKEA's planners flipped the model. The company aligned product design, flat-pack engineering, global sourcing, and warehouse-style stores into a single value promise: "I can picture it in my home, buy it now, and fit it in the car."

IKEA's planning processes coordinate product development, supply chain optimization, store design, and inventory management around their customer value proposition. Their integrated planning ensures that new product designs can be manufactured cost-effectively, shipped efficiently in flat-pack format, and displayed inspirationally in showrooms while maintaining inventory availability.

Immersive showrooms inspire, while self-service aisles and flat-pack boxes translate inspiration into immediate ownership. From the shopper's viewpoint, IKEA removes two key frictions—price anxiety and delivery delay—turning cost-conscious buyers into confident decorators. The result is unshakable brand affinity, 180 million annual visitors, and industry-leading repeat purchase rates.

Financially, the flat-pack model slashes logistics cost per unit, enabling both low prices and healthy profitability. Once again, a company that solves for customer value first finds itself in the stakeholder-financial leadership quadrant, rewarded by the market for meeting real-life needs.

Airbnb: "Live Like a Local"

Traditional hospitality optimized around uniformity and occupancy rates. Airbnb sensed a growing traveler desire for authentic, local experiences. Its planners built a two-sided marketplace that empowered hosts and expanded lodging supply without owning a single property. The key to success meant balancing trust and scale through coordinated planning. Identity verification, reviews, Superhost programs, and responsive support created confidence for guests. Data-driven pricing tools and insurance protected hosts.

Every planning cycle weighs community impact, regulatory shifts, and seasonal demand signals to keep the platform healthy while expanding supply and demand simultaneously.

Airbnb's planning processes coordinate technology development, community management, regulatory compliance, and market expansion around creating authentic travel experiences. Their integrated approach ensures that host onboarding, guest safety, pricing optimization, and legal compliance all work together to strengthen the platform.

For travelers, the payoff is profound: "I feel part of the city, not just a visitor." That emotional resonance fuels repeat bookings and an NPS exceeding traditional hotel chains by double digits. Revenue followed suit, growing from $4 billion to $8 billion in four years pre-IPO, thus securing Airbnb's spot in the stakeholder and financial leader quadrant.

The lesson: Designing value around previously unmet aspirations can redefine an entire industry through coordinated planning that aligns all organizational capabilities.

Owner.com: "Arm owners to take on their Goliaths"

While most restaurant technology companies focus on incremental improvements to delivery or ordering workflows, Owner.com began with a sharper insight: Independent restaurants weren't struggling because they lacked software; they were losing control of their demand, their margins, and their customer relationships. They were struggling because other companies forced them to master digital marketing, instead of focusing on their core product: great food and service.

Owner.com reframed the problem. Restaurants owners didn't need to be digital marketing experts. They needed to own their customers, build direct relationships, and keep the economics required to stay profitable. That customer-centric insight shaped every element of Owner's integrated planning.

The company designed a platform that arms restaurant owners with a direct-to-consumer growth engine: branded websites, commission-free online ordering, automated marketing, reputation management, and loyalty programs. But the real magic lies in how these capabilities work together. Each planning cycle integrates software development, restaurant onboarding, performance analytics, and customer feedback to continuously refine the system around one outcome: helping restaurants grow profitably.

The results speak for themselves. Thousands of restaurants have replaced costly marketplace orders with direct, high-margin transactions. Automated marketing brings lapsed customers back. Smart menus increase average order value. And because the platform is built around outcomes, not features, restaurants experience what feels like an extension of their team rather than a tool they must manage.

These outcomes exist because planning is anchored in restaurant success, not software features. By integrating the full customer lifecycle—discovery, order, repeat visit, referral—into a single coordinated system, Owner.com turns digital fragmentation into predictable, compounding value for operators. The pattern is the same as in every stakeholder–financial leader: Solve the right customer problem, coordinate the organization around that value, and superior financial performance follows. Owner.com didn't help restaurants "do digital" better. It helped them reclaim their business.

Full disclosure: My son Jonathan was one of the early employees at Owner.com and is now the vice president of business operations. Several examples referenced later in the book surfaced as he reviewed early drafts of this book, highlighting situations where the principles of Value-Centric IBP were already showing up in the field, long before either of us labeled them that way. We never discussed these cases beforehand; he simply recognized the patterns as he read. I suppose value-centric thinking might be genetic.

FourKites: "See What's Coming"

FourKites is a supply chain technology company that uses integrated AI to turn real-time data into autonomous action. Since the beginning, Matt Elenjickal, the founder and CEO, has prioritized building products based on direct customer input. The company maintains an active online community where 90% of users share ideas through an idea exchange platform. About one in four of those suggestions ends up on the product roadmap. That feedback loop has produced more than 250 features, including the AI-powered digital workers that several customers are now using to automate routine supply chain tasks.

At the heart of these symbiotic relationships with customers is a focus on measurable business outcomes. And that focus is delivering results. When a manufacturer needed to address $2.69 million in annual detention charges, they weren't looking for better dashboards. They needed to stop hemorrhaging money. FourKites' yard analytics tools helped identify the root causes, and the manufacturer implemented proactive monitoring with weekly operational reviews that cut costs by 98.6% at two facilities.

A beverage company wanted to reclaim hundreds of staff hours consumed by routine customer inquiries. The AI agent that FourKites deployed reduced response times from 90 minutes to seconds and evolved to handle increasingly complex tasks. Similarly, a cold storage provider was burning significant resources on manual appointment scheduling. But after an eight-week pilot achieved 87% automation rates, the value became obvious and FourKites was scaled across their network.

These capabilities existed because FourKites had already worked through similar challenges with other customers. The company wasn't selling generic software and hoping customers would figure out how to use it. They were solving specific, costly operational problems that customers needed fixed. And because those solutions kept delivering fast payback and measurable results, customers stayed engaged in helping FourKites understand what to build next. That's how you create what the business literature calls "sustainable competitive advantage," but what really amounts to a partnership where both sides keep winning.

The Pattern Behind Success

These companies didn't succeed by simply improving what already existed. They succeeded because they exemplify the stakeholder-financial value alignment that the Bain research identified as the key to sustainable competitive advantage. They succeeded because they:

- Started with the customer's point of view, not internal capabilities

- Identified what customers really valued, not just what they said they wanted

- Aligned their entire business—strategy, operations, and planning—to deliver that value consistently across all touchpoints

- Built planning processes that coordinated multiple functions around customer outcomes rather than functional optimization

- Created integrated systems that could adapt and respond to changing customer needs while maintaining operational excellence

It's not just innovation. It's empathetic innovation guided by systematic planning. The only kind that matters in today's competitive environment.

Whether you're running a startup, leading a product team, or managing a legacy business that's ready to evolve, the principles are clear:

- **Look outward before you look inward.** Start with customer needs, not internal capabilities.

- **Focus on jobs-to-be-done, not features.** Understand what job your customer is hiring you to do.

- **Build for relationships, not transactions.** Think lifetime value, not quarterly sales.

- **Plan for customer outcomes, not just operational metrics.** Coordinate all functions around customer value creation.

- **Integrate insights across all functions.** Ensure that customer understanding influences every planning decision.

The customer doesn't sit at the edge of your business model. They sit at the center. And once you see that clearly, it changes everything: your priorities, your processes, your products, your culture, and most importantly, your planning. This is a foundational belief in Value-Centric IBP.

Even still, the transformation from traditional business planning to Value-Centric Integrated Business Planning isn't just about understanding customers better. It's about building systematic capabilities that ensure customer understanding influences every decision, every plan, and every action your organization takes. When done effectively, this transformation creates the sustainable competitive advantages that drive both stakeholder satisfaction and financial performance, just as the Bain study demonstrated.

The customer doesn't just buy your product. They're writing your business plan.

The only question is whether you will read it.

Once you accept that the customer is the business, profit stops being the purpose and becomes the outcome, which forces a deeper examination of how value is actually created, the focus of the next chapter.

Redefining the Purpose: From Profit to Value

Price is what you pay. Value is what you get.
—Warren Buffett

The Fundamental Reality

The purpose of a business is to create a customer. Everything else—payroll, revenue, product roadmaps, capital allocation—depends on that fundamental reality. Yet customers do not appear simply because a company exists. They appear when an offer delivers something they genuinely value.

In every decision, customers weigh the benefits they expect to receive against the money, time, effort, and risk they must bear. They compare that equation with the alternatives available to them.

Firms, therefore, compete on two inseparable levers: the value they create and the cost they incur to create it. When leaders internalize this simple reality, they stop running a product or price business and begin running a value creation business. That pivot changes everything: how opportunities are chosen, how resources are allocated, how capabilities are built, and how success is measured. Organizations that understand this are in the value-creation business. Loyalty, brand gravity, and durable profits follow.

However, understanding value creation and systematically delivering it are two different challenges. Traditional planning processes often optimize for single dimensions, usually cost or functionality, while missing opportunities to create multi-dimensional value that commands premium pricing and drives customer loyalty.

The real challenge lies in translating value understanding into planning decisions that consistently deliver value across all customer touchpoints, competitive situations, and market conditions.

The Twin Engines of Value Creation

Value creation begins with listening. Empathy and execution are the twin engines of value: first, the disciplined work of understanding what customers need, resent, and aspire to; then the operational muscle to translate those insights into scalable delivery.

Value proposition without delivery? That's just a promise with better fonts.

Execution without empathy? That's like building a Formula 1 car nobody knows how to drive: technically impressive, strategically useless.

When empathy and execution reinforce each other, a company develops the reflexes of a value business. It learns to discover unmet needs earlier, design sharper solutions faster, and institutionalize the capabilities that make those solutions dependable. Finance, operations, technology, and people practices exist to support and scale those engines, not to substitute for them.

However, coordinating these support functions around value creation rather than internal efficiency requires planning processes that can balance multiple objectives, serve different customer segments appropriately, and adapt to changing competitive dynamics while maintaining operational excellence.

What Is Value, Really?

Value is the perceived benefit someone receives relative to what they give up. For customers, it's the emotional, functional, and social gain they experience compared with the money, time, effort, or risk they expend. For the business, it's the return realized when expectations are met or exceeded in ways that build loyalty, advocacy, and profitable growth.

Customers don't buy features. They buy fewer headaches, smoother mornings, joyful moments, and bragging rights at the dinner table.

Warren Buffett's line captures the distinction: Price is what you pay; value is what you get. Price is a number at the moment of purchase. Value is a judgment formed afterward, a story the customer tells themselves about meaning, transformation, and experience.

Price vs. Value: The Critical Distinction

Price is what a customer pays at a point in time. Value is what the customer believes they got once the experience unfolds. Price is a number. Value is a story. That story is shaped by meaning, transformation, and confidence, and it accrues across touchpoints before, during, and after a transaction. Measuring value only in dollars is like measuring this book by the weight of its paper.

Consider two watches that keep identical time. One costs ten dollars. The other costs 20 thousand. The expensive watch carries with it a narrative of craftsmanship, legacy, precision, and status. Functionally, the two products do the same job. Emotionally and socially, they do very different work. That difference is value.

Rolex doesn't compete on timekeeping accuracy. A $20 Timex keeps better time than most luxury watches. Instead, Rolex sells stories: the

Submariner worn by James Bond, the Daytona linked with racing legends, the GMT-Master trusted by pilots. Each model carries decades of carefully cultivated narrative about precision, adventure, and achievement. Buying a Rolex is less about telling time and more about joining an exclusive club and owning a piece of horological history.

The functional value (timekeeping) is nearly identical across brands, but the emotional, social, and symbolic value creates a willingness to pay a thousand times more. As a watch collector myself, I appreciate this point deeply.

Because value lives in perception, businesses that default to competing on price often ignite a race they cannot win. Discounts are easy to offer and easy for competitors to match. They attract transactional buyers who leave as readily as they came.

By contrast, competing on value builds preference and resilience. Value-driven firms invest in trust, quality, community, and emotional connection. They design experiences that extend beyond the product itself, until customers do not simply choose the brand but identify with it.

When a business sells on price, it is interchangeable and vulnerable to being replaced. When it sells on value, it becomes irreplaceable.

What Customers Actually Buy

It's a myth that customers always buy the best product. They buy the product they believe is best for them. They buy what resonates: what reflects their values, identity, and aspirations. This is where value becomes personal and where planning becomes complex.

A product's true worth lies not in its features, but in how it fits into the customer's world. Iconic brands understand this. They don't sell toothpaste, phones, or shoes. They sell confidence, connection, and lifestyle. Value is perception, and perception is shaped by story, brand, experience, and relationship.

Different customers perceive value differently based on their contexts, priorities, and alternatives. Strategic business customers might value risk reduction and integration above cost savings, while price-sensitive segments prioritize economic value. Understanding these segment-specific value priorities becomes essential for planning decisions about product development, service levels, and resource allocation.

The Value Equation

Value can be summarized as perceived benefit divided by perceived cost:

Value = Perceived Benefit ÷ Perceived Cost

However, that "benefit" isn't one-dimensional. It's emotional, functional, social, and financial.

Understanding value means understanding the full spectrum of human motivation and context. More importantly for planning purposes, it means understanding how different customer segments weigh these benefit dimensions and how competitive dynamics affect customer perceptions of both benefits and costs.

This equation is deceptively simple, but it changes how performance should be interpreted. Once value is understood as a ratio shaped by perception rather than a static output, improvement no longer comes only from cost reduction or feature enhancement. It comes from deliberately influencing how different customers experience benefit and how that experience compares to available alternatives. This insight underpins why segmentation, measurement, and planning must evolve together.

The Six Dimensions of Consumer Value

To repeat: Value is not a single metric. It's a multidimensional experience. The most successful businesses design for value that speaks to not just what people need, but also who they are, how they feel, and what they aspire to. Let's look at the six core dimensions of value.

1. Functional Value

Does it solve a problem or make life easier or more convenient?

Functional value is the foundation. It's about solving problems and helping customers accomplish tasks more effectively. This is what most companies focus on, and it's where you must excel to stay in the game.

Google Maps delivers exceptional functional value by helping people navigate efficiently. But Google didn't stop there. They understood that navigation is often stressful, so they added features like real-time traffic updates, alternative route suggestions, and estimated arrival times that reduce anxiety and uncertainty.

Uber's Functional Value Revolution

Before Uber, getting a taxi meant standing on street corners hoping one would stop, carrying exact change, and having no idea when you'd arrive.

Uber solved multiple functional problems simultaneously: predictable pickup times, cashless payment, route tracking, and driver accountability. The core functional value wasn't just "transportation." It was "reliable, predictable transportation on demand." This functional innovation created a $90 billion company because it solved real friction points that people experienced daily.

2. Emotional Value

Does it make me feel safe, proud, empowered, or excited?

Emotional value is often what drives purchasing decisions, even in supposedly rational B2B environments. People want to feel confident, proud, secure, excited, or relieved. When you understand the emotions customers want to experience, you can design offerings that deliver those feelings consistently.

Apple has mastered emotional value across their product line. When someone uses an iPhone, they don't just accomplish tasks. They feel like they're part of something innovative and exclusive. The careful attention to design details, the satisfying click of buttons, the elegant packaging—all of these create an emotional experience that goes far beyond functional utility.

Nike's Emotional Transformation

Nike transformed from a running shoe company into an emotional empowerment brand with "Just Do It." The campaign wasn't about shoe technology or price. It was about overcoming self-doubt and achieving personal breakthroughs. Nike understood that people don't buy athletic wear; they buy the feeling of being athletic, capable, and unstoppable. This emotional repositioning helped Nike grow from $877 million in 1988 to over $50 billion today. The shoes became symbols of personal potential rather than mere functional footwear.

Nike's emotional value creation required integrated planning across marketing, product design, athlete partnerships, and retail experiences to ensure consistent emotional messaging across all customer touchpoints.

3. Social Value

Does it help me belong, stand out, or send a message?

Social value addresses how customers want to be perceived by others and which groups they want to belong to. In our connected world, many purchase decisions are influenced by what they signal about the buyer's identity, values, and affiliations.

Patagonia's Environmental Identity

Patagonia doesn't just sell outdoor clothing. It sells environmental activism. The brand's "Don't Buy This Jacket" campaign deliberately discouraged consumption while promoting repair and reuse. This counterintuitive approach created immense social value for environmentally conscious consumers who wanted their purchases to reflect their values.

Patagonia customers aren't just buying jackets; they're joining an environmental movement. This social positioning has created fanatical loyalty and allowed Patagonia to charge premium prices while maintaining strong growth, reaching $1 billion in revenue by building a community around shared values.

Supreme's Exclusivity Economy

Supreme mastered social value through artificial scarcity and cultural relevance. The brand produces limited quantities of simple items—t-shirts, hoodies, accessories—that sell out within minutes. Owning Supreme isn't about the product quality; it's about belonging to an exclusive club of culturally aware consumers.

The social value is so strong that Supreme items often resell for five to 10 times the retail price on secondary markets. When Supreme sold to VF Corporation for $2.1 billion, they weren't buying a clothing company. They were buying a social signaling system.

4. Economic Value

Is the trade-off of time, money, and effort worthwhile?

Economic value isn't just about low prices. It's about optimizing the total cost of ownership and maximizing return on investment. Sophisticated customers understand that the cheapest option upfront often costs more in the long run.

TurboTax charges significantly more than many competitors, but delivers superior economic value by reducing the total cost of tax preparation. When you factor in the time saved, the reduced risk of errors, and the potential for finding additional deductions, TurboTax often provides better economic value than hiring an accountant or using cheaper software.

Southwest Airlines' Economic Value Model

Southwest revolutionized air travel by redefining economic value. While competitors focused on amenities and status, Southwest eliminated frills to offer consistently low prices and reliable service. Their economic value proposition was simple: Get from point A to point B affordably and on time.

No assigned seats, no meal service, no fancy lounges, just economic efficiency. This focus on core economic value helped Southwest remain profitable for 47 consecutive years while traditional carriers struggled with bankruptcy and consolidation.

Dollar Shave Club's Subscription Economics

Dollar Shave Club disrupted the razor industry by reframing economic value. Instead of selling expensive cartridges in retail stores, they offered quality razors delivered monthly for a fraction of the cost. Their viral "Our Blades Are F***ing Great" video communicated economic value with humor: great shaves without the markup.

This economic repositioning was so powerful that Unilever acquired the company for $1 billion just five years after launch, proving that superior economic value can topple entrenched incumbents.

5. Fashion Value

Is it trendy, current, or status-enhancing right now?

Fashion value is about timing, cultural relevance, and desirability. It's especially powerful in consumer goods, lifestyle, and entertainment.

Supreme drops limited products that sell out instantly, driven by hype, not function. TikTok trends influence what people wear, buy, or cook because being "in" carries value.

Even tech products can have fashion value. Think of the first AirPods. Fashion value is often ephemeral, but incredibly potent when aligned with emotional and social value.

Crocs' Fashion Value Resurrection

Crocs were once considered fashion disasters: ugly, plastic shoes for gardeners and healthcare workers. But the brand achieved a remarkable fashion transformation by embracing the "ugly-cool" trend and partnering with high-fashion designers and celebrities. Collaborations with Balenciaga, Bad Bunny, and Justin Bieber transformed Crocs from functional footwear into fashion statements.

The fashion value became so strong that limited editions sell out instantly, and Crocs stock rose over 6,000% from 2009 to 2021. The same functional product gained massive fashion value through cultural repositioning.

Stanley Tumbler's Viral Moment

Stanley's 40-ounce tumbler became a social media phenomenon in 2023, with customers camping out at Target and cups selling for hundreds on resale markets. The functional value (keeping drinks cold) existed for decades, but fashion value exploded when the tumbler became a TikTok status symbol. The fashion value was so powerful that Stanley's revenue jumped from $75 million to $750 million in just three years, proving how quickly fashion value can transform established products.

6. Synergy Value

Does it work better as part of a broader ecosystem or experience?

Synergy value emerges when products work better as part of an ecosystem than they do individually. This dimension has become crucial in our connected world, where customers increasingly expect seamless integration between their tools and devices.

Apple's Ecosystem Lock-In

Apple masterfully created synergy value across its product line. An iPhone works better with AirPods, which connect seamlessly to a Mac, which syncs perfectly with an iPad through iCloud. Each product becomes more valuable when used with others.

This synergy value is so powerful that Apple customers are reluctant to switch even individual products, knowing they'll lose ecosystem benefits. Apple's ecosystem synergy helped the company achieve the highest customer retention rates in tech (over 90%) and become the world's most valuable company.

Amazon's Everything Ecosystem

Amazon built synergy value across seemingly unrelated services. Prime membership includes free shipping, video streaming, music, cloud storage, and grocery delivery. Alexa connects to Prime services, smart home devices, and shopping. Amazon Web Services (AWS) provides infrastructure for both Amazon and competitors.

Each service reinforces the others, creating a web of value that's difficult to replicate. This synergy strategy helped Amazon grow from a bookstore to a $1.7 trillion company by making customers more dependent on the entire ecosystem rather than individual products.

The Power of Multi-Dimensional Value

- Functional + Economic keeps you in the game

- Emotional + Social + Fashion builds brand gravity

- Synergy creates ecosystems that lock in loyalty and multiply value over time

Each value dimension requires different organizational capabilities and planning approaches. Functional value demands operational excellence and cost management. Emotional value requires brand building and experience design. Social value needs community building and cultural relevance.

This is the second major shift this chapter establishes: Value leadership is not about excelling on one dimension, but about making intentional choices across multiple dimensions and accepting the trade-offs that come with those choices. Once value is understood this way, the limits of traditional, functionally optimized planning become obvious. Coordinating these dimensions at scale is precisely the challenge Value-Centric IBP is designed to address.

The Seven Core B2B Value Dimensions

Business-to-business decisions reflect a parallel but distinct set of value dynamics. B2B value creation often requires longer planning horizons, multiple stakeholder alignment, and integration with complex organizational systems.

1. Functional Value

Does it solve the business problem effectively?

This is the most basic requirement. Does your solution deliver on its core promise: better performance, improved productivity, increased output?

Salesforce's CRM Revolution

Salesforce didn't invent customer relationship management (CRM). They reinvented it for the cloud era. Traditional CRM systems required expensive IT infrastructure, long implementation cycles, and complex customization. Salesforce delivered core CRM functionality through simple web browsers with faster deployment and lower upfront costs.

The functional value was clear: manage customer relationships more effectively with less technical burden. This functional improvement helped Salesforce grow from startup to $280 billion market cap by solving fundamental business problems better than existing alternatives.

2. Economic (Financial) Value

Does it improve profitability or lower cost?

B2B decisions are driven by measurable impact, often captured in terms of ROI, total cost of ownership (TCO), payback period, or cost avoidance.

UiPath's Robotic Process Automation

UiPath grew from $1.8 million to $600 million in revenue in just four years by delivering clear economic value through robotic process automation. Their software robots automate repetitive tasks like data entry, invoice processing, and customer onboarding. Customers see immediate ROI: a bot that costs $15,000 annually can replace work that would cost $50,000 in human labor.

The economic value is transparent and measurable, making purchasing decisions straightforward. Deutsche Bank automated 470 processes with UiPath, saving 1.5 million hours annually, an economic value that directly improved their bottom line.

3. Operational/Process Value

Does it streamline operations or reduce friction?

This focuses on efficiency gains: saving time, reducing errors, improving compliance, simplifying processes.

4. Risk Reduction Value

Does it reduce exposure to legal, operational, or reputational risk?

Risk is a big driver in B2B, especially in regulated or high-stakes industries. If your solution reduces uncertainty, it adds real value.

CrowdStrike's Cybersecurity Value

CrowdStrike built a $50 billion company by delivering risk reduction value in cybersecurity. Traditional antivirus software detected threats after they infiltrated systems. CrowdStrike's Falcon platform prevents breaches using AI-powered threat detection and response. For enterprises, this isn't just about technology. It's about avoiding catastrophic business damage. A major data breach can cost millions in fines, lost customers, and reputation damage.

CrowdStrike's value proposition is simple: Pay us to avoid much larger losses. Companies like General Electric and Hyatt chose CrowdStrike not for features, but for the risk protection that enables business continuity.

DocuSign's Compliance and Security Value

DocuSign transformed document signing by providing legal validity, audit trails, and compliance frameworks that traditional paper processes couldn't match. For heavily regulated industries like healthcare and financial services, DocuSign's risk reduction value was paramount. The platform ensures HIPAA compliance, provides tamper-evident signatures, and maintains detailed audit logs.

During COVID, DocuSign's value exploded as companies needed to maintain legal processes remotely. Revenue grew from $975 million in 2020 to $2.1 billion in 2022, driven largely by organizations paying for risk mitigation in digital transactions.

5. Strategic Value

Does it support the company's long-term goals or transformation journey?

Some solutions help clients enter new markets, innovate faster, or gain competitive advantage. These are high-leverage value drivers.

Snowflake's Data Cloud Strategy

Snowflake became a $70 billion company by enabling strategic transformation for enterprises struggling with data silos. Their cloud data platform allows companies to break down departmental barriers, enable real-time analytics, and build AI-powered applications.

For Capital One, Snowflake enabled a strategic shift from traditional banking to data-driven financial services. The bank consolidated dozens of data warehouses into Snowflake's platform, accelerating product development and enabling personalized customer experiences.

This strategic value—transformation rather than incremental improvement—justified premium pricing and rapid adoption across Fortune 500 companies.

Stripe's Platform Strategy for Digital Commerce

Stripe provides strategic value by enabling companies to become digital-first businesses. Rather than just processing payments, Stripe offers the infrastructure for entire digital commerce ecosystems: marketplaces, subscriptions, global expansion, and financial services.

For companies like Shopify, Lyft, and Amazon, Stripe became strategic infrastructure that enabled business model innovation. Stripe's $95 billion valuation reflects not just payment processing fees, but the strategic value of enabling digital transformation for millions of businesses worldwide.

6. Relationship and Service Value

Is the partnership easy, responsive, and trustworthy?

Trust, reliability, and ongoing support matter, especially in long-cycle B2B relationships. This includes account management, onboarding, training, support, and cultural fit.

7. Integration and Ecosystem Value

Does it integrate smoothly into existing systems and teams?

Your solution adds more value if it works with existing platforms, processes, and skillsets to reduce barriers to adoption and increase ROI. In B2B, value isn't just about solving a problem. It's about solving it at scale, reliably, and across multiple geographies, business units, or customer segments.

B2C vs. B2B: Same Humans, Different Frames

While consumer choices may lean more on emotion, identity, and convenience, and enterprise choices lean more on ROI, risk, and strategy, the same people who respond to good storytelling at home do not suddenly become immune to feeling, trust, or design at work.

Key Differences:

- B2C value is more emotional, identity-based, and convenience-driven

- B2B value is more ROI, risk, and strategy-driven

The Human Connection: Both remain deeply human. This is why the best enterprise brands pair rigorous financial impact with emotional intelligence: clear proofs of value, credible brands, confident service, and excellent user experience. After all, people adopt what they understand, believe, and enjoy using.

Even still, B2B and B2C value creation require different planning capabilities, timelines, and coordination mechanisms. B2B value often requires longer relationship development, multiple stakeholder management, and integration with complex enterprise systems. These differences must be reflected in planning processes that account for longer sales cycles, more complex implementation requirements, and different success metrics.

From Price Battles to Value Leadership

Taken together, these ideas point to a fundamental managerial posture. Think of value as a living system, not a static checklist. Lead by listening constantly, adapting frequently, personalizing intentionally, and delivering contextually.

Avoid the race to the bottom on price. Instead, design across the full set of value dimensions relevant to your market, prove the value equation from the customer's point of view, and align capabilities to deliver that value at a target cost.

In crowded marketplaces, most offers shout price. Enduring businesses whisper value and win.

The Value-Centric Mindset:

- Listen constantly to evolving customer needs

- Adapt frequently as contexts change

- Personalize intentionally across different stakeholder perspectives

- Deliver contextually based on environment and timing

- Plan systematically to coordinate value creation across all functions

Preparing for Value-Centric Planning

Measuring value creation across multiple dimensions presents challenges that traditional financial metrics don't capture. Customer lifetime value, Net Promoter Scores, competitive positioning indicators, and relationship health metrics become as important as revenue and cost metrics. Value-Centric IBP integrates these diverse measurement approaches into comprehensive planning frameworks.

Delivering multi-dimensional value at scale requires sophisticated capabilities that traditional planning approaches struggle to coordinate. Personalizing emotional value while maintaining economic efficiency or providing synergy value across complex ecosystems demands integrated planning processes supported by advanced analytics and customer intelligence.

Value creation doesn't occur in isolation. It happens in competitive contexts where customer expectations continuously evolve. What creates emotional value today may become functional expectations tomorrow. This dynamic nature of value requires planning processes that can anticipate and adapt to changing competitive landscapes and customer priorities through systematic scenario planning and competitive intelligence integration.

This foundation of value understanding sets the stage for what comes next. Turning insight into consistent value creation at scale requires more than good intentions or isolated tools; it depends on thoughtful coordination, shared language, and capabilities that develop over time. While the frameworks and operating models of Value-Centric Integrated Business Planning will come later in the book (Part 2), the work we're doing here is essential. It ensures that when we move from understanding value to delivering it, the transition is grounded, coherent, and durable rather than rushed or superficial.

Before we can design systems to deliver value at scale, we need to understand the forces that shape it: how customers, competitors, and the company itself interact to create, sustain, or destroy value in the real world.

CHAPTER 4

The Dynamic Dance of Value: The Three C Model

In the midst of chaos, there is also opportunity.
—Sun Tzu

Business as a Love Triangle

Business doesn't operate in a vacuum. It thrives, or fails, within a dynamic system made up of three living entities: the customer, the corporation, and the competition. Business strategy often hides behind numbers, charts, and dashboards. But at its core, it's about relationships. And relationships are messy, emotional, and full of tension.

If we're honest, business is less like a boardroom negotiation and more like a love story. In fact, a love triangle. The three characters in this triangle are the Customer, the Corporation, and the Competition. Each has their own desires, insecurities, and moves. And the glue that holds (or breaks) these bonds is value.

Value is the attraction, the spark that makes the customer notice you, trust you, and ultimately choose you.

From this point forward, value is never discussed in isolation. It exists only in relationship: between customers with expectations, companies with capabilities, and competitors offering alternatives. Every planning decision that follows in this book assumes this three-way dynamic is always in motion, whether leaders acknowledge it or not.

The Customer: The One You Want to Say "Yes"

Every story starts with them (remember, the business is the customer). They are the hero of this narrative. Your goal is to earn their "yes" to your proposal, to your product, to your promise.

But they are not a passive character. They have expectations, standards, and choices. They are constantly evaluating whether the relationship still serves them.

The Competition: The Rival Suitor

No romance is without a rival. Your competition is always waiting in the wings, flowers and chocolates in hand, ready to whisper, "You deserve better."

Their role is to test the strength of your bond. If your attraction fades, if you stop listening, if you take the relationship for granted, they will step in. And customers, like in life, rarely stay where they feel neglected.

The Corporation: The Persistent Partner

That's you. Your role in this triangle is to be continuously romantic, not in the sentimental sense, but in the practical one: to show you care, to keep the spark alive, to ensure the passion doesn't fade. This means working to understand the customer deeply, adapting as they evolve, and renewing the promise of value again and again.

Like any relationship, there are ups and downs. There will be moments of doubt, misalignment, or even conflict. Customers will question your intentions. Competitors will appear more attractive. The market will test your resilience. But in this love triangle, it is your responsibility to keep the relationship strong. You must not only win their heart once; you must win it continuously.

Value-Centric IBP: The Relationship Playbook

This is where Value-Centric Integrated Business Planning comes in. It is the disciplined process that ensures you don't rely on luck, charm, or old promises. Instead, it helps you:

- Anticipate the customer's evolving needs

- Strengthen the bond by keeping your value proposition fresh

- Recognize early when passion is fading and reignite it before your rival moves in

- Balance attraction with stability, passion with trust, and romance with reliability

The outcome is not just a transaction. It is a relationship. One that, if nurtured, becomes long-lasting, mutually beneficial, and deeply rewarding. In business terms, that translates to loyalty, advocacy, and profitable growth. In human terms, it is called love.

Why Traditional IBP Misses the Point

The Three Cs framework reveals the challenge with traditional IBP processes. They often optimize for internal coordination without systematic consideration of how customer dynamics, competitive actions, and corporate capabilities interact to create or destroy value. Most planning approaches treat these as separate variables rather than recognizing them as interconnected forces that must be balanced simultaneously to achieve sustainable success.

This is the critical failure of traditional planning: It treats customers, competitors, and internal operations as separate inputs instead of interacting forces. Once you see value as something shaped by all three simultaneously, optimizing one dimension in isolation stops looking efficient and starts looking dangerous.

This dynamic interaction becomes particularly critical in Value-Centric IBP because customer value creation depends not just on what you do, but on how what you do compares to competitive alternatives and aligns with evolving customer expectations. The planning challenge lies in coordinating organizational capabilities around customer value creation while anticipating and responding to competitive dynamics that constantly reshape the value landscape.

Let's continue examining the love triangular players. The Corporation that wants commitment, the Customer that wants excitement, and the Competition that wants a rebound opportunity.

The Customer: The Most Powerful Force

Customers have options. They constantly compare, not just between products, but between experiences, perceptions, and values offered by different providers. Their needs evolve, their expectations rise, and their loyalty is earned moment by moment.

If you don't provide what they need, someone else will. It's not personal. It's business reality. The customer sits at the center of the value ecosystem because they ultimately determine which companies survive and thrive. But their power has fundamentally shifted in the digital age, creating new challenges for planning processes that must account for these changed dynamics.

The Digital Transformation of Customer Power

Twenty years ago, companies held most of the information about products, pricing, and alternatives. Today, customers often know more about your offerings, including your costs, competitor comparisons, and peer reviews, than your own sales team. They arrive at purchase decisions 70% complete before ever engaging with your company.

This information asymmetry reversal has profound implications for Value-Centric IBP. Demand planning can no longer assume that marketing and sales control the customer journey. Product planning must account for customers who research extensively and have detailed competitive knowledge. Supply planning must deliver on expectations set by customer research rather than just internal promises.

The Amplification Effect: Every Customer Is a Broadcaster

A single customer's experience doesn't stay with them. It cascades through social networks, review platforms, and communities. One viral TikTok video can make or break a product launch. A detailed Reddit review can influence thousands of purchase decisions. Customers have become broadcasters of brand experience.

This amplification effect means that customer success planning becomes critical for sustainable business performance. A dissatisfied strategic partner doesn't just churn. They potentially influence dozens of prospects in their network. Conversely, delighted customers become powerful marketing assets that traditional advertising cannot replicate.

Friction Intolerance and Instant Alternatives

With unlimited options available instantly, customer tolerance for friction has plummeted. If your website loads slowly, your checkout process has too many steps, or your customer service puts them on hold, they'll simply go elsewhere. The switching cost for many products has dropped to near zero.

This reality requires planning processes that optimize for customer experience alongside operational efficiency. Supply chain planning must prioritize customer experience metrics like delivery speed and reliability, not just cost optimization. Technology planning must ensure seamless customer interactions across all touchpoints.

Cross-Industry Expectation Setting

Here's something that catches most companies off-guard: Fairly or not, customers don't compare you only to direct competitors. They compare your experience to the best experience they've had anywhere. If Amazon can deliver same-day, why can't you? If Uber can show exactly where their driver is, why can't your repair service?

This is where planning quietly breaks down for many organizations. Customer expectations are no longer set by industry peers but by the best experience customers have anywhere. That means competitive awareness must expand beyond "companies like us" to include any experience redefining what "good" looks like.

Customer expectations are set by the highest-performing companies across all sectors. This cross-industry comparison creates planning challenges that traditional IBP approaches struggle to address. Competitive intelligence must extend beyond direct competitors to include any company that shapes customer expectations in your category. Capability development must consider not just industry benchmarks but cross-industry best practices that customers experience elsewhere.

Case Study: The Airbnb Experience Revolution

Airbnb didn't just compete with hotels. They redefined what customers expected from travel accommodation. By understanding that travelers increasingly valued authentic local experiences over standardized amenities, Airbnb tapped into latent customer desires that traditional hospitality had missed.

The platform's power came from recognizing that customers weren't just buying a place to sleep; they were buying stories to tell, Instagram moments to share, and connections to local culture. This deeper understanding of customer motivation allowed Airbnb to create value that hotels couldn't easily replicate, even with superior amenities or lower prices.

Planning Implications: Airbnb's success required integrated planning across technology development, host acquisition, regulatory compliance, and customer experience design. Their planning processes had to balance supply and demand in local markets while maintaining consistent quality standards and navigating complex regulatory environments across different cities and countries.

Segment-Specific Dynamics: Different customer segments respond differently to the Three Cs forces. Business travelers using Airbnb value different factors (reliability, WiFi, workspace) than leisure travelers (uniqueness, local experience, value). Airbnb's planning processes had to account for these varying expectations while maintaining operational efficiency across diverse host and property types.

The Corporation: This Is You

Your mission is to identify and deliver value to your customers in a way that is both meaningful and sustainable. But it's not just about meeting needs. It's about doing so better, faster, or more meaningfully than anyone else. And doing so at a cost structure that allows you to grow, reinvest, and stay ahead.

Business without value is like a bar without drinks: all promise, no reason to stay. The corporation must balance multiple stakeholder interests while remaining laser-focused on customer value creation. This requires operational excellence, strategic clarity, and the agility to adapt as market conditions evolve.

But modern corporations face unprecedented complexity that traditional planning approaches struggle to manage effectively.

Stakeholder Capitalism and Value Creation

Today's corporations must deliver value to customers, employees, shareholders, communities, and the environment simultaneously.

Companies like Patagonia and Unilever have shown that this balance isn't just ethical. It's profitable. They are enhancing pure shareholder primacy with stakeholder capitalism where long-term value creation requires satisfying multiple constituencies. This stakeholder complexity requires planning processes that can balance competing objectives while maintaining customer focus. Financial planning must account for stakeholder value creation alongside traditional profitability metrics. Resource allocation must consider environmental and social impact while optimizing for customer outcomes.

The Competition: Everyone Vying for Your Customer

This is everyone trying to earn your customer's attention, trust, and spend. Competitive pressure is relentless. It doesn't pause for internal reorganizations or strategic planning cycles. The marketplace rewards relevance, responsiveness, and innovation and punishes complacency.

Competition isn't just direct competitors. It includes substitute products, alternative solutions, and even the customer's decision to do nothing. In the digital age, competitive threats can emerge from adjacent industries or entirely new business models that traditional competitive analysis might miss.

The Expanding Competitive Landscape

Direct Competitors: Companies offering similar products to similar customers through similar channels. These are the obvious rivals everyone watches and benchmarks against.

Indirect Competitors: Companies solving the same customer problem through different approaches. Netflix competes with traditional TV, but also with video games, social media, books, and any other entertainment option competing for leisure time.

Substitute Solutions: Companies offering entirely different solutions that fulfill the same customer need. Ride-sharing services like Uber substituted for car ownership in urban areas. Email substituted for postal mail. Smartphones substituted for cameras, GPS devices, and MP3 players simultaneously.

Inaction Competition: Often the biggest competitor is the customer choosing not to buy anything at all. This is why market expansion (growing the overall pie) can be more valuable than market share battles (fighting over the existing pie).

A medtech company launched a remote patient monitoring system for heart-failure patients and initially viewed other monitoring platforms as its main competitors. But adoption data showed that most clinicians were not using any remote patient monitoring solution at all.

The real competitor was inaction: concerns about workflow burden, reimbursement, and patient participation kept providers from adopting any system.

When the company simplified onboarding, clarified reimbursement, and offered turnkey workflows, adoption grew rapidly. The growth came not from taking share from competitors, but from converting clinicians who had previously chosen to do nothing.

Ecosystem vs. Ecosystem Competition

Today's competition, in some cases, is not company versus company. It's value chain against value chain or ecosystem versus ecosystem.

The iPhone competes with Android phones, but really Apple's ecosystem competes with Google's ecosystem across hardware, software, services, and data.

This ecosystem-level competition creates planning challenges that extend far beyond traditional competitive analysis. Organizations must coordinate planning across multiple products, services, and partnerships while competing against similarly complex ecosystem competitors.

Case Study: How Zoom Redefined Video Conferencing Competition

Before the pandemic, Zoom competed in a crowded market with established players like Cisco's WebEx, Microsoft's Skype for Business, and GoToMeeting. The competitive landscape seemed settled. But Zoom understood competition differently. They realized they weren't just competing with other video conferencing tools, they were competing with:

In-Person Meetings: The biggest "competitor" was people choosing to meet face to face instead of virtually. Zoom optimized for ease of use and reliability to make virtual meetings actually preferable to traveling.

Email and Phone: For many business communications, the alternative to video calls was asynchronous email or traditional phone calls. Zoom added features like chat, screen sharing, and recording to make video calls more valuable than these alternatives.

Productivity Tools: Zoom integrated with calendars, project management tools, and other business software to become part of the workflow rather than separate from it.

Consumer Expectations: Zoom competed against consumer apps like FaceTime and WhatsApp video for simplicity and reliability. They brought consumer-grade ease of use to enterprise features.

When the pandemic hit, Zoom was positioned to capture demand because they had defined their competition broadly and built capabilities to win across multiple dimensions. While competitors focused on enterprise features and security compliance, Zoom had built a product that anyone could use instantly and that became the decisive advantage when millions of people suddenly needed to work from home.

The Strategic Equations That Actually Matter

Competitive advantage grows fundamentally when the value you create for your customers exceeds the value that the competition can offer and the price the customer is willing to pay for the value you deliver exceeds the cost of generating it. Sustainable competitive advantage requires winning on two dimensions simultaneously:

Market Success: Your customer value must exceed what competitors and substitutes can offer. This is about being chosen by customers over all available alternatives.

Financial Success: Customer willingness to pay must exceed your costs of creating and delivering that value. This is about building a sustainable business model that can continue serving customers long term.

Many businesses excel at one dimension while failing at the other. Companies that deliver exceptional customer value but can't capture sufficient price to cover costs eventually fail. Organizations that optimize costs and pricing but don't deliver superior customer value get displaced by better alternatives.

The strategic challenge is optimizing both dimensions simultaneously while recognizing that they are interconnected. Better customer value often enables higher pricing. Lower costs can enable better value delivery through investment in customer experience.

Dynamic Strategic Management

Here's what makes this really hard: These strategic relationships are constantly shifting.

Customer Value Evolution: As customers gain experience with your product, their perception of value changes. Early adopters may value innovation and status; mass market customers may value reliability and price. Value also shifts based on context. For example, business travelers value different airline features than leisure travelers.

Corporate Cost Dynamics: Learning curves reduce costs over time. Technology improves efficiency. But complexity can also increase costs as products mature and feature sets expand. Scale can reduce unit costs but increase coordination costs.

Competitive Alternative Changes: Competitors improve their offerings. New entrants arrive with different cost structures. Substitute products emerge from adjacent industries. The competitive landscape is constantly moving.

Customer Price Sensitivity Shifts: Economic conditions, competitive options, and customer maturity all influence willingness to pay. What customers paid premium prices for when it was new and unique may become commoditized as alternatives emerge.

Planning Implications for Strategic Advantage

Value-Centric IBP must continuously monitor and optimize these strategic relationships across different customer segments. Different segments may have different competitive alternatives, value priorities, and price sensitivities, requiring segment-specific optimization strategies. Each IBP cycle should assess whether your strategic position is strengthening or weakening across both market and financial dimensions:

Market Position Analysis: Are you delivering increasing customer value relative to evolving competitive alternatives? Are you maintaining or improving your position as the preferred choice for target customers?

Financial Position Analysis: Are customers willing to pay prices that not only cover your costs but provide returns sufficient for continued investment in value improvement? Can you maintain pricing power as markets mature?

Integrated Optimization: How can improvements in operational efficiency enable better customer value delivery? How can superior customer value justify pricing that supports continued innovation? How can competitive positioning protect both value delivery and pricing power?

The goal is building planning processes that systematically strengthen your position across both strategic dimensions, ensuring that every decision contributes to widening the gap between what you deliver and what alternatives can provide, while maintaining the financial sustainability that enables continued value investment and innovation.

Case Study: Tesla's Multi-Dimensional Value Equation

Tesla succeeded by optimizing a different value equation than traditional automakers:

Customer Value Redefinition: While traditional car companies competed on horsepower, reliability, and price, Tesla redefined value around environmental impact, technology leadership, performance, and brand status. They turned buying a car into making a statement about innovation and environmental consciousness.

Cost Structure Innovation: Tesla vertically integrated battery production, built a direct-sales model bypassing dealers, and treated cars as software platforms updated over the air. This required massive upfront investment but created a fundamentally different cost structure focused on software and energy rather than just mechanical engineering.

Competitive Alternative Repositioning: Tesla didn't position against other car brands. They positioned against the entire fossil fuel transportation system. Their competition was oil companies, gas stations, and the environmental costs of traditional transportation. This reframing made price comparisons with traditional cars less relevant.

The result: Tesla achieved the highest market valuation in automotive history by solving a different value equation than everyone else in the industry.

Planning Complexity: Tesla's approach required planning processes that could coordinate automotive manufacturing, battery technology, charging infrastructure, software development, and direct sales across multiple markets while competing against established automotive ecosystems with different competitive advantages and cost structures.

Orchestrating the Dance

Business is not a solo performance; it's a dance. And the Three Cs—customer, corporation, competition—are always on the floor, whether you like it or not. The question isn't whether you can control them (you can't), but whether you can orchestrate your moves so that together they create value greater than the sum of their parts.

Customers will continue to raise expectations, comparing you not just to your rivals but to the best experience they've ever had anywhere. Corporations must translate purpose into capabilities, balancing operational discipline with relentless customer focus. Competition will always be lurking, often in unexpected forms, ready to rewrite the rules of the game.

Sustainable advantage comes from managing all three forces in harmony. Value-Centric IBP provides the choreography: integrating customer insight, corporate capability, and competitive awareness into a systematic rhythm. When it works, the result is elegant. Customers feel understood, companies grow profitably, and competitors are left scrambling to catch up. Miss a beat, though, and the music changes quickly. Customers switch with a swipe, competitors exploit the gap, and corporations stumble into irrelevance.

The lesson is simple: Don't just plan inside-out, plan outside-in and all-around.

In the dynamic dance of value, survival belongs to those who listen to the music, anticipate the steps, and never forget that the customer always leads.

Understanding the dance is essential, but advantage comes from choosing your moves, which means defining the value you will offer and the strategic position you will defend.

CHAPTER 5

Strategy as Chess: Competing on the Board of Value

Strategy without tactics is the slowest
route to victory. Tactics without
strategy is the noise before defeat.
— **Sun Tzu**, *The Art of War*

The Game Where the Rules Keep Changing

I like playing chess occasionally. It's the only meeting where silence is considered strategy.

Business competition is much like a game of chess. Each company begins with a similar set of resources: talent, technology, capital, capabilities. And like chess pieces, each has distinct strengths, limitations, and roles to play. The marketplace is the board. The customer is the prize. And the rules—cost structures, regulations, technology trends, consumer behavior—are the boundaries within which this game plays out.

But here's where the analogy becomes both illuminating and insufficient: Unlike chess, the rules of business competition are constantly changing.

Imagine a chess game where players could, on their turn, not only move a piece but modify the rules themselves. Suddenly, the king can move three spaces. Pawns can jump backward. Checkmate isn't the end of the game. The traditional player, no matter how skilled, is thrown off balance. Their mastery of the old rules becomes a limitation in this new, fluid, unpredictable game.

In business, the most transformative companies don't just play better. They play differently. They change the rules entirely.

How Market Rules Get Rewritten

Emerging technologies create new possibilities for value delivery or cost structure optimization. Cloud computing eliminated the need for companies to own their IT infrastructure. Mobile devices enabled location-based services and always-on connectivity.

Shifting customer expectations raises the bar for entire industries. Amazon's next-day delivery made "7 to 10 business days" seem antiquated across all e-commerce. Uber's transparent pricing made traditional taxi meters feel like black boxes.

Regulatory changes open new competitive possibilities or close existing ones. GDPR changed how technology companies handle customer data. Financial services deregulation enabled new business models.

Platform business models create network effects that fundamentally alter competitive dynamics. Facebook didn't just compete with other social networks. They changed how people think about connection and information sharing.

New entrants with no legacy constraints can optimize for current customer needs without being limited by previous investments or business model assumptions.

Examples of Rule-Changing Companies

Amazon changed retail rules by redefining delivery speed and customer convenience. While competitors optimized traditional store operations, Amazon built fulfillment networks that made next-day delivery the new standard.

Airbnb reimagined hospitality without owning a single room. Instead of competing with hotels on amenities, they created a new category based on authentic local experiences and peer-to-peer trust.

Tesla didn't just build electric vehicles. They redefined the automotive distribution model, skipped dealerships, and rewired customer expectations around software updates, charging infrastructure, and brand experience.

Apple turned phones into ecosystems, transforming customers into platform participants. They shifted competition from hardware specifications to integrated experiences across devices and services.

Red Oceans vs. Blue Oceans: Understanding the Battlefield

Traditional competitive strategy often leads companies into what strategists describe as "red ocean" thinking: bloody battles over the same customers with increasingly similar offerings. In traditional red ocean strategy, companies compete within the accepted boundaries of an industry by improving on the very factors that rivals already contest. Customer value is framed largely as incremental enhancement— better features, higher quality, faster delivery—while cost is managed through efficiency programs, scale effects, and lean operations.

The governing logic is a trade-off: Firms typically choose between offering more value at higher cost or lowering cost while holding value to an acceptable level. Because the industry's value drivers are taken as given, management attention gravitates to benchmarking, best practices, and share-shifting moves that squeeze cost out of the current formula rather than questioning whether the formula itself still creates distinctive value for customers.

W. Chan Kim and Renée Mauborgne's Blue Ocean Strategy provides a powerful framework for understanding how companies can escape competitive battles and create new market space. The breakthrough comes when companies shift to "value innovation": simultaneously raising customer value while lowering costs through disciplined focus. Rather than accepting trade-offs between value and cost, they eliminate factors customers don't truly value while creating new factors that address unmet needs.

The Practical Path: Build Shared Value Before Chasing Oceans

Let me be direct about something most strategy discussions gloss over: Reinventing a market and creating a true blue ocean is rare and difficult. Only a small minority of companies manage to reconstruct industry boundaries rather than compete within them.

The practical path begins earlier and much closer to home. It starts by developing a precise understanding of customer value—what outcomes specific segments truly prize—and pairing it with an equally rigorous view of the value the company realizes from serving those segments, including profitability, customer lifetime value, reference power, and learning.

Value-Centric Integrated Business Planning mirrors this progression: Fund the segments where customer value and corporate value are mutually highest, and reinvest savings from eliminated low-value activities into the capabilities that create the greatest shared value.

Blue oceans are the destination. Shared value is the compass that keeps you on course.

Treating Value as a Living System

Treating value as a living system has operational consequences that change how you actually run the business.

Discovery becomes continuous. Instead of annual surveys and sporadic focus groups, organizations instrument the experience and listen across channels: usage telemetry, service interactions, reviews, field interviews, and community feedback.

Planning shifts from rigid forecasts to dynamic learning. Integrated Business Planning no longer reconciles volume to capacity in the abstract; it reconciles value: which segments experience the greatest benefit, where the firm realizes the strongest return, and how resources should be redeployed accordingly.

Product roadmaps become vehicles for focus rather than feature accumulation. Teams visualize the current "value curve," identify which factors customers truly prize, and eliminate or reduce the rest to free resources for a small number of high-impact moves.

Supply chains become experience chains. Service levels, lead times, and inventory buffers are tiered to segment value so that the customers who value speed, certainty, or customization most receive it consistently, while the cost-to-serve remains aligned with economics.

Finance evolves from cost policing to value investing. Scorecards track perceived value, adoption, retention, expansion, referrals, and customer lifetime value by segment, and funds flow to the combinations that expand mutual value for customer and company.

From Principles to Practice:
Ten Systematic Approaches

This Section's Executive Takeaway

The key takeaway of this section is that competitive advantage comes from orchestrating a small number of reinforcing transformation levers.

For Implementation Teams

The following ten patterns provide a practical taxonomy for designing those moves and translating value innovation into capability roadmaps and execution priorities.

Understanding value as a living system is one thing. Systematically transforming that understanding into competitive advantage is another. Through analyzing successful market transformations across industries, ten distinct patterns emerge, ten systematic approaches that companies use to escape red ocean competition and create new market space. These aren't just theoretical frameworks. They're proven pathways that real companies have used to rewrite the rules of competition in their favor.

Each approach offers a different mechanism for value innovation, but all share three common characteristics that make them particularly powerful when integrated with disciplined business planning processes:

Customer Job Amplification: They make the customer's core job dramatically easier, faster, or more satisfying than any alternative. A customer job is the fundamental task or outcome the customer is trying to achieve—independent of any specific product or feature— and amplification occurs when the new solution improves that job so meaningfully that older approaches are no longer acceptable.

Cost Structure Realignment: They eliminate costs associated with factors customers don't value while investing in factors that create disproportionate customer impact.

Competitive Moat Creation: They establish sustainable advantages through network effects, switching costs, data accumulation, or ecosystem development.

These ten approaches aren't mutually exclusive. In fact, the most successful transformations orchestrate multiple approaches that reinforce each other. But understanding each mechanism individually helps you identify which levers offer the greatest potential for your specific competitive context.

Let me walk you through each transformation approach, understanding both the mechanism by which it creates value and the practical implications for implementation.

Transformation 1: Value Dimension Reconstruction

Value dimension reconstruction means competing on entirely new dimensions customers didn't realize mattered, rather than incrementally improving existing factors. For example, instead of building a "better taxi," Uber eliminated uncertainty (will one come?), friction (carrying cash), and anxiety (is this fair pricing?) while creating transparency (real-time tracking) and convenience (seamless payment).

Spotify demonstrated this approach in music by reconstructing competition entirely. Traditional music industry competition focused on catalog size, audio quality, and price per album. Spotify eliminated physical ownership and album-based purchasing while creating personalized recommendations, mood-based discovery, and collaborative playlists. The result: Spotify didn't just compete in the music industry. They redefined what music consumption could be, making customers stop thinking about owning music and start expecting instant access to anything, perfectly curated for their context.

Transformation 2: Customer Journey Redefinition

Customer journey redefinition redesigns the entire end-to-end customer job, not just individual touchpoints. The mechanism is mapping the complete customer journey from initial need recognition through outcome achievement and then eliminating steps entirely rather than just optimizing them.

Amazon transformed traditional retail's "browse-compare-decide-purchase-wait" journey into "see-want-arrives tomorrow," eliminating the entire concept of "going shopping" and making it feel antiquated. They didn't just make shopping faster. They made the distinction between wanting something and having it nearly disappear.

Tesla applied this approach to automotive purchases by transforming the traditional journey of research, dealer visits, negotiation, financing arrangement, and dealership service into a streamlined experience of online configuration, transparent pricing, direct purchase, over-the-air updates, and mobile service. Tesla eliminated the entire dealer experience, which customers consistently rated as one of the worst parts of car ownership, and transformed car buying from a dreaded negotiation into a premium technology purchase experience.

Transformation 3: Ecosystem Value Creation

Ecosystem value creation makes each product more valuable when used with others, creating network effects and switching costs that feel like benefits rather than limitations. The key is designing complementary products and partnerships that increase value exponentially rather than additively.

As previously mentioned, Apple mastered this transformation by evolving from a computer company into an ecosystem where each product enhances every other product. Device integration means iPhone + AirPods + Apple Watch + Mac work seamlessly together. Service integration through iCloud syncs everything automatically. Experience integration with handoff features lets you start tasks on one device and continue on another. Purchase integration means buy once, use everywhere for apps and media.

The switching cost isn't replacing one device. It's rebuilding an entire integrated lifestyle. Apple customers often buy products they wouldn't consider individually because they increase the value of their existing Apple products.

Let's talk again about how Salesforce does this. Salesforce demonstrated similar ecosystem power by evolving from CRM software to a platform ecosystem. Their AppExchange offers third-party applications that extend functionality. Integration hubs connect other business tools. Trailhead training increases user proficiency and platform stickiness. Customers become invested not just in Salesforce software but in the entire ecosystem of apps, customizations, integrations, and skills built around it.

Transformation 4: Experience Innovation

Experience innovation creates emotional, identity, and community value that reframes how customers think about the entire category. The mechanism is designing signature moments, rituals, and community connections that make functional benefits feel transformational.

Starbucks didn't just sell better coffee. They created a "third place" social category. Physical experience includes comfortable seating, WiFi, ambient music, and a distinctive aroma. Service ritual involves personalized ordering, name-calling, and customization options. Community building happens through local store culture, rewards programs, and seasonal experiences. Identity expression emerges when carrying a Starbucks cup becomes a lifestyle signal.

Starbucks transformed coffee from a commodity beverage into a daily ritual and social experience, creating emotional and social value that justified premium pricing even when competitors offered similar coffee quality.

Let's look at Nike again through this lens. Nike evolved this approach further by transforming from athletic equipment to inspiration and identity. Product experience delivers performance gear that makes athletes feel capable. Digital experience provides apps that track progress and celebrate achievements. Community experience includes running clubs, challenges, and social sharing. Retail experience creates stores designed as inspiration destinations, not just shopping locations. Nike customers don't just buy shoes. They buy membership in a community of athletes and the identity of someone who "Just Does It."

Transformation 5: Pricing and Business Model Innovation

Pricing and business model innovation aligns payment structure with realized customer value through subscriptions, usage-based pricing, outcome-based contracts, or creative bundling. The mechanism is charging customers in ways that feel fair and aligned with the value they receive while reducing purchase risk and capturing more value from high-usage customers.

Adobe transformed from selling expensive software licenses to subscription services. Before: $2,000-plus upfront for Creative Suite with expensive upgrades every few years. After: $20 to $50 per month for always-current software with cloud services included. This change eliminated the high upfront barrier for new customers while creating predictable revenue and enabling continuous product improvement. Customers gained always-current software, cloud storage, and collaboration features.

Rolls-Royce demonstrated outcome-based innovation with "Power by the Hour." Traditional model: Sell engines, charge separately for maintenance and parts. Power by the Hour: Airlines pay a fixed rate per flight hour while Rolls-Royce handles everything. This shifted risk from airlines to Rolls-Royce while aligning incentives: Rolls-Royce makes more money when engines are reliable and efficient, not when they break down.

Transformation 6: Risk Transfer and Assurance

Risk transfer and assurance reduces perceived customer risk through guarantees, trials, warranties, or performance-based contracts. The mechanism is taking on risks that you can manage better than customers, reducing barriers to purchase, and increasing customer confidence.

Zappos eliminated online shoe shopping risk through extraordinary return policies. A 365-day return policy means a full year to return shoes with no questions asked. Free shipping both ways eliminates any cost to try shoes or return them. 24/7 customer service is available whenever customers have concerns. Size/fit guarantees include multiple sizes available to ensure perfect fit.

Zappos took on inventory and logistics costs to eliminate customer uncertainty about fit and satisfaction. This enabled them to sell shoes online when most people thought shoes required in-person fitting, proving that strategic risk absorption can transform customer behavior and open entirely new markets.

Transformation 7: Data Network Effects and Personalization

Data network effects and personalization make products improve as more users and data flow through them, creating personalized experiences that become more valuable over time. The mechanism is collecting usage data that improves the product for all users while creating individual customer value that increases switching costs.

Netflix transformed entertainment discovery through data-driven personalization. Content recommendations improve with every view, rating, and search. Personal profiles give each family member personalized suggestions. Viewing data informs original programming decisions. Interfaces and previews adapt to individual preferences. The more you watch, the better Netflix gets at predicting what you'll enjoy. The collective viewing data helps Netflix create content audiences want before they know they want it.

Waze demonstrated community-powered network effects by creating navigation that improves through crowd-sourced data. Real-time traffic comes from user reports creating accurate traffic condition maps. Route optimization uses collective driving patterns to improve suggestions. Hazard alerts from community reports warn about accidents, police, and road conditions. Local knowledge contributions share information about business hours, prices, and conditions. Every Waze user contributes data that makes the service better for everyone while receiving personalized routing based on their travel patterns.

Transformation 8: Modularity and Platformization

Modularity and platformization recompose offerings into modules or primitives that enable customers and partners to build customized solutions. The mechanism is creating stable interfaces and self-serve provisioning that allow others to build on your platform while you capture value from the ecosystem they create.

Shopify modularized e-commerce into composable services. The core platform handles basic store setup and management. The app ecosystem provides thousands of extensions for specialized functionality. Integrated payment processing solutions simplify transactions. Fulfillment services handle warehousing and shipping. Developer tools include APIs and SDKs for custom integrations. Businesses can start simple and add capabilities as they grow, with third-party developers creating specialized solutions Shopify couldn't build economically.

Stripe demonstrated payment primitives by breaking payment processing into modular components. Payment processing handles core transaction capabilities. Billing and subscriptions manage recurring payments. Marketplace tools enable multi-party payment splitting. Financial services build on payment data. Developer APIs provide tools for custom integration. Developers can combine Stripe's modules to create exactly the payment experience their application needs without building everything from scratch.

Transformation 9: Distribution and Access Innovation

Distribution and access innovation fundamentally changes how customers discover, evaluate, and access your solution. The mechanism is bypassing traditional channels or creating new ones that reduce customer effort while improving your economics.

Zoom grew through product-led growth rather than traditional sales. Their freemium model provides full functionality for small meetings with upgrades for scale. User-driven adoption occurs when individual contributors start using Zoom then convert organizations. Meeting network effects happen when non-Zoom users join meetings and experience the product. Viral sharing through easy meeting links creates organic user acquisition. Zoom's product quality drove adoption without traditional enterprise sales processes, reducing customer acquisition costs while creating bottom-up organizational adoption.

Let's return to Tesla again. As mentioned, Tesla eliminated automotive dealerships entirely through a direct-to-consumer model. Online configuration lets customers design their car on Tesla's website. Transparent pricing eliminates negotiation and dealer markup. Experience centers provide test drives and education without sales pressure. Home delivery brings cars directly to customers. Mobile service handles maintenance and repairs at customer locations. Tesla created a premium purchase experience while capturing dealer margins and controlling the entire customer relationship.

Transformation 10: Cost-Structure and Asset Model Innovation

Cost-structure and asset model innovation delivers "good-enough plus dramatically cheaper" through fundamental redesign of production and delivery models. The mechanism is eliminating cost layers that don't create customer value while investing in automation, standardization, or asset-light models.

Dollar Shave Club, which we looked at earlier, is a great example of this. Dollar Shave Club eliminated retail distribution costs through direct-to-consumer sales. No retail markups or shelf space competition reduces costs. A subscription model creates predictable demand enabling efficient manufacturing. Simple products with few SKUs reduce complexity and inventory costs. Automated fulfillment handles recurring shipments with minimal customer service. Dollar Shave Club delivers quality razors at a fraction of traditional costs by eliminating retail distribution and simplifying the product line.

Again, let's look at Airbnb. Airbnb created a hospitality company without owning real estate. Their platform model means hosts provide accommodations while Airbnb provides technology and trust infrastructure. Variable costs through revenue sharing replace fixed property costs. Community-driven quality emerges from host and guest reviews creating quality control. Local experiences come from hosts providing authentic knowledge hotels can't match. Airbnb achieved global scale without the capital requirements of traditional hospitality companies while often providing more authentic experiences than hotels could offer.

The Orchestration Insight

Value transformation isn't about choosing between these ten levers. It's about orchestrating them systematically to create compound competitive advantages. Think guacamole: Avocado is good, but when you add lime, garlic, and salt, suddenly everyone's willing to pay extra.

The most successful companies deploy multiple levers that reinforce each other, creating value systems that competitors struggle to replicate.

Netflix combined journey redefinition (seamless streaming), data network effects (personalized recommendations), pricing innovation (subscription model), and ecosystem creation (content production) to transform entertainment consumption entirely.

Amazon orchestrated ecosystem value creation (Prime benefits), journey redefinition (one-click commerce), cost structure innovation (fulfillment automation), and platform modularity (Amazon Web Services) to become infrastructure for modern commerce.

Apple integrated ecosystem value creation (device integration), experience innovation (retail stores), risk transfer (Genius Bar support), and distribution innovation (direct relationships) to create premium technology experiences.

The key insight: Each transformation lever becomes more powerful when combined with others. Journey redefinition enables pricing innovation. Data network effects strengthen ecosystem value. Experience innovation supports premium pricing. Cost structure innovation funds investment in other transformations.

Your Strategic Path Forward

Your value transformation strategy should identify two to three primary levers that address your customers' biggest pain points while leveraging your unique capabilities, then systematically layer additional transformations that reinforce your primary advantages.

Don't try to implement all ten levers simultaneously. That's a recipe for diluted efforts and mediocre results across the board. Start with understanding which customer jobs you can make dramatically better through one or two transformation approaches. Build competitive moats around those approaches. Then systematically add complementary transformations that compound your advantages.

The companies that win aren't those with the most sophisticated strategies or the longest list of initiatives. They're the ones that execute a few transformations exceptionally well, building sustainable advantages that competitors can't easily replicate. Because in the end, strategy isn't about having the best plan. It's about changing the game in ways that make your unique strengths devastatingly effective and your competitors' traditional advantages increasingly irrelevant.

The chessboard keeps changing. The question is whether you're reacting to changes others make or creating changes that force others to react to you.

Choosing your moves on the chessboard is essential, but without a way to read the board, evaluate position, and assess momentum, even the best strategy loses its edge. This brings us to Chapter 6, which focuses on measuring customer value.

CHAPTER 6

Measuring Customer Value: A Framework for Value-Centric Segmentation

*Not everything that can be counted counts, and
not everything that counts can be counted.*
—William Bruce Cameron

When Loyalty Lies to You

Customer loyalty is often celebrated as the ultimate testimony of a company's worth and customer value measure. When customers keep coming back, it signals that something meaningful is happening, that the relationship is built on attraction, satisfaction, and trust.

But loyalty, as powerful as it is, carries two limitations that can mislead you badly if you're not careful. First, it can be deceptive. Some customers stay not because they love you, but because the cost of leaving feels too high. That's not loyalty, that's captivity. And captivity is fragile. As soon as switching costs drop or alternatives emerge, you notice your partner's suitcases by the door and the relationship ends abruptly.

Second, loyalty is a lagging indicator. By the time it shows up in renewal rates, churn statistics, or lifetime value numbers, the underlying story has been unfolding for months. A loyal customer who leaves isn't just a data point. It's an alarm bell. Something in the value equation broke, and you only noticed once it was too late.

Loyalty confirms the past, but it doesn't predict the future. This is why the true discipline lies in measuring customer value directly. Loyalty is the applause at the end of the concert; value is the music itself. If you want to keep the audience clapping, you need to understand the notes, the rhythm, and the moments that make people lean in.

This is the first trap value-centric leaders must avoid: mistaking outcomes for causes. Loyalty tells you what already happened; value measurement helps you understand what is happening now and what is likely to happen next. Everything that follows in this chapter is about shifting measurement upstream, before relationships break. Upstream value measurement is critical. It allows you to see not just who stayed, but why they stayed and more importantly, why they might leave.

The Measurement Challenge: Why This Is So Hard

The measurement of customer value represents one of the most complex challenges in business. Unlike operational metrics that track concrete activities or financial measures that quantify monetary flows, customer value exists in the perceptual realm where individual experiences, contextual factors, and dynamic expectations create measurement complexities that traditional business analytics struggle to address effectively. Let me walk you through why this is so difficult.

The Individual Nature of Value

Customer value manifests differently for each individual customer based on their unique needs, preferences, circumstances, and mental models of what constitutes valuable outcomes. Two customers purchasing identical products for similar use cases may experience dramatically different value levels based on their expectations, alternative options, and personal evaluation criteria.

Enterprise software customers demonstrate this clearly. Two companies in similar industries with comparable employee counts might evaluate the same CRM system completely differently. One might value customization capabilities and integration flexibility above all else, while another prioritizes ease of use and rapid deployment. Their value perceptions depend on internal capabilities, existing technology infrastructure, organizational culture, and strategic priorities that demographic or firmographic data cannot capture.

This individual variation requires measurement approaches that can identify and account for these differences rather than assuming homogeneous value perceptions within defined segments.

The Dynamic Nature of Value Evolution

Customer value perceptions change continuously as customer needs evolve, competitive landscapes shift, and contextual factors influence evaluation criteria. What enchanted customers yesterday may become baseline expectations today, while new value dimensions may emerge that weren't previously considered important. Put in another way: What delighted yesterday becomes today's "meh" and tomorrow's "why is this still a thing?" Value priorities shift as customers mature and markets move.

At this point, a key implication should be clear: Any measurement system that assumes stable value priorities will fail over time. Measuring customer value is not a one-time exercise. It is an ongoing capability that must evolve as customers, competitors, and contexts change.

An example of this: Early smartphone buyers valued mobile internet magic. Later, camera quality, battery life, and ecosystem integration dominated. Companies that continued measuring value using original criteria missed these evolution patterns and struggled to maintain competitive positioning.

Customer lifecycle patterns often create predictable value priority changes as customers become more sophisticated users or as their business contexts evolve. New customers might prioritize ease of implementation and learning support, while experienced customers might value advanced capabilities and customization options.

Competitive environment changes also affect value priorities as new alternatives become available or as market standards evolve. The emergence of cloud computing shifted enterprise customer priorities from ownership and control toward accessibility and scalability, requiring software vendors to adjust their value propositions and measurement approaches.

The Perceptual Reality of Value

Customer value exists in customer minds rather than in objective reality, creating measurement challenges that go beyond capturing customer opinions to understanding the cognitive processes through which customers form value judgments.

Customer perceptions may not align with objective product performance or competitive comparisons, but these perceptions determine customer behavior regardless of their relationship to measurable reality.

Brand perception demonstrates this complexity clearly. Apple customers often report high value perceptions despite paying premium prices for products that competitive analysis suggests provide equivalent or inferior functionality compared to alternatives. Here the value perception incorporates brand associations, ecosystem benefits, status considerations, and design aesthetics that objective product comparisons cannot capture.

Perceptual value measurement requires approaches that understand customer mental models rather than just capturing satisfaction ratings. This might involve qualitative research that explores customer reasoning processes, behavioral analysis that infers value perceptions from customer actions, or mixed-method approaches that combine quantitative measurement with qualitative understanding.

The Contextual Influence on Value

Customer value perceptions are significantly influenced by contextual factors including timing, circumstances, competitive alternatives, and environmental conditions that affect how customers experience and evaluate your offerings. The same product or service may create dramatically different value perceptions depending on when and how customers encounter it. For example, the hotel Wi-Fi is either life-saving or irrelevant depending on whether you present tomorrow or are already on the beach.

Business travel services demonstrate contextual influence clearly. The same hotel room might create high value perceptions for a business traveler who needs reliable internet and proximity to meetings, while creating low value for a leisure traveler who prioritizes recreational amenities and scenic location. The hotel's objective characteristics remain constant, but contextual factors determine value perceptions.

The Relative Aspect of Value

Customer value perceptions are inherently comparative, with customers evaluating your offerings against available alternatives rather than in absolute terms.

Taken together, these characteristics—individual, dynamic, perceptual, contextual, and relative—explain why simplistic dashboards consistently disappoint. Customer value cannot be captured by a single metric without losing the very insight leaders need to make better decisions.

Relative value measurement requires understanding customer consideration sets and the specific alternatives against which customers compare your offerings. B2B customers might compare you against direct competitors, internal solutions, or doing nothing, with different comparison contexts creating different value perceptions for identical offerings.

Competitive benchmarking should extend beyond feature comparisons to understand how customers perceive value trade-offs between different approaches to solving their problems.

Building a Practical Measurement Framework

This Section's Executive Takeaway

Customer value can't be managed through a single metric or survey. Leaders need an integrated view that connects perception, behavior, and economics so investment decisions are guided by what truly drives retention, growth, and competitive advantage. The purpose of measurement is not precision for its own sake, but decision-grade insight that reveals where to double down, where to fix, and where to exit.

For Implementation Teams

This section goes deeper into the specific measurement components, data sources, and analytical structures required to build this capability in practice.

Because value lives in perception and behavior, the dashboard must combine both. Surveys capture sentiment, expectation, and willingness to pay. Qualitative interviews reveal the "why" behind the numbers. Behavioral signals—adoption depth, repeat usage, expansion, referrals, renewals—demonstrate whether value is real in practice.

Financial metrics translate those signals into economics through retention, churn, and lifetime value. All of this is read through the lens of cost-to-serve, because sustainable value couples customer delight with operational discipline.

Multi-Dimensional Value Scoring

Hopefully by now you can see that customer value rarely exists as a single dimensional construct that can be measured through simple satisfaction ratings or Net Promoter Scores. Effective measurement requires multi-dimensional approaches that capture the various ways customers experience and evaluate value while providing aggregate scores that enable strategic decision-making.

This is where measurement becomes decision-grade. Multi-dimensional scoring doesn't exist to satisfy analytics teams; it exists to enable trade-offs between segments, investments, service levels, and pricing, based on what customers actually value.

Just to be clear: Multi-dimensional scoring systems should reflect the specific value dimensions that matter to your customer base rather than using generic measurement frameworks that might miss important value drivers.

A SaaS platform might measure value dimensions, including functionality completeness, ease of use, performance reliability, integration capability, support quality, and innovation pace, with different weights reflecting the relative importance of each dimension. Weighted scoring approaches enable customization for different customer segments or use cases where value dimension importance varies significantly. Enterprise customers might weight integration capability and security more heavily, while small business customers might prioritize ease of use and affordability.

Statistical approaches like factor analysis, principal component analysis, or structural equation modeling help identify underlying value constructs and validate measurement models. These approaches can reveal whether your assumed value dimensions represent distinct concepts in customer minds or whether customers perceive value through different mental models than your measurement framework assumes.

Jobs-to-Be-Done Value Mapping

Customer value measurement should begin with understanding the fundamental jobs customers are trying to accomplish and how your offerings help them achieve desired outcomes.

The most powerful framework for understanding what customers truly value emerged from Harvard Business School professor Clayton Christensen's research into why customers choose one product over another. The Jobs-to-Be-Done theory rests on a simple but profound insight: Customers don't buy products or services; they hire them to get a job done. A job represents the progress a customer wants to make in a particular context. That progress can be functional (solving a practical problem), emotional (achieving a feeling), or social (how they want to be perceived by others).

Think about the last time you bought a cup of coffee. Were you buying coffee? Perhaps. But more likely, you were buying caffeine to make the 8:00 a.m. meeting survivable.

The same product can be hired for completely different jobs by different customers or even by the same customer in different contexts. Understanding these jobs unlocks innovation opportunities that purely feature-focused thinking misses entirely.

Jobs-to-Be-Done analysis reveals value dimensions that customers might not articulate directly but that significantly influence their satisfaction and loyalty. Small business customers purchasing accounting software might describe their job as "managing financial records," but deeper analysis might reveal underlying jobs like "making confident business decisions," "reducing compliance anxiety," or "appearing professional to stakeholders."

The jobs perspective helps identify value dimensions that transcend specific product categories or competitive alternatives. Customers hiring rideshare services might be accomplishing jobs related to convenient transportation, but they might also be hiring these services for social status, environmental responsibility, or personal safety outcomes that traditional transportation analysis would miss.

From Measurement to Strategic Segmentation

This Section's Executive Takeaway

Once value is measured correctly, segmentation stops being a marketing exercise and becomes a strategic one. Customers who look similar on paper often differ radically in what they value, how they decide, and how profitable they can become. Value-based segmentation allows leadership to allocate resources, shape offerings, and design go-to-market strategies around what actually drives choice and long-term advantage.

For Implementation Teams

This section details how to translate value insight into actionable segmentation models and operational targeting.

Traditional segmentation approaches based on demographics, firmographics, or purchase history fail to predict customer behavior and lifetime value with sufficient accuracy for competitive advantage. Companies increasingly discover that customers who appear similar in traditional segmentation schemes often have dramatically different value perceptions, satisfaction levels, and growth potential.

This is the pivot point of the chapter. Once value is measured correctly, segmentation stops being a descriptive exercise ("who they are") and becomes a strategic one ("why they choose and how they decide"). Everything that follows builds on this shift.

Why Traditional Segmentation Falls Short

Most organizations still segment customers using demographic, firmographic, or geographic criteria. While these approaches tell you who your customers are, they reveal little about why they buy, what keeps them loyal, or how to serve them more effectively.

Take the enterprise software market as an example: Two Fortune 500 manufacturing companies might have identical employee counts, revenue, and geographic footprints, yet require fundamentally different value propositions.

Company A, a pharmaceutical manufacturer, values security and compliance above all else. They operate in a heavily regulated environment where data breaches can result in billion-dollar fines and product recalls. This company will pay premium prices for robust governance features, extensive audit trails, and white-glove support that ensures regulatory compliance. Their buying process involves legal, compliance, and IT security teams, often taking 12 to 18 months from initial contact to contract signature. They measure success through risk mitigation metrics: uptime percentages, security certifications, and compliance audit results.

Company B, an automotive parts manufacturer, prioritizes operational efficiency and cost reduction. They compete in commodity markets where margins are razor-thin, and every efficiency gain directly impacts profitability. This company wants streamlined functionality at competitive pricing, with fast implementation and minimal training requirements. Their buying process is led by operations and procurement teams focused on ROI calculations and implementation timelines. They measure success through operational metrics: productivity improvements, cost savings, and time-to-value.

Traditional demographic segmentation would place these companies in the same bucket, leading to generic marketing messages, inappropriate pricing strategies, and misaligned product development priorities.

Value-based segmentation reveals the fundamental differences in their needs, enabling targeted approaches that resonate with each company's actual decision criteria and success metrics.

The Power of Value-Based Segmentation

Value-based segmentation identifies what customers truly care about—speed, trust, price, experience, innovation—and groups them accordingly.

Netflix exemplifies this approach brilliantly: Rather than segmenting simply by demographics, they identify viewing behavior patterns and content preferences. Their "Binge Watchers" segment values extensive content libraries and seamless streaming experiences, while their "Casual Viewers" prioritize easy discovery and family-friendly options. This segmentation drives everything from content acquisition strategies to user interface design, enabling Netflix to serve over 230 million subscribers with highly personalized experiences.

Strategic alignment represents the first major benefit. When you understand what each customer group truly values, you can better match your offers to their priorities, leading to stronger product-market fit and more effective resource allocation.

HubSpot demonstrates this through their segmentation of marketing teams. Their "Growth-Stage Marketers" segment values scalability and automation, receiving product features focused on lead nurturing and campaign management. Their "Enterprise Marketers" segment values integration and customization, accessing advanced attribution models and custom reporting capabilities.

Pricing optimization becomes significantly more sophisticated with value-based segmentation. Rather than using one-size-fits-all pricing, you can implement value-based pricing strategies that capture fair value while respecting segment-specific price sensitivities.

Adobe's previously mentioned transition from perpetual licenses to Creative Cloud subscriptions illustrates this perfectly. They identified that professional agencies valued access to the latest features and collaborative tools, making them willing to pay monthly subscriptions for continuous updates. Individual freelancers valued cost predictability and basic functionality, leading to simplified pricing tiers. Students represented a future-value segment, receiving substantial discounts in exchange for long-term brand loyalty.

Operational focus emerges naturally from value-based segmentation, enabling clear prioritization of high-value segments for product development, marketing investment, and customer success efforts.

Competitive differentiation represents perhaps the most sustainable benefit. By understanding what different customer groups value most deeply, you can move beyond price competition and create defensible market positions.

Zoom's success during the pandemic wasn't just about video conferencing technology. It was about understanding different segments' varying needs. Their "Education" segment valued ease of use and reliability for teachers managing virtual classrooms. Their "Healthcare" segment required HIPAA compliance and advanced privacy controls. Their "Enterprise" segment needed administrative controls and integration capabilities. By serving each segment's specific needs better than generic competitors, Zoom built market leadership that extended far beyond price considerations.

Common Value-Based Segments Across Industries

While every business develops unique segments reflecting their specific market and value proposition, certain patterns emerge consistently across industries.

In consumer markets:

Price-conscious customers represent a significant segment. Walmart built a global empire by deeply understanding this segment's needs: not just low prices, but reliable value, convenient locations, and broad selection. Their "Always Low Prices" promise resonates because price-conscious customers value predictability; they want confidence that they're getting good value without spending time researching alternatives.

The key insight is that price-conscious doesn't mean cheap; these customers often have sophisticated value calculations that consider total cost of ownership, convenience, and reliability.

Quality seekers prioritize durability, craftsmanship, and reliability over price considerations. Patagonia exemplifies how to serve this segment effectively: Their customers willingly pay premium prices because they value products that last for years, support for repairs and maintenance, and alignment with environmental values.

Experience-driven customers value emotions, aesthetics, and community over functional benefits. As previously discussed, Starbucks transformed coffee from a commodity into an experience by understanding this segment's needs. Their customers aren't just buying caffeine; they're purchasing a social experience, workspace, and identity association.

Convenience-first customers prioritize speed, availability, and low effort above other considerations. Amazon Prime's success stems from deep understanding of this segment: They value time savings more than cost savings, prefer integrated solutions over best-of-breed options, and will pay premiums for reduced friction.

Identity-aligned customers seek self-expression, values alignment, and status through their purchases. Nike's success with sneaker enthusiasts demonstrates sophisticated understanding of this segment: Limited edition releases, collaborations with artists and athletes, and community-building initiatives all reinforce customers' identity and status within their peer groups.

In business-to-business markets:

Cost optimizers, typically found in mature industries or companies facing margin pressure, make decisions based on clear ROI calculations and operational efficiency improvements.

Risk minimizers, often found in heavily regulated industries like healthcare and financial services, prioritize security, compliance, and vendor stability over other considerations.

Growth accelerators, typically high-growth companies or organizations undergoing digital transformation, value scalability, time-to-market, and competitive advantage.

Innovation leaders actively seek cutting-edge capabilities that provide competitive advantages. They're willing to invest in unproven technologies and accept higher risks in exchange for potential competitive advantages.

Integration-focused customers, typically large enterprises with complex technology environments, prioritize compatibility, seamless workflows, and minimal disruption.

Implementing Measurement: Start Simple, Build Sophistication

This Section's Executive Takeaway

Perfect measurement is neither possible nor necessary. What matters is building a learning system that improves over time, moving from basic visibility to predictive insight and adaptive decision-making. Organizations that start early, even imperfectly, develop a compounding advantage in understanding customers and allocating resources ahead of competitors.

For Implementation Teams

What follows outlines a staged roadmap for building this capability, including tools, methods, and analytical maturity levels.

The key is simply to begin the journey of customer value measurement. At the start, precision isn't what matters most; momentum is. The simple act of measuring marks the beginning of understanding. Start small. Track something basic. Then refine, expand, and build sophistication over time. What begins as a rough sketch of value will gradually evolve into a detailed portrait, one that guides decisions with clarity and confidence.

Stage 1: Foundation Building

Foundation building establishes basic customer value measurement capabilities through simple, reliable approaches that provide immediate insights while building organizational confidence in measurement value.

Core Measurement Implementation: Begin with an internal assessment of the value the business believes customers are realizing. This creates a baseline mental model of customer value perceptions, essentially forming a hypothesis about what matters most to customers and how well the company thinks it delivers.

Introduce simple satisfaction measurement using established frameworks like Net Promoter Score (NPS), Customer Satisfaction (CSAT), or Customer Effort Score (CES). These approaches provide a quick baseline understanding of customer perceptions while offering comparative benchmarks against industry standards.

Basic demographic and behavioral segmentation provides initial customer grouping that enables targeted measurement analysis without requiring sophisticated analytical capabilities.

Initial Business Value Correlation: Connect customer satisfaction metrics with basic business metrics like retention rates, expansion revenue, or support ticket volume to establish proof of concept for customer value-business value relationships. Simple correlation analysis often reveals surprising insights that justify continued measurement investment.

Stage 2: Sophistication Development

Sophistication development expands measurement capabilities through multi-dimensional frameworks, enhanced analytical approaches, and integrated data collection that provides deeper customer understanding.

Multi-Dimensional Value Framework Implementation: Develop customer value measurement frameworks that capture multiple value dimensions specific to your customer base and value proposition rather than relying solely on general satisfaction measures.

As already mentioned, Jobs-to-Be-Done analysis reveals underlying customer motivations and outcome expectations that satisfaction surveys might miss. Understanding why customers choose your solution and what success looks like from their perspective enables more accurate value measurement.

Enhanced Analytical Capabilities: Statistical modeling approaches, including regression analysis, factor analysis, and cluster analysis, enable more sophisticated understanding of customer value patterns and their relationship with business outcomes.

Predictive modeling development enables forecasting of customer behavior changes based on value perception trends. Early warning systems for retention risk or expansion opportunities provide proactive relationship management capabilities.

Integration Expansion: Multi-channel measurement integration combines survey data with behavioral analytics, support interactions, and usage patterns to provide comprehensive customer understanding without requiring customers to provide all information through direct feedback.

CRM integration ensures that customer value insights reach customer-facing teams while enabling relationship management strategies that reflect value perception patterns.

Stage 3: Optimization and Adaptation

Optimization focuses on measurement framework refinement based on implementation experience while developing adaptive capabilities that enable continuous improvement as customer needs and competitive dynamics evolve.

Dynamic Measurement Adaptation: Measurement framework evolution based on customer feedback, analytical insights, and changing market conditions ensures that measurement approaches remain relevant and accurate as circumstances change.

Real-time measurement capabilities enable rapid response to customer value changes while providing continuous feedback on improvement initiative effectiveness.

Advanced Analytics Implementation: AI and machine learning approaches often provide superior predictive accuracy for complex customer value patterns compared to traditional statistical models. Advanced analytics can identify non-linear relationships and interaction effects that simpler approaches miss.

Customer lifetime value modeling that incorporates value perception trends enables more accurate customer investment decisions while providing better understanding of how value improvements translate into business outcomes over time.

The Hard Reality: Perfect Measurement Is a Myth

I will be honest and direct: You will never achieve perfect customer value measurement. Value is too individual, too dynamic, too perceptual, and too contextual to be captured perfectly by any measurement system. The complexities are real and unavoidable.

If this feels uncomfortable, that's a feature, not a flaw. Organizations that wait for certainty never develop insight; those that measure imperfectly learn faster and adapt sooner.

But perfect measurement isn't the goal. Useful measurement is the goal. Organizations that wait for perfect measurement systems never start measuring. They remain blind to customer value perceptions while competitors who measure imperfectly gain insights that drive better strategic decisions.

The organizations that win are those that start measuring despite imperfection, learn from their measurement experiences, and systematically improve their measurement capabilities over time.

Perfect measurement is a myth. Useful measurement is a competitive advantage. Aim for the latter, brag like the former.

Moving Forward: From Measurement to Advantage

Measuring customer value effectively requires acknowledging its inherent complexity while building systematic approaches that provide actionable insights for strategic decision-making. The key to success lies not in achieving perfect measurement but in developing measurement capability that evolves with your understanding of customer value. By starting with foundation-building approaches and systematically expanding sophistication over time, organizations can develop customer value measurement that drives strategic decisions, improves customer outcomes, and creates sustainable business value.

Organizations that master customer value measurement gain the ability to predict customer behavior, optimize resource allocation, and differentiate their market positioning based on deep understanding of what customers truly value.

In an increasingly competitive business environment, this capability represents a source of sustainable competitive advantage that competitors cannot easily replicate. Because in the end, you can't optimize what you don't measure. And you can't measure what you don't understand. Start with understanding—even imperfect understanding—and the optimization follows.

The music is playing. You just need to learn to hear it.

Once you can hear the music of customer value clearly, the next step is ensuring that what customers value also creates value for the business.

CHAPTER 7

Measuring Business Value Creation Beyond Revenue and Profit

*Measurement is the first step that leads to control
and eventually to improvement. If you can't
measure something, you can't understand it.
If you can't understand it, you can't control it.
If you can't control it, you can't improve it.*
—H. James Harrington

When Great Numbers Hide Bad News

In 2018, Amazon's stock price dropped 20% in a single quarter despite reporting revenue growth of 43% and beating earnings expectations. The market reaction puzzled many observers: How could such strong financial performance trigger such negative investor response?

The answer revealed a sophisticated understanding of business value that goes far beyond traditional financial metrics. Investors weren't concerned about Amazon's current financial performance. They were worried about leading indicators predicting future competitive advantage: Prime membership growth was slowing, one-day delivery infrastructure investments were increasing costs, and Amazon Web Services growth rates were moderating.

The market understood that Amazon's long-term success depended on business value dimensions that traditional accounting couldn't capture: customer ecosystem development, competitive moat strengthening, and strategic option creation.

Amazon's executives weren't surprised by the market reaction because they had spent years developing measurement systems tracking business value across multiple dimensions. They measured customer lifetime value expansion, ecosystem development metrics, operational capability improvement, and strategic option creation. They knew that Prime membership growth and delivery infrastructure investments would create compound value that quarterly financial statements couldn't reflect.

This illustrates a critical reality facing modern businesses: Traditional financial measurement systems provide essential but incomplete insights into business value creation. Companies relying solely on revenue and profit metrics often make strategic decisions that optimize short-term financial performance while destroying long-term competitive advantage.

The companies that consistently outperform markets and competitors have developed sophisticated measurement systems tracking value creation across financial, strategic, operational, innovation, and data dimensions. More importantly, they understand how different customer segments contribute to these various forms of business value, enabling systematic optimization of customer portfolios and strategic investments.

This chapter explores how to measure business value comprehensively and then systematically correlate those measurements to customer value segments, creating the foundation for Value-Centric IBP that optimizes mutual value creation.

If Chapter 6 measured value through the customer's eyes, this chapter measures it through the business's long-term survival lens. The goal isn't to replace revenue and profit. It's to keep them from blinding you to the leading indicators that determine whether you'll still have revenue and profit next year.

From Industrial Age Accounting to Strategic Value Metrics

Traditional business measurement evolved during the industrial age when competitive advantage came primarily from scale, efficiency, and resource control. Traditional accounting treats value moats like expenses and algorithms like hobbies.

Financial metrics like revenue, profit margins, and return on assets provided adequate insight into business performance because value creation was relatively straightforward: Companies that produced goods more efficiently than competitors generated superior returns.

The information age fundamentally changed value creation dynamics. Today's most valuable companies—Apple, Microsoft, Amazon, Google—create value through intangible assets, network effects, data advantages, and ecosystem development. These value creation mechanisms don't appear clearly in traditional financial statements, creating measurement gaps that can mislead strategic decision-making.

Here's the shift to hold onto: In modern markets, the most important sources of value are often invisible to traditional accounting until it's too late. That's why the rest of this chapter focuses on measuring what finance statements *don't* show clearly: moats, options, ecosystems, and capability momentum.

Leading Indicators vs. Lagging Indicators: The Critical Distinction

The fundamental principle of effective business value measurement is understanding the difference between leading indicators that predict future performance and lagging indicators that confirm past results. Leading indicators are the weather forecast. Lagging indicators are the puddles in your shoes. Use both: Steer with the windshield, not the rearview mirror, but keep the mirror, because of the auditors.

Leading indicators provide early signals of value creation trends, enabling proactive management decisions. Net Promoter Score and usage engagement predict future revenue and retention before they appear in financial results. Win/loss rates, time to close, and premium pricing sustainability predict market share changes before they show up in revenue reports.

Lagging indicators confirm value creation results and validate strategic decisions. Revenue growth, profit margins, ROIC, and stock price performance demonstrate cumulative impact. Market share changes, retention, and competitive displacement confirm positioning effectiveness. Quality scores, cost per unit, and delivery performance validate operational capability development.

Leading indicators enable course correction; lagging indicators provide accountability. This distinction is the difference between steering and post-mortems. Lagging indicators tell you what happened; leading indicators tell you what's about to happen, so you can intervene while you still have choices.

The Strategic Risk of Traditional Metrics

Here's what makes traditional metrics dangerous: They can show great performance while your competitive position quietly deteriorates.

Cutting R&D can juice margins now while starving tomorrow. Yes, profits go up. So does your risk of becoming irrelevant. Reducing service costs may improve this quarter's operating line while quietly torching lifetime value. Minimizing platform investment may please finance and terrify anyone who understands network effects.

I've watched companies report record profits while their competitive moats eroded. The numbers looked great until suddenly they didn't, and by then it was too late to rebuild what had been destroyed.

This is why "good numbers" can be a false sense of security. If your metrics reward short-term performance while your moat is thinning, your dashboards will look healthiest right before the business becomes vulnerable.

The Multi-Dimensional Reality of Modern Business Value

Business value measurement must capture the complete economic impact of customer relationships including revenue generation, cost implications, strategic benefits, and risk factors affecting long-term organizational success. Traditional metrics like customer lifetime value provide foundations but often miss important value dimensions that comprehensive analysis requires.

Financial Value Components: All Dollars Are Not Created Equal

Direct financial value includes revenue generation, profitability, and cash flow impacts that customers create through their purchasing behavior and payment patterns. However, comprehensive business value assessment requires understanding indirect financial impacts that might not appear in traditional customer accounting.

All dollars are not created equal. Some arrive predictably; others show up late and eat all the snacks.

Revenue quality varies significantly between customers based on predictability, growth potential, and margin characteristics.

Subscription customers often provide higher quality revenue than transaction customers due to predictability and lower acquisition costs, while enterprise customers might provide higher margin revenue than small business customers.

Cost-to-serve variations can dramatically affect customer profitability even when revenue appears similar. High-maintenance customers requiring extensive support, custom development, or special handling might generate lower net value despite higher gross revenue. You may think you got a "whale" customer, but in reality sometimes it's just a very expensive goldfish. Understanding these cost patterns enables more accurate business value assessment.

Payment behavior affects cash flow and financial risk in ways that traditional revenue metrics don't capture. Customers who pay quickly, require minimal collections effort, and maintain consistent payment patterns provide higher business value than customers who create administrative overhead and cash flow uncertainty.

Strategic Value Assessment: The Invisible Multipliers

Strategic value encompasses the indirect benefits that customers provide beyond direct financial impact, including market position enhancement, competitive intelligence, innovation catalysts, and reference value that supports broader business objectives.

Market influence varies dramatically between customers with some providing disproportionate impact on market perceptions, competitive positioning, and ecosystem development. A few good logos can reshape category perception.

Technology companies often find that certain high-profile customers provide strategic value, exceeding their direct financial contribution through market validation and competitive advantages.

Innovation partnership potential represents strategic value for customers who can provide product development insights, testing opportunities, or co-innovation capabilities that enhance organizational competitiveness. These relationships often provide value extending beyond the specific customer relationship to benefit the entire customer base.

Reference and advocacy value includes the marketing and sales benefits that satisfied customers provide through testimonials, case studies, referrals, and word-of-mouth marketing. Some customers provide significant business value through their advocacy activities even when their direct purchasing is relatively modest.

Ecosystem effects occur when certain customers attract other valuable customers or enable platform network effects creating value beyond individual relationships. Platform businesses often find that certain customers provide disproportionate strategic value through their ability to attract complementary participants.

Risk and Sustainability Factors: What Keeps You Up at Night

Business value assessment should include risk factors affecting the sustainability and predictability of customer value creation. High-risk customers might provide lower long-term business value even when short-term financial returns appear attractive.

Concentration risk affects business value when individual customers represent disproportionate shares of revenue, making the organization vulnerable to relationship changes or customer business problems. If one customer sneezes and you catch a cold, you might be overexposed.

Diversification benefits often make smaller customers more valuable than their direct financial contribution might suggest.

Competitive vulnerability varies between customers based on their switching costs, satisfaction levels, and alternative options. Customers who are vulnerable to competitive displacement provide lower business value because of the uncertainty and potential replacement costs they represent.

Economic sensitivity affects customer business value during market downturns or industry contractions. Customers in recession-resistant industries or with stable business models might provide higher long-term value than customers in cyclical or volatile markets.

Establishing Comprehensive Business Value Measurement Process

This Section's Executive Takeaway

Modern business value is driven by leading indicators—moats, ecosystem strength, capability momentum, and strategic optionality—not just revenue and margin. Leaders must ensure their organizations are measuring what predicts future advantage, not just what reports past performance, and aligning decisions with segments that create both customer and business value over time.

For Implementation Teams

This section goes deeper into the data foundations, indicator systems, analytical methods, and governance required to operationalize multidimensional business value measurement in practice.

Understanding the multiple dimensions of business value is one thing. Building systematic processes to measure them reliably is another, and it's where most organizations struggle. The measurement challenge isn't just technical. It requires data infrastructure, analytical capability, organizational alignment, and sustained commitment to tracking metrics that traditional accounting systems ignore. But the organizations that build these capabilities create competitive advantages that compound over time.

Building the Data Foundation

Effective business value measurement starts with establishing data collection systems that capture information across all value dimensions: financial, strategic, operational, and risk factors. This requires integrating data from multiple sources that traditionally operate independently:

- Customer relationship management systems track interaction history and satisfaction metrics.

- Enterprise resource planning systems capture transaction patterns and profitability.

- Support systems reveal cost-to-serve patterns.

- Product usage analytics show engagement and adoption trends. Market research provides competitive positioning insights.

The challenge is creating unified customer records that combine these disparate data sources into comprehensive profiles showing both what customers buy and how they create multidimensional value. Many organizations discover their current systems can't provide the data integration needed for sophisticated business value assessment.

Start with what you can measure today, even if incomplete. Revenue quality metrics like contract duration, renewal rates, and expansion patterns provide foundational insights. Cost-to-serve analysis combining support tickets, customization requests, and payment behavior adds profitability context. Reference activity tracking through case study participation, referral generation, and advocacy actions captures strategic value dimensions.

Build incrementally toward comprehensive measurement rather than waiting for perfect data availability.

Implementing Leading Indicator Tracking

Leading indicators require continuous monitoring rather than periodic reporting. Traditional quarterly business reviews reveal trends too late for proactive management. By the time retention problems show up in churn reports, you've already lost customers.

Effective leading indicator systems track early warning signals across multiple dimensions:

Customer engagement metrics reveal satisfaction trends before they affect retention. Product usage frequency, feature adoption rates, support interaction sentiment, and community participation patterns all predict future relationship health. Declining engagement often precedes churn by quarters, providing intervention opportunities that reactive metrics miss.

Competitive positioning indicators track relative value perception and vulnerability to displacement. Win/loss analysis, pricing pressure patterns, feature comparison requests, and alternative evaluation activities reveal competitive threats before they materialize in lost business. Understanding why you win or lose provides strategic intelligence that revenue reports can't capture.

Strategic value signals identify customers providing disproportionate non-financial value. Reference activity levels, innovation collaboration engagement, ecosystem participation, and market influence indicators reveal strategic relationships worth protecting even when direct financial returns appear modest.

The measurement cadence should match decision-making rhythms. Weekly tracking for operational metrics enables immediate intervention. Monthly review for tactical indicators guides resource allocation adjustments. Quarterly assessment for strategic patterns informs capability investment decisions.

Developing Analytical Capabilities

Raw measurement produces data. Analytical capabilities transform data into insights that drive better decisions.

The correlation challenge requires understanding relationships between customer value delivery and business value creation while accounting for time delays, non-linear effects, and multiple influencing factors. Simple correlation analysis often misleads because customer value improvements take months or years to translate into measurable business value changes.

Cohort analysis enables temporal relationship assessment by tracking how customer value changes affect business outcomes over time for specific customer groups. This approach identifies the time horizons required for customer value improvements to generate business value returns, which is essential for evaluating investment effectiveness and setting realistic expectations.

Predictive modeling transforms historical patterns into forward-looking insights. Machine learning approaches often provide superior accuracy for complex customer value-business value relationships compared to traditional statistical models. Random forest algorithms, neural networks, and ensemble modeling can capture non-linear relationships and interaction effects that linear models miss.

Build models that forecast business value from customer value signals. Validate predictions using holdout samples and time-based testing that ensure models can predict future outcomes rather than just fitting historical data. If a model can't predict the past accurately, it won't predict the future reliably.

Feature engineering improves predictive accuracy by creating derived variables that capture customer value patterns more effectively than raw measurements. Trend calculations reveal trajectory rather than just current state. Ratio variables compare performance across dimensions. Interaction terms capture how multiple factors combine to influence outcomes.

The goal isn't analytical sophistication for its own sake. It's building prediction capabilities that enable proactive management based on leading indicators rather than reactive responses to lagging results.

Creating Organizational Alignment

The hardest part of establishing business value measurement isn't technical. It's organizational. Different functions optimize for different outcomes, creating measurement conflicts that undermine systematic value optimization. Finance focuses on revenue, margins, and cash flow, traditional metrics deeply embedded in accounting systems and management processes. Sales optimizes for deal closure and revenue attainment, often prioritizing transaction value over customer lifetime value. Customer success emphasizes satisfaction and retention metrics that might conflict with profitability targets. Product teams track feature adoption and usage engagement without always connecting to business value creation.

These functional perspectives aren't wrong. They're incomplete. Comprehensive business value measurement requires integrating insights across functional boundaries to reveal how different value dimensions interact and compound.

This demands executive sponsorship that elevates business value measurement beyond functional silos. Someone senior must own the question: "What is this customer relationship actually worth to our business across all dimensions?" That ownership enables the difficult conversations about measurement methodology, data integration requirements, and strategic trade-offs that comprehensive value assessment demands.

Start with pilot programs demonstrating value before scaling enterprise-wide. Select customer segments where comprehensive measurement can reveal insights that traditional metrics miss. Build proof points showing how multidimensional value assessment improves resource allocation decisions, retention strategies, or portfolio optimization. Use those successes to build organizational momentum toward comprehensive adoption.

Implementing Continuous Improvement

Business value measurement isn't a one-time project. It's an ongoing capability requiring continuous refinement as markets evolve, competitive dynamics shift, and organizational strategies adapt.

Measurement methodologies should evolve based on analytical learning and strategic requirements. Regular reviews assess whether current metrics still predict business outcomes effectively. Measurement frameworks adjust as new value dimensions emerge or existing dimensions lose predictive power.

Data quality improvement never ends. Automated validation catches inconsistencies and anomalies. Regular audits verify measurement accuracy across data sources. Continuous enhancement expands coverage of value dimensions and customer segments.

Analytical model updates maintain prediction accuracy as customer behaviors and market conditions change. Quarterly retraining using recent data prevents model drift. Annual comprehensive reviews evaluate whether fundamental model architecture still captures current value creation dynamics.

The organizations that build sustainable competitive advantages through business value measurement treat it as a core capability requiring ongoing investment and continuous improvement, not a project with an end date.

The Customer-Business Value Matrix: Where Strategy Gets Real

Understanding these multiple dimensions of business value and establishing measurement systems to track them is necessary but not sufficient for strategic advantage. The critical insight comes from recognizing that business value and customer value are two distinct dimensions that don't always align and that the intersection between them determines strategic positioning and competitive sustainability.

Up to here, we've been building measurement capability. Now we turn measurement into strategy. The matrix that follows is where customer value (what they feel) and business value (what you capture) intersect, and that intersection determines which relationships you protect, which you fix, which you monetize, and which you stop funding.

In 2019, Uber faced a strategic crisis hidden within their explosive growth numbers. While they had successfully created high customer value through convenient, affordable transportation, they were simultaneously destroying business value through unsustainable unit economics. Every ride generated customer satisfaction but company losses. The fundamental misalignment between customer value delivery and business value capture was burning through billions in investor capital.

Meanwhile, Apple was demonstrating the opposite dynamic with their services business. App store customers received high value through curated app access and seamless integration, while Apple captured 30% margins with minimal incremental costs. High customer value aligned perfectly with high business value, creating sustainable competitive advantage that strengthened over time.

These contrasting examples illustrate a critical strategic reality that most companies struggle to navigate: Not all customer value creation is equally valuable to the business, and not all business value capture is sustainable without genuine customer value delivery.

Some companies create high customer value while destroying business value, burning cash to delight customers in unsustainable ways. Others capture high business value while delivering low customer value, exploiting customers through lock-in and limited alternatives until disruption inevitably arrives. The companies that achieve lasting competitive advantage systematically identify and optimize the intersection where high customer value and high business value reinforce each other.

This requires moving beyond measuring business value in isolation to understanding how different customer segments simultaneously create value for customers and capture value for the business. The framework for this strategic analysis is the Customer-Business Value Matrix, a tool that plots customer segments across two dimensions to reveal where sustainable competitive advantage actually lives and how to systematically optimize your customer portfolio.

The Framework: Two Dimensions That Matter

The Customer-Business Value Matrix plots customer segments based on two critical dimensions:

Customer Value (Y-Axis): The total value customers believe they receive across functional, emotional, social, and future security dimensions, minus the total costs they invest in price, time, effort, and risk. This represents the customer's perception of net value delivered.

Business Value (X-Axis): The total value the company captures across financial returns, strategic positioning, competitive advantages, learning opportunities, and capability development. This represents the company's comprehensive return on investment.

This framework creates four distinct strategic quadrants, each requiring different capability development priorities and Value-Centric IBP management approaches.

Quadrant I: Value Partners (High Customer Value / High Business Value)

You are in a healthy and loving relationship.

These are the customers who adore you and make your CFO smile. These customers perceive high value from your offerings while generating significant business value through their relationships. Value Partners represent the ideal customer relationships that should receive premium investment and protection efforts.

Value Partners often become reference customers, innovation partners, and growth catalysts, providing value beyond their direct financial contribution. These relationships require consistent investment in relationship quality, capability development, and value delivery enhancement to maintain their strategic position.

Strategic Significance: These represent the optimal position where customer delight systematically generates superior business returns. Activities in this quadrant create customer experiences so valuable that customers willingly pay premium prices while the business captures multiple forms of value simultaneously.

Competitive Characteristics:

- High customer lifetime value with expanding usage over time

- Premium pricing power that customers accept willingly

- Multiple revenue streams from single customer relationships

- Competitive advantages that strengthen with scale and usage

- Network effects and ecosystem development potential

- Low customer acquisition costs through organic referrals and advocacy

Protection strategies for Value Partners should focus on preventing competitive displacement while expanding relationship depth and breadth. Account management intensity, executive engagement, and proactive service delivery help maintain these critical relationships.

Quadrant II: Retention Risk (Low Customer Value / High Business Value)

They're the partner who says, "We need to talk."

Translation: You are about to be dumped. Do something!

These customers make you money but don't feel much love back. These customers generate significant business value despite perceiving relatively low value from your offerings. Retention Risk relationships represent significant improvement potential but also competitive vulnerability.

Retention Risk customers often indicate value delivery problems or competitive disadvantages requiring immediate attention. Their high business value justifies investment in value improvement initiatives, but their low customer value perception creates retention risk requiring urgent action.

Strategic Significance: These generate significant business returns but provide limited customer value relative to alternatives. While profitable in the short term, they are strategically vulnerable because they depend on customer lock-in, limited alternatives, or market inefficiencies rather than genuine value creation.

Competitive Characteristics:

- High short-term profitability and cash generation

- Customer retention through switching costs rather than satisfaction

- Vulnerability to competitive disruption from higher-value alternatives

- Declining customer satisfaction and engagement over time

- Defensive rather than offensive competitive positioning

- Limited growth potential due to customer resistance and market maturity

Improvement strategies should focus on understanding and addressing the specific value gaps creating low customer value perception while maintaining the business value they currently provide. Value delivery enhancement, service improvement, and competitive differentiation might convert Retention Risk into Value Partners.

Quadrant III: Margin Diluters (High Customer Value / Low Business Value)

You're in a one-sided relationship. They're thrilled; you're drained. How does that feel?

These customers perceive high value from your offerings but generate relatively low business value due to size, profitability, or strategic limitations. Margin Diluters represent relationships that provide satisfaction and advocacy benefits without significant financial returns.

Margin Diluters often provide strategic value through reference activities, market validation, and ecosystem effects that might justify continued investment despite low direct business value. However, their low business value requires efficient service approaches that maintain satisfaction without excessive cost.

Strategic Significance: These customers have significant customer satisfaction and loyalty but fail to generate proportional business returns. While customers love these offerings, the business model fails to capture adequate value from the customer satisfaction created.

Competitive Characteristics:

- High customer satisfaction scores and Net Promoter Scores
- Strong customer retention and engagement metrics
- Difficulty generating profitable revenue streams
- Unsustainable cost structures relative to direct revenue generation
- High customer acquisition costs relative to monetization capability
- Vulnerability to competitive attack from better-monetized alternatives

Optimization strategies should focus on increasing business value through expansion opportunities, service efficiency improvements, or strategic value enhancement. Some Margin Diluters might transition to Value Partners through business growth or relationship development.

Quadrant IV: Value Destroyers (Low Customer Value / Low Business Value)

You are in a relationship and both of you do not know why! Nobody's happy.

These customers perceive low value while generating low business value, representing the least attractive relationships in your customer portfolio. Value Destroyers require careful evaluation to determine whether improvement or disinvestment provides better strategic outcomes.

Value Destroyers might result from poor market fit, competitive disadvantages, or service delivery problems creating mutual dissatisfaction. Some might be recoverable through targeted improvement efforts, while others might require relationship termination to optimize resource allocation.

Strategic Significance: These customers fail to create value for either themselves or the business. They represent strategic dead-ends that consume resources without generating returns for any stakeholder and require immediate strategic attention.

Competitive Characteristics:

- Low customer satisfaction and high churn rates

- Negative or minimal business returns on invested resources

- Resource consumption without value creation for any stakeholder

- Competitive disadvantage in customer acquisition and retention

- Limited strategic options for improvement without fundamental restructuring

- Clear candidates for elimination or complete business model transformation

Decision frameworks should evaluate improvement potential, resource requirements, and opportunity costs to determine optimal strategies for Value Destroyers. Some might benefit from service level reduction, pricing adjustments, or migration to self-service models that reduce cost-to-serve while maintaining minimal relationship value.

The Correlation Challenge: Time, Complexity, and Prediction

This Section's Executive Takeaway

Value creation and value capture are separated by time, not accounting periods. The most important strategic investments often look unattractive in early quarters, only becoming decisive later through compounding effects. Leaders must therefore champion measurement systems that make long-term value visible—or risk killing the very initiatives that would have created enduring advantage.

For Implementation Teams

This section addresses the analytical rigor required to model time lags, non-linear effects, and predictive relationships between customer value and business value.

Understanding the relationship between customer value perceptions and business value creation requires sophisticated analytical approaches that can handle time delays, non-linear relationships, and multiple influencing factors.

Time Lag Consideration: Planting Trees Takes Time

Customer value improvements often require months or years to translate into measurable business value changes, creating analytical challenges for correlation analysis that must account for temporal relationships rather than assuming immediate impacts. In other words, planting trees now may not create shade by Friday.

Investment recovery periods vary based on the type of customer value improvement and the customer segment characteristics. Enhanced onboarding experiences might show business value impact within quarters, while product development improvements might require years to demonstrate full business value through customer expansion and retention.

Leading indicator identification helps predict business value changes before they manifest in financial metrics. Customer satisfaction improvements, engagement increases, or value perception enhancements might predict future business value changes that correlation analysis can model.

Cohort analysis enables temporal correlation assessment by tracking how customer value changes affect business outcomes over time for specific customer groups. This approach helps identify the time horizons required for customer value improvements to generate business value returns.

Predictive Modeling Development: Looking Forward, Not Just Back

Correlation analysis should enable predictive modeling that can forecast business value changes based on customer value measurement results. These models enable proactive management of customer relationships and resource allocation optimization based on predicted rather than just historical outcomes.

Machine learning approaches often provide superior predictive accuracy for complex customer value-business value relationships compared to traditional statistical models. Random forest, neural network, and ensemble modeling approaches can capture non-linear relationships and interaction effects that linear models miss.

Build models that forecast business value from different customer value segments. Validate out-of-sample and over time. If a model can't predict the past, it's not shy; it's wrong.

Model validation requires testing predictive accuracy using holdout samples or time-based validation approaches that ensure models can predict future outcomes rather than just fitting historical data.

Feature engineering might improve predictive accuracy by creating derived variables that capture customer value patterns more effectively than raw measurement data. Trend calculations, ratio variables, and interaction terms often improve model performance for customer value prediction.

If this feels like more rigor than most organizations apply today, good. That's the point. The matrix is demanding because the trade-offs are real, and the companies that face them early win.

Making This Actually Work

This Section's Executive Takeaway

Measuring business value at this level is not an analytics project; it is an enterprise capability that requires ownership, cross-functional alignment, and sustained executive sponsorship. Without this, even the best models will never change decisions.

For Implementation Teams

This section details the operating cadence, governance, data confidence, and change-management disciplines required to embed the Customer-Business Value Matrix into real planning and investment processes.

Let me be direct about something: Implementing the Customer-Business Value Matrix isn't a weekend project. It requires systematic customer scoring and placement using consistent methodologies that enable reliable quadrant assignment while accounting for measurement uncertainty and temporal variation. Statistical confidence intervals and placement stability analysis help ensure matrix reliability.

You need data infrastructure capturing both customer value perceptions and business value metrics at sufficient granularity to enable meaningful segmentation. Many companies discover their current systems can't provide the data needed for sophisticated correlation analysis.

You need organizational alignment around using the matrix for resource allocation decisions. Finance wants to optimize revenue. Sales wants to close deals. Customer success wants to help everyone. The matrix requires making difficult trade-offs that not everyone will initially support.

But the organizations that build these capabilities create competitive advantages that compound over time. They systematically migrate customers toward Value Partner status. They identify and address Retention Risk vulnerabilities before competitors exploit them. They optimize Margin Diluter relationships for efficiency or conversion. They make data-driven decisions about Value Destroyer relationships.

Moving Forward: The Integration Challenge

Business value extends far beyond financial metrics to include strategic positioning, operational excellence, innovation capability, and data advantages. Comprehensive measurement across all dimensions enables better strategic decisions and competitive advantage development.

Revenue and profit tell you how you did. Value metrics tell you whether you'll still be around to brag about it.

Different segments contribute different types and levels of value. The Customer-Business Value Matrix aligns resource allocation with mutual value creation, expanding Partners, converting Retention Risks, monetizing Diluters, and pruning Destroyers.

Monitor quadrant populations, migrations, and portfolio returns. Adjust strategies as evidence evolves. The matrix isn't static. Customer positions change based on your actions, competitive moves, and market evolution.

Integrating this matrix with Value-Centric IBP turns planning from rearview reporting into proactive advantage-building. Product planning prioritizes features for Value Partners. Demand planning forecasts segment-specific patterns. Supply planning differentiates service levels by quadrant. Financial planning optimizes investment across the portfolio. Do that consistently and your leading indicators won't just predict success; they'll compound it.

Because in the end, sustainable competitive advantage comes from systematically optimizing the intersection of customer value delivery and business value capture. The companies that measure both dimensions comprehensively and act on those insights will consistently outperform those that optimize revenue and profit alone.

Seeing where customers sit in the matrix is diagnostic; shifting their position is strategic. Chapter 8 explores how companies design deliberate customer migration strategies that increase mutual value while pruning relationships that erode it.

Customer Migration Strategies: Moving Customers to Value Partner Status and Strategic Value Portfolio Pruning

The art of leadership is saying no,
not yes. It is very easy to say yes.
—Tony Blair

The Discovery That Changed Everything

In the mid-2000s, Salesforce's analytics team uncovered a surprising pattern. Traditional customer characteristics—company size, industry, or contract value—were poor predictors of retention and expansion. Instead, the most valuable customers shared one behavioral trait: They integrated Salesforce with multiple complementary applications.

The numbers told the story. Customers using three or more integrated applications had retention rates above 95%, expanded their Salesforce usage three to five times faster, and referred new business at much higher rates than isolated CRM users. These integrations transformed Salesforce from a departmental tool into critical infrastructure, making competitive displacement almost impossible.

The strategic response was bold. In 2005, Salesforce launched AppExchange, the first on-demand business application marketplace. By making integration as easy as installing an app, Salesforce empowered customers to tailor solutions, partners to reach new markets, and itself to capture higher retention, faster growth, and greater competitive resilience.

The results validated the strategy:

- By 2008, AppExchange hosted 800-plus apps; by 2012, over 2,000 apps with retention rates above 95%.

- By 2020, the ecosystem grew to 5,000-plus apps and 10 million installations, generating billions in partner revenue.

- Integrated customers delivered three to five times higher lifetime value and were effectively locked in, not by constraint, but by the real benefits of ecosystem integration.

The AppExchange story reveals a truth that challenges much conventional business thinking: Sustainable competitive advantage often comes from systematically identifying and amplifying the intersection where customer value delivery and business value capture reinforce each other.

Salesforce didn't just build better CRM features. They created an ecosystem where helping customers solve more problems through integration simultaneously made those customers more valuable and more loyal. They turned customer success into competitive advantage through systematic capability building around proven value patterns.

When the Data Tells You to Let Customers Go

In 2007, Sprint faced a customer service crisis that perfectly illustrated the Value Destroyer quadrant. Analysis revealed that approximately 1,000 subscribers (less than 0.02% of their customer base) were generating a disproportionate share of customer service costs through excessive support calls.

These customers weren't just unprofitable. They were actively destroying value across multiple dimensions. Their constant service demands consumed support resources that could serve other customers. They frustrated customer service representatives, contributing to employee turnover. Their complaints amplified on social media and forums, damaging Sprint's brand. Most critically, the support capacity they consumed degraded service quality for the broader customer base.

Sprint's analysis was sound: These relationships were economically impossible to maintain. Despite extensive support interventions, premium service offers, and technical solutions, the call patterns persisted. The customers weren't satisfied. Sprint couldn't serve them profitably. The broader customer base suffered from degraded service capacity.

Sprint made a decisive decision: They sent letters to roughly 1,000 customers, professionally terminating their contracts and encouraging them to find providers better suited to their needs.

The public reaction was swift and devastating. Media coverage focused on the customer rejection angle: "Sprint Fires Customers," "Wireless Provider Tells Subscribers to Get Lost." The story became a viral example of corporate insensitivity. Sprint's brand took significant reputational damage that persisted for years.

Sprint's strategic reasoning was correct: These relationships destroyed value for all parties. Their execution was disastrous. The public communication created a PR nightmare that overshadowed sound analysis. The story became about "firing customers" rather than "optimizing mutual value creation."

The lesson: Value Destroyer relationships often require decisive action, but that action must be executed with professionalism, discretion, and strategic sophistication.

Around the same time, Best Buy faced a similar challenge with more strategic sophistication. In 2004, CEO Brad Anderson publicly acknowledged that Best Buy had identified customers they internally called "devil customers," shoppers systematically destroying shareholder value despite generating sales revenue.

Best Buy's analytics revealed that approximately 20% of customers generated the majority of profits (their "angels"), while another 20% destroyed value through behaviors that made serving them economically impossible. These "devil customers" engaged in systematic practices that exploited Best Buy's service model: serial returners who treated Best Buy as a free rental service, cherry-picking deal hunters who bought only loss-leader items, and extreme rebate manipulators who consumed extensive support resources while generating minimal profit.

The analysis showed these customers consumed disproportionate resources through return processing, rebate support, and inventory disruption while providing revenue but negative margins when costs were properly allocated.

Best Buy's response differed fundamentally from Sprint's approach. Rather than terminating customers publicly, they implemented a sophisticated multi-year strategy to optimize their customer portfolio through systematic differentiation.

The crucial difference: Best Buy never publicly "fired" customers. They made their stores, marketing, and service models progressively more attractive to profitable customers and progressively less attractive to unprofitable ones, allowing natural customer migration rather than forced termination.

The results validated the approach. Between 2003 and 2008, Best Buy's revenue grew from $27.4 billion to $45.0 billion while gross margin percentage increased from 23.9% to 24.8%, indicating they were growing revenue while simultaneously improving customer mix quality. Customer satisfaction increased for profitable segments as resources shifted toward "angel" customers. "Devil customer" behaviors declined naturally as unprofitable segments gradually migrated to competitors offering the deep discounts and loose return policies they sought.

Most significantly, Best Buy achieved portfolio optimization without reputational damage. While Sprint became a cautionary tale, Best Buy's customer-centricity strategy strengthened their competitive position and contributed to surviving Amazon's disruption when many analysts predicted their demise.

This chapter explores the sophisticated strategies and systematic processes for customer portfolio optimization, both the growth strategies for migrating existing customers toward Value Partner status and the equally important discipline of strategic customer redirection, i.e., "pruning," when mutual value creation isn't achievable.

The Hidden Costs of Serving Everyone

Most companies measure customer relationships primarily through revenue metrics: monthly recurring revenue, average contract value, and customer lifetime value calculated on revenue alone. This narrow focus obscures the true economics of customer relationships and often leads to strategic decisions that optimize for revenue growth while destroying long-term competitive advantage.

Trying to serve everyone is how you end up serving no one particularly well, like a restaurant attempting sushi and Texas BBQ out of the same fryer. Low-value customers overconsume resources. High-value customers quietly wonder if the grass is greener. Product roadmaps drift toward the loudest voices instead of the most valuable outcomes. Feature bloat ensues. Nobody's thrilled.

Companies that fail to optimize their customer portfolios systematically face a series of compounding strategic disadvantages that become more severe over time. Let's look into those disadvantages.

Resource dilution across mismatched customers forces your best people to spend time on customers who can never achieve mutual value creation. Your customer success team becomes glorified technical support for customers who won't expand. Your product team builds features for customers who will churn anyway. Your executives spend strategic thinking time on accounts that will never be strategic.

Product roadmap drift toward low-value customers happens because these customers complain the loudest about missing features. They're unsatisfied, so they're vocal. Meanwhile, your Value Partners quietly use your product effectively and don't demand much. If you're not careful, you optimize your product for customers who will never be happy while neglecting those who are already succeeding.

Competitive positioning erosion occurs when trying to serve everyone forces you to compromise on the distinctive capabilities that make you valuable to your best customers. You can't be the premium solution and the budget solution. You can't be the enterprise-grade platform and the simple tool for beginners. Trying to be both means you're neither.

Brand confusion in the market results from mixed customer experiences. When Value Partners rave about your solution while Value Destroyers complain publicly, prospects don't know what to believe. Your brand becomes muddled rather than clear and distinctive.

Team morale degradation happens when talented people spend their days fighting losing battles with customers who can't succeed. Customer success managers become cynical. Product managers become frustrated. Sales teams become demoralized closing deals they know won't work out.

Finding More Value Partners: The Systematic Approach

The most successful customer portfolio optimization starts with understanding what makes Value Partner relationships work and then systematically finding more customers with those characteristics.

The Anatomy of Mutual Value Creation

Value Partners aren't just satisfied customers or high-revenue accounts. They represent a specific type of customer relationship where the value equation works optimally for both parties.

Value Partners typically generate three to five times higher lifetime value than average customers through higher retention, expansion, and referral rates. They provide market credibility, competitive intelligence, and innovation insights that benefit your entire business strategy. They require less support relative to revenue generated and provide valuable feedback that improves products for all customers.

But what actually makes someone a Value Partner?

Value Partners hire your solution to solve jobs that are critical to their success, where failure has significant consequences and success creates substantial benefits. They're not experimenting or trying something nice-to-have. They need what you do to work.

They have organizational characteristics that enable them to maximize value from your solution while minimizing implementation friction. They have the technical sophistication, organizational processes, and cultural attitudes that let them use your product effectively.

They understand and appreciate the total value your solution provides, not just obvious functional benefits. They recognize subtle advantages and are willing to pay for superior outcomes.

They have characteristics that indicate potential for expanding relationships and creating strategic value beyond immediate transactions. They're growing, they're sophisticated, and they see you as a strategic capability rather than a tactical tool.

Market Intelligence and Target Identification

This Section's Executive Takeaway

Portfolio optimization is a growth strategy, not a cleanup exercise. The goal is to deliberately acquire and protect Value Partners—customers where retention, expansion, and advocacy compound—while avoiding patterns that dilute focus and erode differentiation.

For Implementation Teams

This section goes deeper into the practical targeting, scoring, and go-to-market motions that help you identify Value Partner candidates early and build a repeatable pipeline of high-fit customers.

The first step in finding more Value Partners is understanding exactly what characteristics predict Value Partner potential before someone becomes a customer. Use predictive analytics to identify prospects that mirror the characteristics of your best Value Partners and apply propensity models to score them based on their likelihood of delivering similar long-term value.

From there, craft marketing messages and content that speak directly to Value Partner priorities, distribute them through the channels most likely to reach high-potential buyers, and reinforce credibility with thought-leadership pieces that attract prospects who already share a Partner mindset.

Support this with lead-generation campaigns designed to surface Value Partner-like behaviors, then qualify and prioritize those leads through a systematic scoring process that ensures sales teams focus first on the prospects with the greatest potential to become high-value, loyal customers.

HubSpot identified that their Value Partners were growing technology companies with complex sales and marketing processes. They used predictive analytics to identify similar companies before they began looking for marketing automation solutions with the goal of achieving higher conversion rates and customer lifetime values.

Owner.com identified a Value Partner segment among restaurants with strong web traffic but relying almost entirely on third-party ordering platforms and paying high commissions as a result. These operators were generating their own demand but losing margin and customer loyalty to intermediaries. By giving them their own direct ordering platform, Owner.com helped these restaurants improve profitability, strengthen retention, and rebuild direct customer relationships—clear hallmarks of high-need, high-potential Value Partner customers. Recognizing these patterns allowed Owner.com to refine its targeting, tailor its sales proposition to the segment's specific pain points, and prioritize capabilities that delivered the greatest mutual value.

The key insight: Don't wait for prospects to raise their hands. Go find the ones who look like your best customers and engage them proactively with messages designed specifically for their needs and characteristics.

Competitive Displacement Strategies

Some of your best potential Value Partners are currently stuck in mediocre relationships with competitors. They're achieving okay results but not thriving. They're staying because switching seems risky or difficult, not because they're delighted. These situations create opportunities for competitive displacement that can rapidly expand your Value Partner base.

Develop a systematic competitive intelligence program that pinpoints when rivals are failing to serve Value Partner customers, monitoring competitor satisfaction, retention patterns, pricing moves, and product or service shifts that open displacement opportunities.

Use these insights to design targeted campaigns aimed at reaching dissatisfied potential Value Partners, supported by switching incentives and migration programs that reduce risk and effort for those considering a move.

Reinforce the message with competitive comparison tools and clear proof points that highlight your differentiated strengths for Value Partner needs, and build robust reference programs that showcase successful competitive displacements to create both credibility and momentum in winning over high-value accounts.

Tesla systematically targeted luxury car buyers who were environmentally conscious but unsatisfied with existing electric vehicle options. They created targeted campaigns highlighting performance, technology, and environmental benefits that existing luxury car manufacturers couldn't match. The competitive displacement wasn't about being cheaper. It was about being better aligned with what these customers actually valued.

Migration Strategies by Source Quadrant

This Section's Executive Takeaway

Not every customer can—or should—be "saved." Migration requires different interventions depending on where a segment sits in the Customer-Business Value Matrix, and the most important leadership decision is where to invest for conversion versus where to redirect with integrity.

For Implementation Teams

This section provides a quadrant-by-quadrant set of migration plays: what to fix, what to redesign, and what capabilities are required to move customers toward Value Partner status (or exit relationships that destroy mutual value).

Different customer types require fundamentally different migration approaches. Understanding which quadrant someone starts in determines your migration strategy.

From Margin Diluters to Value Partners: The Business Model Innovation Challenge

Margin Diluters represent perhaps the most frustrating category in the Customer-Business Value Matrix. These customers genuinely love your solution, achieve meaningful results, and often become vocal advocates. The problem is that your business model doesn't capture adequate value from their satisfaction, making the relationships unsustainable despite high customer satisfaction.

The migration challenge is complex: You must either help Margin Diluters become more valuable to your business or develop better ways to capture value from their satisfaction without degrading their experience. If you can lower cost-to-serve while increasing business value, do it, but make sure the customer doesn't notice anything missing. Think of it like cutting calories without losing flavor.

Here are some effective ways for helping Margin Diluters become more valuable to your business and gain more value from it.

Usage Expansion and Sophistication Development

Analyze how Margin Diluters use your solution compared to Value Partners. Often, the difference isn't in satisfaction but in sophistication of usage and depth of integration with their business processes.

Slack discovered this pattern with many of their Margin Diluters—small teams that loved using Slack for basic communication but hadn't adopted advanced features like workflow automation, app integrations, or enterprise security capabilities. Rather than accepting limited revenue from these relationships, Slack invested in education and success programs that helped small teams expand their usage sophistication.

The results were remarkable: Teams that initially used Slack for basic chat often evolved into power users who relied on Slack for project management, vendor communication, customer support, and strategic collaboration. As their sophistication increased, so did their willingness to pay for premium features and enterprise capabilities.

Customer Capability Development Programs

Margin Diluters often have limited organizational capabilities for maximizing value from sophisticated solutions. Investment in customer capability development can transform satisfied but low-value customers into Value Partners.

HubSpot developed this approach through their Academy program: comprehensive marketing education that helped small businesses develop the strategic capabilities needed to use marketing automation effectively. Customers who completed Academy programs showed significantly higher retention, expansion, and satisfaction rates because they had the organizational capabilities needed to achieve better results.

This isn't just training on your product. It's training on the business capabilities customers need to succeed with your product. HubSpot taught marketing strategy, not just software operation.

Strategic Value Recognition and Positioning

Margin Diluters sometimes fail to recognize the strategic potential of your solution because they use it for tactical rather than strategic purposes. Education and consulting that helps customers understand broader applications can increase both customer value and business value.

The migration isn't about selling more. It's about helping customers recognize value they're already getting but haven't fully appreciated.

Business Model Innovation for Value Capture

When Margin Diluters can't become more valuable through usage expansion, the solution often lies in developing new ways to capture value from their satisfaction and success. Convert Margin Diluters relationships into platforms that generate value through ecosystem participation rather than just direct usage. Consider creating formal programs that enable Margin Diluters to generate business value through referrals, case studies, and community leadership rather than just revenue.

Some customers will never pay you enough to justify the relationship. But if they can help you acquire customers who will, the economics work differently.

From Retention Risk to Value Partners: The Customer Experience Revolution

Retention Risk customers generate good business value but receive limited customer value relative to alternatives. These relationships are profitable in the short term but strategically vulnerable because they depend on customer lock-in, limited alternatives, or market inefficiencies rather than genuine value creation.

The migration challenge is inverse to Margin Diluters: You must dramatically improve customer value delivery while maintaining or improving business value capture. This requires systematic customer experience innovation rather than business model changes. Consider the following systematic customer experience innovations to migrate this segment.

Customer Experience Analysis and Pain Point Resolution

Conduct comprehensive customer experience analysis to identify specific factors that create frustration, effort, or dissatisfaction.

Microsoft faced this challenge with their enterprise software licensing. Customers continued using Microsoft products due to integration requirements and switching costs, but licensing complexity, audit anxiety, and upgrade hassles created significant dissatisfaction.

Microsoft's move to simplified cloud subscriptions eliminated major customer pain points while improving business model predictability.

The key insight: Your Retention Risk customers are staying despite frustrations, not because of satisfaction. Remove the frustrations and they become advocates rather than captives.

Proactive Value Addition and Experience Enhancement

Identify opportunities to add genuine value that customers didn't expect or request. The goal is to exceed customer expectations in ways that transform their perception of the relationship from necessary evil to strategic advantage.

Owner.com provides a clear example of moving customers from Retention Risk to Value Partner. By predicting ROI for every restaurant on the platform, the company identifies when customers are not receiving sufficient value and proactively makes adjustments across pricing, feature development, and hands-on business support to restore positive economics. Sales, product, and customer success teams are all aligned around this process. This disciplined, customer-first approach systematically converts at-risk customers into loyal advocates who generate strong mutual value.

Often, Retention Risk relationships can be transformed through superior service delivery that reduces customer effort while improving outcomes. This requires investment in customer success capabilities and process innovation.

Competitive Vulnerability Mitigation

Retention Risk customers are vulnerable to competitive displacement from alternatives offering superior customer value. Migration strategy must address this vulnerability through competitive differentiation based on customer experience rather than just switching costs.

Increase customer retention through switching costs that feel like benefits rather than barriers. The goal is integration and customization that genuinely improves customer results rather than just creating exit friction. For example: Instead of blocking customers from leaving, a logistics platform introduced AI-enabled custom workflows, automated alerts, and integrations that eliminated hours of manual work. These tailored capabilities made the platform more valuable the longer customers used it, so customers stayed not because exit was hard, but because staying delivered superior results they couldn't get elsewhere.

Develop capabilities and value propositions that competitors cannot easily replicate while addressing customer experience concerns. This often requires significant investment in capabilities that serve Retention Risk customers better than alternatives.

The transformation isn't about making it harder to leave. It's about making it more valuable to stay.

From Value Destroyers to Value Partners: The Triage and Transformation Challenge

Value Destroyer relationships fail to create value for either customers or businesses. Migration to Value Partner status requires fundamental transformation of both the customer relationship and the value delivery model. Most importantly, it requires honest assessment of whether transformation is possible or whether strategic redirection would serve both parties better. Let's look more into what such an assessment would entail.

Transformation Feasibility Assessment

Before investing in Value Destroyer transformation, companies must systematically assess whether transformation is feasible and likely to succeed. This assessment requires brutal honesty about customer characteristics, relationship dynamics, and business model alignment.

Are the problems preventing mutual value creation due to fundamental misalignment between customer needs and your solution capabilities, or are they due to execution issues that could be addressed?

Does the customer have the leadership, resources, and organizational capabilities needed to transform their relationship with your solution? Transformation often requires significant customer investment and change.

Can your business model serve this customer type profitably while delivering genuine value, or would serving them well require business model changes that would compromise your ability to serve your target market?

Are there alternative solutions that would serve this customer better? If competitors have fundamental advantages for serving this customer type, transformation may be less valuable than strategic redirection.

Relationship Reset and Transformation (High Feasibility Only)

For Value Destroyers with genuine transformation potential, success requires a fundamental relationship reset rather than incremental improvement. Design limited pilot programs that test new approaches to value delivery before making major commitments. This allows both parties to validate transformation potential without excessive risk.

At Owner.com, a clear example of identifying Value Destroyer relationships emerged from analyzing discount-driven customers. When the team reviewed retention data, they found that restaurants who only signed up because of an end-of-month discount had significantly lower long-term ROI and much higher churn. These weren't the customers Owner.com wanted to build around. Even more telling, relying on discounts suggested that the company hadn't effectively demonstrated the value of the platform, undercutting trust and weakening the relationship from the start. By eliminating discounting from the sales process, Owner.com avoided attracting low-value customers and reinforced a discipline of selling to operators who understood, needed, and could fully benefit from the value the platform provides.

Establish clear success metrics and accountability systems that enable both parties to track transformation progress and make data-driven decisions about relationship continuation.

Make specific commitments about resources, timeline, and deliverables for transformation efforts while establishing clear exit criteria if transformation doesn't succeed.

Strategic Redirection When Transformation Isn't Viable

For Value Destroyers without realistic transformation potential, strategic redirection often serves both parties better than continued unsuccessful relationship attempts.

One of the most counterintuitive aspects of customer portfolio optimization is that helping customers find better solutions elsewhere often creates more value for all parties than continuing unsuccessful relationships. The conventional business wisdom suggests that losing customers is always bad, but sophisticated companies understand that strategic customer redirection is a sign of mature market understanding and ethical business practice. Resources invested in serving customers who can't achieve success could be redirected toward serving other customers exceptionally well. This creates more total value in the market while enabling both parties to optimize their outcomes.

Companies that help customers find better solutions build reputations for integrity and customer focus that often lead to future business when customer needs evolve or when they refer others who are better fits.

Customer Migration as Competitive Strategy

Customer migration and portfolio optimization represent sophisticated competitive strategies that create advantages beyond just better customer relationships. Companies that master these capabilities often achieve strategic advantages that competitors struggle to replicate.

Reputation and Market Positioning Advantages

Companies known for helping customers achieve exceptional success attract better prospects and command premium pricing. This reputation effect creates competitive advantages that compound over time as more Value Partners generate referrals and market credibility.

Capability Development Focus

Focused customer portfolios enable specialized capability development that creates competitive advantages. Companies serving specific customer types exceptionally well consistently outperform companies trying to serve everyone adequately.

Ecosystem and Partnership Development

Clear customer focus enables better partnership development with companies serving complementary customer types. Strategic customer redirection often leads to referral partnerships and ecosystem relationships that create mutual value.

The Hard Reality of Portfolio Pruning

I will be direct and honest about something most business books don't say clearly enough: Helping customers leave is one of the hardest things leadership teams do. Sales leaders worry about missing revenue targets. Customer success teams feel like they're abandoning people who need help. Finance sees immediate revenue reduction before long-term benefits materialize. The emotional resistance is real and understandable. These are real relationships with real people who trusted you enough to become customers.

But continuing relationships that don't work serves nobody well. The customer isn't getting the value they need. Your team is frustrated. Your resources are being consumed by relationships that can't succeed.

Strategic redirection isn't about giving up on customers. It's about being honest that you're not the right solution for everyone and having the integrity to help customers find better alternatives.

The companies that do this well build reputations for integrity that become competitive advantages. Customers remember when you prioritized their success over your revenue. Prospects notice when you're honest about who you can serve well.

Moving Forward: Implementation Takeaways

Customer migration and portfolio pruning aren't about serving fewer customers. They're about serving the right customers exceptionally well. Saying "no" becomes a growth lever when it protects the capacity to say an emphatic "yes" to Value Partners.

Invest where odds are real: Score migration potential and concentrate resources on high-probability upgrades. Not every customer can become a Value Partner. Focus your investment on those who can.

Redirection is service: Helping misfit customers succeed elsewhere builds trust and often future demand. The customers you help find better solutions remember that integrity.

Optimize the portfolio, not just revenue: The goal is compounding mutual value, not maximal headcount. A smaller portfolio of Value Partners often outperforms a larger portfolio of mixed customers.

Build the muscles: Assessment, success, education, model innovation, and change management. These capabilities take time to develop but create sustainable competitive advantages.

Wire it into IBP: Make migration paths, off-ramps, and capability bets explicit in your planning cycles. Portfolio optimization can't be a one-time project. It needs to be built into how you plan and operate.

Do this consistently and you'll earn a reputation for outcomes, not features; for focus, not FOMO. Competitors will try to copy your product. Copying your portfolio discipline is the hard part. Because in the end, the companies that win aren't the ones serving the most customers. They're the ones creating the most value for the right customers and having the courage to redirect the rest.

Choosing the right customers sets direction; having the capability to serve them well determines the outcome. Chapter 9 turns to the organizational muscles required to make that choice stick.

Strategic Capability Identification: A Methodology for Competitive Value Creation

The essence of strategy is choosing what not to do. But it is just as important to choose what to do exceptionally well.
—Michael Porter

Get Better

One day my wife gave me a card that said: "Get better!"

I told her, "But I'm not sick."

She smiled and replied, "Thank God, but you can always get better."

As usual, she was right. In business and in life, continuous improvement isn't optional. It's a survival strategy.

Customer value is not static, and neither should be your internal capabilities. The most successful organizations continuously evolve their competencies to match the changing needs and strategic importance of their customer segments.

Amazon demonstrates this perfectly: Prime members receive white-glove logistics capabilities and exclusive access to content. Marketplace sellers get sophisticated analytics and advertising tools. Small businesses access simplified interfaces and automated services. Enterprise customers receive dedicated account management and custom integration support. This segmented capability development enables Amazon to serve vastly different customer needs while maintaining operational efficiency and profitability across all segments.

Identifying which capabilities to develop, enhance, or eliminate represents one of the most critical strategic decisions organizations face. The wrong capability investments can consume years of effort and millions of dollars while providing little competitive advantage. The right capability choices can create sustainable market leadership and exceptional returns.

Netflix's early decision to invest in streaming technology and data analytics capabilities, rather than expanding their DVD distribution network, positioned them to dominate entertainment while Blockbuster collapsed. That's not just good luck. That's strategic capability identification done right.

This chapter explores how to build and align your core competencies and operational strengths to match the different needs and strategic importance of customer segments identified through the customer value matrix framework. The goal is transforming your organization from a one-size-fits-all service provider into a value-optimized machine that excels at serving your most important customers while efficiently managing less strategic relationships.

This is where the book turns from understanding value to building the muscle that delivers it. Customer value and business value tell you where you win; capabilities are how you keep winning on purpose, repeatedly, and at scale.

The Value Creation Hierarchy: From Waste to Moat

Different capabilities create varying levels of value and competitive protection. Understanding this hierarchy helps you prioritize investments and avoid wasting resources on activities that don't contribute to strategic objectives. The Value Creation Hierarchy progresses from waste elimination through value creation to competitive moat development.

Think of this hierarchy as a filter for attention. If you treat every capability as equally strategic, you'll spread resources thin and call it "transformation." The hierarchy forces a more uncomfortable and more useful question: Which work creates real advantage, and which work just keeps us busy?

Waste Elimination: The Foundation Nobody Talks About

Waste represents activities, processes, or resources consuming organizational energy without creating customer value or competitive advantage. Identifying and eliminating waste frees up resources for value-creating investments while improving operational efficiency.

Toyota's legendary production system identifies seven types of waste: overproduction, waiting, transportation, inappropriate processing, unnecessary inventory, unnecessary motion, and defects. However, waste in modern organizations often wears a suit and attends meetings.

Process waste occurs when organizations maintain bureaucratic procedures that slow decision-making without adding value. Many large companies require multiple approval layers for routine decisions, creating delays and frustration without improving outcomes. Spotify's squad-based organization structure eliminates much of this waste by empowering small teams to make decisions quickly without extensive hierarchical approval.

Communication waste emerges when information flows inefficiently through organizations, requiring multiple meetings, emails, and reports to accomplish simple coordination. Think endless meetings and reply-all email threads. Some meetings could be replaced by a two-line Slack message. Others could be replaced by silence.

Technology waste appears when organizations maintain redundant systems, unused software licenses, or overly complex technical architectures requiring excessive maintenance. It's like subscribing to three gyms and still not working out.

Resource allocation waste occurs when talented people spend time on activities that don't leverage their expertise or contribute to strategic objectives. Sales representatives doing administrative work instead of selling or engineers spending excessive time in status meetings instead of developing products, represent common forms of resource waste. The opportunity cost is enormous. It's like having a BMW idling in the driveway while you pedal a tricycle to work.

Value-Enabling Capabilities: The Foundation That Enables Everything Else

Value-enabling capabilities don't directly create customer value but make other value-creating activities possible or more effective. These capabilities often receive insufficient attention because their contributions are indirect, yet they're essential for sustainable competitive advantage.

Amazon Web Services' global infrastructure represents a value-enabling capability that makes their cloud services possible while enabling rapid geographic expansion. Without this foundation, none of their customer-facing capabilities would work.

Platform capabilities enable other parts of an organization to create value more effectively. Salesforce's platform architecture allows thousands of third-party developers to create applications that enhance customer value while reducing Salesforce's own development burden. The platform itself doesn't directly serve customer needs, but it enables an ecosystem of value creation that competitors find difficult to replicate.

Data and analytics capabilities enable evidence-based decision-making and personalization across an organization. Google's data collection and analysis capabilities don't directly serve user needs, but they enable highly relevant search results, targeted advertising, and product improvements that create substantial customer and business value.

Talent development capabilities ensure the organization can attract, develop, and retain people capable of creating customer value. Netflix's culture of high performance and creative freedom enables them to attract exceptional content creators and technologists who develop compelling original programming and innovative platform features.

Learning capabilities enable continuous improvement and adaptation to changing market conditions. Organizations with strong learning capabilities can identify emerging customer needs, evaluate new technologies, and adjust strategies based on feedback and results. This meta-capability enables all other capabilities to improve over time.

Value-Added Capabilities: What Customers Actually Notice

Value-added capabilities directly enhance customer experiences or outcomes in ways that customers recognize and appreciate.

These capabilities typically influence customer purchase decisions, satisfaction levels, and loyalty behavior. However, here's the catch: Value-added capabilities may not provide sustainable competitive advantage if competitors can easily replicate them.

Service capabilities that improve customer convenience, responsiveness, or problem resolution create immediate customer value. Zappos' exceptional customer service creates customer loyalty and word-of-mouth marketing, though competitors could potentially develop similar service capabilities with sufficient investment and cultural change.

Product features that address specific customer needs or preferences create value that customers can directly experience and evaluate. Tesla's over-the-air software updates provide ongoing value enhancement that customers appreciate, though other automotive manufacturers are developing similar capabilities.

Process improvements that reduce customer effort, increase reliability, or accelerate outcomes create value through better experiences. Amazon's one-click ordering and Prime delivery create customer value through convenience and speed, though the underlying capabilities could theoretically be replicated by other retailers.

Quality enhancements that improve product reliability, durability, or performance create customer value through better outcomes. Apple's build quality and reliability create customer value influencing purchase decisions and reducing support costs, though achieving similar quality levels requires significant investment in design and manufacturing processes.

Differentiating Value: Actually Standing Out

Differentiating value emerges when capabilities enable you to serve customer needs in ways that competitors cannot easily match. These capabilities provide competitive advantages influencing customer choice and enabling premium pricing. But be warned: Differentiating capabilities may eventually become commoditized as competitors develop similar abilities.

Here's the trap: Many companies stop at "value-added" and assume they're safe. But customers noticing you is not the same as competitors being unable to copy you. The hierarchy is moving you toward the only place strategy ultimately cares about: differentiation that lasts.

Innovation capabilities that enable rapid development and launch of new products or features create differentiating value by giving customers access to capabilities they can't find elsewhere. Google's search algorithm innovations consistently provide more relevant results than competitors, creating clear differentiation that drives market share and advertising revenue.

Speed capabilities that enable faster delivery, implementation, or response create differentiating value in markets where time matters to customers. FedEx's overnight delivery capability created significant differentiation when it launched, though competitors eventually developed similar services that reduced the competitive advantage.

Customization capabilities that enable tailored solutions for specific customer needs create differentiating value by addressing unique requirements that competitors' standard offerings cannot meet. Salesforce's customization capabilities enable enterprise customers to configure their CRM systems for specific industry requirements and business processes.

Expertise capabilities that provide superior knowledge, insights, or problem-solving create differentiating value through better outcomes for customers. McKinsey's strategy consulting expertise enables them to command premium pricing by helping clients solve complex problems that other consultants cannot address effectively.

Value Moat: The Sustainable Competitive Protection

Let's return to this foundational concept explored earlier in the book: While reinventing markets and creating blue oceans is rare and difficult, the practical path for most companies begins with understanding customer value precisely and building competitive moats around the segments where mutual value is highest. Even if you were able to do it, the competition is catching up and you need to protect it.

Something to keep in mind: A moat isn't a slogan. It's a system. It's what remains standing after competitors copy your features, match your prices, and hire away your people. If your advantage disappears under pressure, you didn't have a moat. You had a moment.

Warren Buffett popularized the concept of economic moats: sustainable competitive advantages that protect businesses like medieval moats protected castles. But digital-age moats are built differently than industrial-age moats.

Traditional Moats (Industrial Age):

- Scale economies: Lower unit costs through volume

- Network effects: Value increases with more users

- Brand power: Customer loyalty based on trust and recognition

- Regulatory barriers: Legal protection from competition

- Geographic advantages: Physical proximity to customers or resources

Digital-Age Moat Types:

Data Moats: Proprietary data that improves products and experiences over time. Google's search algorithm gets better with every query. Netflix's recommendation engine improves with every view. The more customers use the product, the more valuable it becomes.

Learning Moats: AI and machine learning systems that create compound advantages. Tesla's Autopilot system improves as more cars collect driving data. The competitive advantage accelerates rather than erodes over time.

Ecosystem Moats: Integrated platforms where switching costs are high but feel like benefits. Leaving Apple means losing iCloud integration, familiar interfaces, and seamless device interaction. The "cost" of switching feels like losing value, not just changing products.

Speed Moats: Organizational capabilities to innovate and adapt faster than competitors. Amazon's ability to rapidly enter new markets and experiment with new services creates competitive advantages difficult to replicate.

Community Moats: Customer networks that create value beyond the core product. Peloton's community of riders, instructors, and shared experiences creates switching costs that go beyond exercise equipment functionality.

True value moats provide lasting protection against competitive threats while enabling premium pricing and market leadership. They emerge from complex combinations of people, processes, technology, and culture that have developed over years or decades.

Network effects create value moats when your product or service becomes more valuable as more people use it. Facebook's social network becomes more valuable to each user as more of their friends and family join the platform. Competitors cannot easily replicate this value because users have strong incentives to remain where their networks already exist.

Scale economies create value moats when size advantages enable cost structures or capabilities that smaller competitors cannot match. Amazon's logistics scale enables delivery speeds and costs that smaller e-commerce players cannot replicate without massive infrastructure investments that may not be economically viable.

Learning curve advantages create value moats when experience accumulation enables performance improvements that competitors cannot quickly match. Intel's semiconductor manufacturing expertise represents decades of learning that enables them to produce more advanced chips than competitors who lack similar experience.

Switching costs create value moats when customers face significant expenses or risks in changing to competitive solutions. Enterprise software providers like SAP create value moats through deep integration with customer business processes that would be extremely expensive and risky to replace. For Apple iPhone customers, leaving isn't just buying a new phone. It's explaining to your family why you turned the group chat green. Some costs are financial. Others are emotional.

Brand and reputation create value moats when customer loyalty and trust enable premium pricing and preferential consideration that competitors cannot easily overcome. Luxury brands like Rolex create value moats through decades of reputation building that new entrants cannot quickly replicate.

Data assets create value moats when accumulated information enables capabilities or insights that competitors cannot match without similar data access. Google's search data enables algorithm improvements and advertising targeting that competitors cannot replicate without comparable data sources.

Integrating Capabilities Into Core Competencies

The most powerful competitive advantages emerge when individual capabilities combine into integrated core competencies that create value moats. This integration process requires deliberate organizational design, cultural development, and strategic focus aligning multiple capabilities toward common objectives.

This is where capability thinking becomes strategic instead of departmental. Individual functions can build good capabilities; only organizations build core competencies. When the parts reinforce each other, like a jazz band instead of a set of soloists, you get a kind of advantage competitors can't replicate by copying one instrument.

Core competencies represent integrated combinations of capabilities that create distinctive value for customers and sustainable competitive advantages for organizations. They emerge when multiple capabilities are woven together in ways that competitors find difficult to understand, replicate, or substitute.

Google's core competency is its unparalleled ability to organize and deliver information instantly. By fusing search algorithms, massive data infrastructure, machine learning, and global-scale computing into a single capability, Google creates speed, relevance, and personalization no rival can match. This competency powers not just Search, but Maps, Ads, YouTube, Android, and AI—proving its reach across multiple markets and its central role in customer value.

Core competencies must meet three essential criteria established by C.K. Prahalad and Gary Hamel, two of the most influential strategic thinkers of the last half-century: They must provide potential access to multiple markets, contribute significantly to customer value in target markets, and be difficult for competitors to imitate.

Apple's competency in user experience design meets all three criteria: It enables success across computers, phones, tablets, and services; creates substantial customer value through intuitive, elegant interfaces; and has proven extremely difficult for competitors to replicate despite decades of attempts.

Amazon's logistics competency integrates warehouse management, inventory optimization, transportation networks, demand forecasting, and technology systems into a comprehensive capability that enables rapid, cost-effective delivery. While competitors can develop individual logistics capabilities, replicating the integrated system requires massive investment and years of organizational learning.

Medtronic, the largest medical device company in the world, integrates biomedical engineering, clinical expertise, and regulatory mastery into therapies that consistently improve patient outcomes—a core competency of the company. This combination enables Medtronic to scale solutions across cardiac care, diabetes, surgery, and neuromodulation—offering trusted, clinically validated products that competitors struggle to replicate. Its strength lies in uniting science, evidence, and workflow design into a capability that spans multiple markets and delivers meaningful value to patients and clinicians.

The key to developing integrated competencies lies in identifying how different capabilities can reinforce each other while creating customer value that exceeds the sum of individual parts. The magic happens when capabilities stop working in isolation and start playing like a jazz band. This requires strategic thinking that goes beyond functional excellence to consider how organizational elements work together to create distinctive value propositions.

The Integrated Capability Identification Framework

This Section's Executive Takeaway

Capabilities are how you turn value insight into repeatable advantage. The goal is not to be good at everything, but to deliberately build a small set of integrated competencies that your best customers value and competitors can't easily copy. Use the value hierarchy to stop funding busywork, reinforce what differentiates you, and invest where customer value and business value compound.

For Implementation Teams

This section goes deeper into the step-by-step method for identifying, benchmarking, and prioritizing capabilities—translating segment needs into requirements, mapping competitors, scoring and sequencing investments, and building a practical roadmap.

Up to this point, we've built the logic: Value tells you where to play, and capabilities determine whether you can win there repeatedly. Now comes the harder part: making those capability choices explicit, defensible, and actionable. The Integrated Capability Identification Framework given below walks through four interconnected analytical phases designed to produce clear capability priorities and a roadmap you can actually execute.

Phase 1: Competitive Landscape Mapping and Analysis

Comprehensive competitive analysis forms the foundation for capability identification because it reveals which abilities enable market success and where competitive gaps create opportunities for differentiation.

However, effective competitive analysis goes far beyond identifying direct competitors to include adjacent players, potential entrants, and substitute solutions that might address similar customer needs.

Competitive Ecosystem Identification

Begin by mapping your complete competitive ecosystem rather than focusing only on obvious direct competitors. The ecosystem includes direct competitors offering similar solutions, indirect competitors addressing the same customer needs through different approaches, adjacent players who might expand into your market, potential new entrants with relevant capabilities, and substitute solutions that customers might choose instead of your category.

Uber's original competitive analysis had to consider not just taxi companies but also public transportation, car rental services, and car ownership as alternative solutions to urban mobility needs.

Direct competitors require detailed analysis of their business models, customer segments, value propositions, and operational capabilities. However, the most strategic insights often emerge from studying indirect competitors who serve similar customer needs through different approaches.

When Zoom entered the video conferencing market, they competed not just against WebEx and GoToMeeting but also against travel budgets, phone conferences, and in-person meetings. Understanding these broader competitive dynamics revealed opportunities for simplicity and reliability that traditional video conferencing vendors had overlooked.

Adjacent market players represent potential future competitors who might leverage existing capabilities to enter your market. Adjacent competitors sneak in from unexpected places. Banks dismissed fintechs as toys until Square and Stripe started taking their lunch money.

Amazon's entry into cloud computing wasn't obvious to traditional IT vendors, but their infrastructure management capabilities and scale economics created competitive advantages that established players couldn't easily match. Monitoring adjacent players helps identify emerging competitive threats and capability requirements before they become direct market pressures.

Capability-Based Competitive Positioning

Once you've identified the competitive ecosystem, analyze how different players create competitive advantages through specific capabilities. This analysis should focus on understanding which capabilities enable market success rather than just cataloging what competitors do.

Value chain analysis reveals how competitors organize activities to create and deliver customer value. Different competitors may excel at different parts of the value chain, creating opportunities for focused capability development.

In the smartphone market, Apple excels at design and user experience integration, Samsung leads in display technology and manufacturing scale, while Google dominates mobile software and services. Understanding these capability-based positions helps identify where your organization might develop distinctive advantages.

Business model analysis examines how competitors monetize their capabilities and create sustainable competitive advantages. Some competitors may rely on scale economies, others on network effects, premium positioning, or operational efficiency.

Netflix's subscription model enables different capabilities than traditional movie studios' project-based approach, allowing Netflix to invest in data analytics and original content development that creates sustainable competitive advantages.

Technology capability assessment identifies which technological abilities enable competitive success and how technology strategies differ across competitors. This analysis should consider not just current technology implementations but also development trajectories and platform capabilities that might enable future advantages.

Tesla's early investment in battery technology and electric powertrain capabilities created competitive advantages that traditional automotive manufacturers are still struggling to match.

Competitive Performance Analysis

Understanding how capability differences translate into competitive performance provides insights into which capabilities generate the highest returns and which represent necessary but insufficient competitive requirements.

Market share evolution reveals which competitors are gaining or losing position and often indicates which capabilities are becoming more or less important. The rapid growth of cloud-based software companies at the expense of on-premise vendors demonstrates how cloud infrastructure and SaaS capabilities became essential for competitive success in enterprise software markets.

Customer acquisition metrics show how effectively different competitors convert prospects into customers and which capabilities drive acquisition success. Some competitors may achieve lower acquisition costs through superior digital marketing capabilities, while others rely on strong sales organizations or partner channels.

Customer retention and expansion patterns indicate which competitors create the strongest ongoing value and switching costs. High retention rates often correlate with superior customer success capabilities, while high expansion rates may indicate effective upselling capabilities or products that naturally grow with customer needs.

Pricing power analysis reveals which competitors can command premium pricing and which capabilities enable pricing advantages. Premium pricing often indicates distinctive capabilities that customers value and that competitors cannot easily replicate. Apple's ability to maintain premium pricing in consumer electronics reflects design and brand capabilities that create customer willingness to pay higher prices.

Phase 2: Customer Value Matrix Analysis for Capability Requirements

Customer value analysis reveals which capabilities matter most to different customer segments and where gaps exist between current delivery and customer expectations. This analysis must go beyond general customer satisfaction surveys to understand specifically which capabilities drive value perception, purchase decisions, and long-term loyalty for different types of customers.

Segment-Specific Value Driver Analysis

Each customer segment in your value matrix has different priorities, success criteria, and capability requirements. Value Partners typically value sophisticated capabilities that enable deep integration and co-innovation, while Retention Risk customers prefer simple, efficient capabilities that minimize complexity and effort.

Understanding these differences prevents the common mistake of developing expensive capabilities that only matter to low-value customers while neglecting abilities that Value Partners consider essential. Investing in the wrong capabilities is like buying flowers for someone who just told you they want pizza. You'll spend money, but you won't get love.

Value Partners' value drivers often center on capabilities that enable partnership rather than just vendor relationships. These customers typically value innovation collaboration capabilities, strategic account management, custom integration support, and access to roadmap influence that helps them achieve competitive advantages.

Microsoft's enterprise customers don't just buy software; they expect partnership capabilities that include joint business planning, dedicated support resources, and influence over product development priorities.

The analysis should identify specific capabilities that Value Partners consider non-negotiable versus nice-to-have. Non-negotiable capabilities represent minimum requirements for maintaining these relationships, while nice-to-have capabilities create opportunities for differentiation and deeper partnership.

Margin Diluters typically value capabilities that accelerate their success and enable expansion of their relationship with your organization. These capabilities often include comprehensive onboarding, proactive success management, expansion planning, and usage optimization that helps customers achieve better outcomes.

Slack's Margin Diluters customers value capabilities that help them expand team adoption and integrate workflows, rather than advanced enterprise features they're not ready to use.

Understanding the capability requirements for converting Margin Diluters customers into Value Partners provides crucial insights for development prioritization. These conversion capabilities often involve deeper product functionality, enhanced support, and strategic consulting that helps customers achieve transformational rather than incremental outcomes.

Retention Risks require capabilities focused on relationship recovery, value communication, and addressing specific pain points that created dissatisfaction. The capability requirements often involve enhanced customer success, proactive issue resolution, and customization options that address unique customer needs.

Value Destroyers prefer capabilities that minimize effort and complexity while providing adequate functionality for their basic needs. These customers often value self-service capabilities, automated support, standardized processes, and simple pricing that reduces decision-making complexity. Over-investing in sophisticated capabilities for this segment typically generates poor returns and may actually create negative value by increasing complexity.

Capability Gap Assessment by Segment

Once you understand what each segment values, assess how well your current capabilities meet those requirements compared to competitive alternatives. This gap analysis should be specific and actionable, identifying not just where gaps exist but which gaps matter most for competitive success and customer retention.

Perception gap analysis compares how customers rate your capabilities against their importance ratings and competitive alternatives. Customers may highly value certain capabilities but perceive your organization as weak in those areas, creating vulnerability to competitive displacement.

Performance gap analysis examines objective measures of capability effectiveness compared to customer requirements and competitive benchmarks. This analysis might reveal that your customer service response times are slower than customer expectations, your product features lack functionality that competitors provide, or your onboarding process takes longer than customers prefer.

The analysis should prioritize gaps based on their impact on customer relationships and competitive position. Some gaps may seem significant but have minimal impact on customer decisions or satisfaction, while others may appear minor but represent critical vulnerabilities.

For example, in many industries, gaps that look strategically important turn out to have little influence on customer decisions, while small operational flaws create real vulnerability. A national retailer once prioritized a major loyalty program overhaul because customers said rewards mattered, yet post-launch data showed no improvement in sales. The real issue was a slow checkout process that added 20 seconds per transaction and drove shoppers to competitors. A logistics provider invested heavily in expanding its analytics dashboard, believing shippers wanted deeper insights, but churn decreased only after fixing a minor tracking delay that had been creating anxiety during late deliveries. Similarly, a SaaS company spent months building advanced customization options requested by enterprise clients, only to learn that the primary retention driver was a simple onboarding bottleneck that made new users feel stuck on day one. The takeaway: Across industries, the pattern is consistent: Some gaps look big but don't move the needle, while others appear small but represent the true friction points that matter most to customers.

Value Opportunity Identification

Beyond addressing gaps, the analysis should identify opportunities to create new value through capabilities that exceed current customer expectations or enable outcomes that customers haven't yet imagined. These breakthrough opportunities often provide the foundation for sustainable competitive advantages and customer loyalty that extends beyond functional requirements.

Unmet need identification reveals customer challenges that current solutions, including your own, don't adequately address. These unmet needs often represent opportunities for capability development that could create significant competitive advantages. For example, Netflix identified that customers wanted on-demand access to content without physical media constraints, leading to streaming capabilities that transformed the entertainment industry.

Adjacent value opportunities consider how current customer relationships might expand through capabilities that address broader customer needs. Amazon's evolution from e-commerce to cloud computing emerged from recognizing that their internal infrastructure capabilities could address enterprise customer needs beyond retail purchases.

Integration opportunities identify how capabilities might combine to create value that exceeds the sum of individual parts. Apple's success stems largely from integration capabilities that combine hardware, software, and services into cohesive experiences that competitors with single-focus capabilities cannot match.

Phase 3: Capability-Competitive Intersection Analysis

The intersection of competitive dynamics and customer value requirements reveals which capabilities will create the most significant competitive advantages for your specific situation. This analysis identifies where capability investments can simultaneously address competitive pressures and customer needs while creating sustainable advantages that competitors cannot easily replicate.

Competitive Capability Benchmarking

Systematic benchmarking of competitor capabilities provides the foundation for understanding where you need to achieve parity versus where you can create differentiation. The benchmarking should be comprehensive and specific, measuring not just capability existence but effectiveness, efficiency, and customer impact. Benchmarking is important. But remember: Parity doesn't win markets. If you're only trying to keep up with competitors, you'll always be looking at their backs.

Direct capability comparison examines how your abilities stack up against competitors in specific functional areas. This comparison should consider both quantitative measures (response times, feature counts, pricing) and qualitative assessments (user experience, reliability, strategic value).

Capability maturity assessment evaluates not just current competitive positions but trajectory and development velocity. Some competitors may currently lag in specific capabilities but are investing heavily and improving rapidly, while others may have strong current positions but are not keeping pace with evolving requirements.

White Space Opportunity Mapping

White space analysis identifies capability areas where no competitor currently excels, creating opportunities for differentiation and market leadership. These white spaces often emerge from changing customer needs, technological possibilities, or business model innovations that create new forms of value creation.

Capability gap mapping plots all competitors across key capability dimensions to identify areas where everyone underperforms relative to customer requirements. These universal gaps often represent opportunities for significant competitive advantage through superior capability development.

Technological opportunity assessment considers how emerging technologies might enable new capabilities that could reshape competitive dynamics. Artificial intelligence, automation, and data analytics continue creating opportunities for capabilities that didn't exist previously, enabling new forms of customer value and competitive advantage.

Business model innovation opportunities examine how different approaches to capability delivery might create competitive advantages. For example, the shift from product sales to subscription models has enabled different types of customer success and retention capabilities that create ongoing competitive advantages.

Competitive Response Analysis

Understanding how competitors are likely to respond to your capability investments helps prioritize investments that will maintain competitive advantages over time. Some capability areas may be easily replicated, while others create sustainable competitive protection through complexity, scale requirements, or first-mover advantages.

Replication difficulty assessment evaluates how easily competitors could develop similar capabilities, considering factors like development time, resource requirements, technological barriers, and organizational change needs. Capabilities that require years of development and substantial organizational change provide more sustainable competitive advantages than those that can be quickly implemented.

Netflix's early streaming investment prompted various competitive responses including Hulu's ad-supported model, Amazon's content creation investment, and Disney's direct-to-consumer platform development. Understanding these potential responses helps you prepare for competitive reactions rather than being surprised by them.

Phase 4: Strategic Capability Prioritization Matrix

This Section's Executive Takeaway

Prioritization is where strategy becomes real: You're making explicit trade-offs about where to build advantage and where to accept limits. The output should be a short list of capabilities that earn disproportionate investment because they protect your moat and serve your highest-value segments.

For Implementation Teams

This section details a practical scoring and resourcing approach to translate capability choices into an executable investment plan and multi-year roadmap.

The final phase synthesizes insights from competitive analysis and customer value assessment into actionable capability development priorities.

This prioritization must balance multiple considerations including competitive impact, customer value creation, development feasibility, resource requirements, and strategic fit with your organization's broader objectives.

Multi-Criteria Capability Scoring

Effective capability prioritization requires systematic evaluation across multiple dimensions that capture both strategic importance and implementation feasibility. The scoring framework should be specific to your organization's situation while being comprehensive enough to support difficult resource allocation decisions. Multi-criteria scoring helps, but don't turn it into a bureaucratic monster.

Customer impact scoring evaluates how much each capability would improve customer satisfaction, retention, and expansion for different segments. Value Partner capabilities should receive higher weightings because these customers provide disproportionate business value, while Value Destroyer customer capabilities receive lower priority unless they address major efficiency opportunities.

Competitive advantage scoring assesses how much each capability would improve your competitive position, considering both defensive necessity and offensive opportunity. Capabilities that address current competitive vulnerabilities receive priority for protecting existing business, while capabilities that could create new competitive advantages get prioritized for growth opportunities.

Development feasibility scoring considers the complexity, time, and resources required to develop each capability to competitive levels. Some capabilities may provide substantial value but require development timelines or resource investments that exceed organizational capacity or strategic patience.

Strategic alignment scoring evaluates how well each capability supports your organization's broader strategic objectives and business model. Capabilities that align with existing strengths and strategic direction typically receive higher priority than those requiring significant organizational changes or new competencies.

Financial impact scoring estimates the revenue, cost, and profitability implications of each capability investment. This analysis should consider both direct financial benefits and indirect effects like improved customer retention, pricing power, and operational efficiency.

Resource Allocation Framework

Capability development requires substantial resource commitments across people, technology, and organizational change. The allocation framework must balance ambitious capability goals with realistic resource constraints while ensuring that investments reinforce each other rather than compete for attention and resources.

Investment sequencing determines the optimal order for capability development, considering dependencies, resource constraints, and competitive timing. Some capabilities may need to be developed sequentially because they build on each other, while others can be pursued in parallel if resources permit.

Resource requirement analysis details the specific investments needed for each capability including talent acquisition, technology infrastructure, process changes, and organizational development. The analysis should be realistic about total costs including ongoing maintenance and evolution requirements.

Timeline planning balances capability development speed with quality and organizational capacity. Attempting to develop too many capabilities simultaneously often results in poor execution across all areas, while developing capabilities too slowly may allow competitors to establish advantageous positions.

Implementation Roadmap Development

The capability identification process culminates in detailed implementation roadmaps that guide organizational capability development over multiple years. These roadmaps must be specific enough to enable execution while remaining flexible enough to adapt as competitive and customer dynamics evolve.

In the next few chapters, we'll explore how this roadmap will be incorporated as part of Value-Centric IBP.

From Analysis to Action

The capability identification methodology provides a systematic approach for determining which abilities your organization should develop to create competitive advantages and customer value. However, the methodology's effectiveness depends on rigorous analysis, honest assessment of organizational capabilities, and sustained commitment to capability development over multiple years.

If this chapter feels demanding, good. Capability choices are expensive, slow to build, and brutally hard to unwind, so they deserve more rigor than intuition, politics, or last year's priorities.

The most successful organizations treat capability identification as an ongoing strategic process rather than an annual planning exercise. Competitive landscapes and customer needs evolve continuously, requiring regular reassessment of capability priorities and adjustment of development plans.

Remember that capability development is ultimately about creating sustainable competitive advantages that enable superior customer value delivery. The analysis and prioritization frameworks are tools for making better strategic decisions, but execution excellence remains essential for translating capability investments into competitive success.

Organizations that combine rigorous capability identification with exceptional implementation will create the sustained competitive advantages that drive long-term market leadership. The organizations that win are those that continuously reassess, reprioritize, and reinvest in capabilities that create value and protect moats. Strategy isn't about doing everything; it's about doing the right things exceptionally well and knowing when to stop doing the wrong things. Or, as my wife would remind me: "Get better!"

That brings us to the end of the foundation. In Part 2, we move from insight to action, applying everything we've built to Value-Centric Integrated Business Planning and the practical realities of running the business. And if these ideas spark questions, challenges, or reflections of your own, I welcome the conversation. Value-Centric IBP is not just a framework, it's a journey, and I'm always glad to engage with leaders who are exploring how to put it into practice in their own organizations.

PART 2

The Engine of Value

*Operationalizing Value Through
Integrated Business Planning*

CHAPTER 10

From Traditional IBP to Value-Centric Transformation

Plans are worthless, but planning is everything.
—Dwight D. Eisenhower

When Good Planning Isn't Good Enough Anymore

Let me share with you what I've watched happen over and over: A company implements Oliver Wight IBP perfectly. They've got their five-step process humming. Cross-functional meetings happen like clockwork. Forecast accuracy improves. Everyone's aligned. The CFO is happy.

Then one day they wake up and realize their perfectly optimized supply chain is efficiently delivering products that customers are increasingly indifferent about. A competitor, maybe one with messier operations, is stealing market share because they actually understand what customers value.

This isn't a failure of traditional IBP. It's a limitation baked into its DNA.

Oliver Wight built something remarkable for its time. The framework brought order to chaos, got functions talking to each other, and turned operational guesswork into disciplined planning. For decades, that was exactly what companies needed because operational excellence was competitive advantage.

But somewhere between the 1980s and now, the game changed.

The World That Created Traditional IBP

Think about competing in the '80s and '90s. If you could deliver consistently, keep costs down, and maintain quality, you won. Toyota became legendary not through customer intimacy but through operational brilliance. The message was clear: Get your operations right and customers will come.

Traditional IBP made perfect sense in that world. It solved the real problem companies faced: How do you get sales, operations, finance, and leadership aligned around a single plan? How do you translate market demand into production schedules without either stockouts or bloated inventory?

The five-step process—Product Management Review, Demand Review, Supply Review, Financial Integration, Executive Review—created a systematic way to coordinate across functions. Manufacturing companies especially loved it because their competitive edge really did come from supply chain optimization, inventory management, and production efficiency.

And here's the thing: All of that still matters. You can't win with bad operations.

But you also can't win with *only* good operations anymore.

What Changed (And Why It Matters)

Digital transformation didn't just make things faster. It fundamentally shifted competitive dynamics. Customers now have near-perfect information, low switching costs, and endless alternatives. Social media makes your service failures instantly visible. Subscription models mean you have to earn customer loyalty every single month.

In this environment, operational efficiency became table stakes. Customers expect reliable delivery and competitive pricing the way they expect electricity to work when they flip a switch. Nobody gives you credit for meeting basic expectations.

Real competitive advantage moved upstream: superior customer understanding, personalized experiences, innovations that address unmet needs, relationships that create emotional attachment.

Netflix illustrates this perfectly. Their initial advantage came from logistics: better DVD delivery than Blockbuster. But they didn't win long term through operational excellence. They won through technological innovation and data analytics that understood what you wanted to watch before you did, through content personalization that made their service indispensable, through original programming that competitors couldn't replicate. Could they have done this with lousy operations? No. But operational excellence alone would have made them a better Blockbuster, not a market-transforming company.

The Integration Problem Nobody's Solving Well

So, companies try to bolt customer focus onto their existing IBP processes. They add NPS scores to executive dashboards. They invite customer success to demand planning meetings. They talk about "putting customers first."

And mostly, it doesn't work.

Here's why: You can't just add customer metrics to processes designed around operational optimization. The underlying logic doesn't change. When customer value conflicts with operational efficiency, and sometimes it does, which wins?

Most organizations send horribly mixed signals. They tell people customers come first, then punish anyone who misses their cost targets to serve a customer better. Employees learn to optimize what gets measured and rewarded, which is usually still the operational metrics.

Value-Centric IBP isn't about choosing between operational excellence and customer focus. It's about integrating them so deeply that the question becomes meaningless. You optimize for value creation, which requires both operational capability and customer understanding.

But I'm getting ahead of myself. Let's talk about why this journey takes time and why you can't skip steps.

Why You're Reading This in Chapter 10

You might wonder why we're only now getting to Value-Centric IBP after nine chapters. If this is the answer, why didn't we start here?

Because you can't build the roof before the foundation. Everything we've covered so far isn't throat-clearing or theoretical background. It's a prerequisite capability you absolutely must have before Value-Centric IBP makes any sense.

We started, in Chapters 2 to 5, by defining what customer value actually means because most companies have only fuzzy notions about this. Without understanding the economic, functional, emotional, and social dimensions of customer value, your "customer-focused" planning is just guesswork dressed up in better language.

Then, in Chapters 6 and 7, we tackled measurement, which proved harder than it looks. You need systematic ways to capture and quantify customer value realization across different dimensions. This isn't optional prep work. It's the data foundation that makes customer-centric planning possible rather than aspirational.

After that, in Chapter 8, we developed frameworks for measuring business value creation because sustainable advantage requires alignment between what customers value and what generates returns for you. The uncomfortable truth is that some things customers want aren't economically viable, and you need frameworks to navigate these tensions rather than pretending they don't exist.

The correlation between customer and business value, captured in the Customer-Business Value Matrix in Chapter 7, became pivotal. This framework moves you beyond false choices between customer satisfaction and profitability. It provides an analytical foundation for resource allocation that optimizes both simultaneously.

Customer value segmentation recognized that different customer groups define, realize, and maximize value in fundamentally different ways. As covered in Chapter 8, treating all customers the same isn't customer-centric. It's customer-ignorant.

And in Chapter 9, we identified the capabilities required to maintain and expand customer value because good intentions don't create competitive advantage. You need operational capabilities, organizational structures, analytical competencies, and cultural foundations that enable consistent value delivery at scale.

Only with all these pieces in place does Value-Centric IBP make sense. It's not planning *instead of* these capabilities. It's the integration framework that brings them together into coherent decision-making.

Think of it like learning to drive. You need to understand how the car works, practice individual skills like steering and braking, learn to read traffic, and develop spatial awareness. Only then does "driving" become a fluid, integrated activity rather than overwhelming cognitive chaos.

Value-Centric IBP is the "driving," the focus of Part 2. Everything we covered up to this point in Part 1 prepared you for it.

The Change Management Reality Check

I want to emphasize that each stage of this journey requires questioning established assumptions, developing new competencies, and often restructuring how you operate and make decisions. This isn't a six-month project. It's organizational transformation that touches everything: how you understand markets, serve customers, and compete for advantage. It requires patience, persistence, and genuine commitment to continuous learning.

The stakes matter because the competitive gap compounds over time. Companies still optimizing primarily for operational efficiency while competitors focus on value creation will fall behind despite superior internal metrics. Their cost per unit might be lower, but their revenue per customer will be worse.

Conversely, companies that successfully evolve their IBP to integrate customer value considerations create advantages that compound: stronger customer relationships, enhanced pricing power, and superior innovation aligned with actual market needs.

The question isn't whether customer-centric planning matters. The question is whether you'll build these capabilities before your competitors do.

What Traditional IBP Does Well
(And Where It Falls Short)

Let's give credit where due: Oliver Wight IBP represents sophisticated planning that has generated enormous value. Understanding its strengths helps us appreciate what to preserve during evolution.

The Real Strengths

Traditional IBP's greatest contribution is systematic cross-functional coordination. It forces sales, marketing, operations, finance, and leadership to actually talk to each other regularly. It eliminates the classic pattern where sales makes promises operations can't keep, operations builds products finance can't afford, and finance sets budgets that ignore market reality.

The monthly cycle creates planning discipline that prevents drift. Without this rhythm, urgent operational issues consume all the oxygen that should go to strategic thinking. Traditional IBP's structured cadence ensures planning gets regular executive attention.

The five-step process provides comprehensive coverage while maintaining logical flow from product strategy through demand, supply, financial integration, and executive decision-making. This structure prevents important considerations from falling through organizational cracks.

Scenario planning lets you evaluate multiple futures rather than betting everything on a single forecast. When that forecast inevitably proves wrong, you have contingency plans ready rather than panicking. Financial integration ensures operational plans translate into realistic projections. This prevents the common problem of attractive-sounding plans that prove financially unsustainable once you account for capital requirements and cash flow realities.

Where It Falls Short

But traditional IBP's operational focus creates blind spots in customer-centric competitive environments.

Product planning emphasizes lifecycle management without systematically considering how products create value for different customer segments. You end up making feature decisions based on technical elegance or development ease rather than customer value impact.

Demand planning treats customers as interchangeable volume. It optimizes for forecast accuracy without considering that serving low-value customers at the expense of high-value relationships might hit your forecast while destroying value.

Supply planning emphasizes standardized efficiency over customer experience. Service levels get set at "acceptable average" rather than "delightful for important customers, adequate for others."

Financial planning focuses on short-term profitability in ways that undervalue long-term customer relationships. Traditional ROI calculations miss the compounding value of customer loyalty, brand equity, and competitive positioning.

Perhaps most critically, traditional IBP lacks systematic customer input. Planning decisions rely on internal assumptions about customer needs rather than actual customer insights. Sales provides some customer voice, but it's filtered through their particular lens and priorities.

Value-Centric IBP: Evolution, Not Revolution

Value-Centric IBP doesn't throw out traditional planning discipline. It preserves cross-functional coordination and process rigor while fundamentally reorienting around customer value creation and competitive differentiation. The philosophical shift changes your primary organizing principle from operational efficiency to customer value creation. Operational efficiency remains important—you can't deliver value poorly—but decisions get evaluated first for customer value impact and competitive positioning, with operational considerations enabling rather than driving strategy.

This recognizes that sustainable advantage increasingly comes from superior customer relationships rather than just operational excellence. Competitors can often replicate operational improvements. Deep customer relationships based on superior value delivery create switching costs and loyalty that protect your position.

The Architecture of Value-Centric IBP

Traditional IBP has five core processes. Value-Centric IBP adds two critical dimensions: customer value optimization and capability development integration.

Think of it as expanding from two-dimensional planning (operational coordination across functions) to three-dimensional planning (operational coordination, customer value optimization, and competitive capability building—all integrated).

Customer-Business Value Matrix Integration

Every IBP process now incorporates customer and business value considerations. Product planning considers which features create the most value for your Value Partners and Retention Risk customers, not just which features are easiest to build or loudest requests suggest.

Demand planning segments forecasts by customer value, predicting not just volume but the mix of high-value versus low-value demand. This enables better resource allocation, so you can prepare to serve the demand that matters most.

Supply planning differentiates service levels based on customer value. Your Value Partners get priority access to constrained resources. Your Value Destroyers get efficient but appropriate service.

Financial planning integrates customer lifetime value and capability development ROI into investment decisions. Executive review explicitly considers customer value and capability implications of major choices.

Capability Development Integration

The second dimension ensures every IBP process includes assessment, planning, and resource allocation for capability enhancement. This transforms capability development from isolated projects into systematic organizational improvement. Product planning integrates capability roadmaps identifying which new abilities you need for future innovations. Demand planning considers how capability improvements might affect market demand and competitive positioning.

Supply planning incorporates capability development resource requirements into capacity planning, ensuring capability work doesn't get starved by operational pressures. Financial planning treats capability investments as strategic expenditures creating future advantage, not just costs reducing current profit.

The integration matters because capability development operates on longer horizons than typical planning cycles. Monthly IBP focuses on quarterly results. Meaningful capability development takes 18 to 36 months. Successful integration balances short-term excellence with long-term capability building.

Reimagining the Five Steps

This Section's Executive Takeaway

Value-Centric IBP does not replace traditional planning discipline; it reorients it. The five-step cycle remains, but every decision is now anchored in customer value, segment economics, and capability advantage rather than volume and efficiency alone. For leaders, the shift is from asking "Are we aligned and on plan?" to "Are we investing, prioritizing, and constraining the organization in ways that grow the right customers and protect long-term competitive advantage?"

For Implementation Teams

The following section translates Value-Centric IBP into operating reality. It shows how each step of the traditional IBP cycle changes in practice: how customer segmentation, value migration, capability roadmaps, and competitive priorities are embedded into product, demand, supply, financial, and executive reviews.

Let me walk you through how Value-Centric IBP transforms each planning step. I'll focus on what actually changes rather than repeating textbook descriptions.

Step 1: Product Management Review: From Lifecycle to Customer Journey

Traditional product review focuses on product lifecycles: which products to develop, maintain, harvest, or discontinue. Financial projections and technical feasibility drive decisions. Customers influence this through sales feedback, but indirectly.

Value-Centric product review starts by analyzing customer positioning in your value matrix. How are customers distributed across quadrants?

What migration patterns do you see? These movements signal strategic opportunities and threats.

You evaluate which product enhancements or new offerings will drive favorable migrations: moving Margin Diluters toward Value Partners, protecting Value Partners from becoming Retention Risks, deciding whether to improve or exit Value Destroyer relationships.

Critically, you integrate capability roadmaps. For each planned product enhancement, you map which organizational capabilities are required, not just technical development abilities, but go-to-market capabilities, customer support requirements, operational scaling needs.

You identify capability gaps: abilities you don't currently have but need. Some gaps get filled quickly through hiring or training. Others require sustained development over multiple planning cycles. You integrate these development timelines with product plans.

This often reveals that capability development, not feature development, is your critical path. The code might be ready in three months, but the sales team won't have the skills to sell it effectively for nine months. That's your real constraint.

Step 2: Demand Review: From Forecasting to Value-Driven Growth

Traditional demand review forecasts sales volumes based on historical patterns, market trends, and sales input. The goal is accuracy, enabling efficient supply planning.

Value-Centric demand review segments forecasts by customer value categories, not just products or regions. You forecast different behaviors based on value matrix positioning. Value Partners typically show stable demand with expansion potential. Margin Diluters exhibit variable demand depending on your value delivery improvements.

Retention Risks demonstrate consistent but limited growth. Value Destroyers indicate declining demand requiring intervention or exit.

You model migration patterns: How will customers move between quadrants based on your actions, competitive moves, and market evolution? How will your capability deployments and product launches influence demand across segments?

You assess competitive value impact: How are competitor value propositions affecting demand patterns across your quadrants? Where are they creating threats? Where are they missing opportunities?

This approach forecasts not just volume but value. You might predict lower total unit volume but higher revenue because you're shifting mix toward Value Partners and away from Value Destroyers.

Step 3: Supply Review: From Efficiency to Value-Driven Fulfillment

Traditional supply review matches capacity to demand while optimizing costs and standardizing service levels.

Value-Centric supply review maintains efficiency while recognizing that different customer segments justify different cost structures and service experiences. You allocate capacity based on customer value matrix positioning. When resources are constrained, Value Partners get priority. When you have excess capacity, you can serve Margin Diluters or Value Destroyers, but you don't build capacity based on their demand.

You assess capability constraints: Which strategic capabilities limit your ability to serve different segments optimally? Innovation capabilities might constrain Value Partner service. Cost management capabilities might limit Margin Diluter profitability.

You develop constraint elevation strategies: investments, partnerships, or resource reallocations that address capability limitations. Some constraints get resolved through technology investment. Others require talent acquisition. Still others need process improvements or organizational changes.

Resource allocation balances constraint management with value matrix objectives. You don't just optimize for efficiency. You optimize for value creation within constraint realities.

Step 4: Financial Review: From Budgets to Value Investment Optimization

Traditional financial review translates operational plans into financial projections supporting budgets and investment decisions based on revenue growth, margin improvement, and ROI.

Value-Centric financial review balances short-term performance with long-term customer value creation by explicitly modeling how customer investments generate future returns. You analyze customer value ROI: profitability by segment, incorporating both direct costs and value delivery investments. You measure returns on technology, process improvements, and capability development that enhance customer value.

You prioritize competitive investment: capital allocation based on competitive advantage potential and customer value impact, not just operational ROI. Long-term value creation balances short-term profitability with capability development and market positioning.

You track value matrix investment: capital allocation based on customer quadrant positioning and migration potential. Investments protecting and expanding Value Partners typically generate highest returns. Margin Diluter conversion investments require careful ROI analysis. Retention Risk optimization focuses on business model improvements, enhancing monetization without compromising satisfaction.

The financial review integrates value matrix metrics with traditional indicators, ensuring balanced optimization rather than short-term financial pressure undermining strategic customer relationships.

Step 5: Executive Review: From Performance to Strategic Value Creation

Traditional executive review aligns functions around a single operating plan, addresses conflicts, and ensures accountability, primarily for financial performance and operational metrics.

Value-Centric executive review transforms into strategic leadership, guiding organizational evolution toward customer-focused competitive advantage. Executives become accountable for customer value creation and competitive positioning alongside financial performance.

You assess strategic coherence: Do operational plans and resource allocations align with value matrix optimization objectives? Do functions collaborate around customer value delivery or optimize individual metrics?

You evaluate capability development progress: Are strategic capability initiatives advancing? Are they integrated with operational plans? Do resource allocations reflect strategic priorities?

You review value matrix performance: Are customers migrating favorably between quadrants? Is competitive positioning improving? Are investments generating expected returns?

The executive review balances value matrix progress with financial performance and competitive dynamics, ensuring operational decisions reinforce customer value optimization and competitive positioning.

The Organizational Reality

Implementation lens: How structure, governance, and decision rights must change to support value-centric planning

Effective Value-Centric IBP requires organizational structures that facilitate collaboration while maintaining accountability. Traditional functional organization often perpetuates silos that suboptimize customer value.

I won't bore you with detailed organizational charts, but the principle matters: You need cross-functional teams organized around customer segments, not just functional hierarchies. An executive steering committee provides strategic direction and resource allocation authority. A value planning council facilitates monthly planning cycles and cross-functional integration. Segment-focused working groups handle specific customer segment planning and optimization.

The key is matrix accountability: People report functionally for skill development and resource management but work cross-functionally for customer value delivery. This creates tension—matrix organizations always do—but it's productive tension that prevents suboptimization.

Process and Facilitation: Where Theory Meets Reality

Implementation lens: How meeting design, cadence, and facilitation discipline determine whether Value-Centric IBP becomes real or remains theoretical

I've watched countless organizations implement sophisticated planning frameworks that fail because meeting discipline collapses or discussions wander into unproductive territory. Value-Centric IBP requires specific facilitation approaches ensuring customer value and competitive considerations actually drive decisions.

The Monthly Rhythm

Operational design focus: cycle structure, handoffs, and escalation logic

Week one focuses on customer value and market analysis. You review segment performance: How are customers realizing value? What trends do you see in satisfaction, retention, expansion? Where are the gaps?

You synthesize competitive intelligence: What are competitors doing? How is the market evolving? What threats and opportunities are emerging?

Week two integrates operational planning. You do demand and capacity planning, incorporating segment-specific patterns and value realization dynamics. You review capability development progress and adjust investment priorities. You integrate financial analysis with value-based ROI assessment.

Week three drives strategic alignment and decision-making. You integrate functional plans, resolving conflicts based on customer value impact. You prepare executive briefings, identifying major decisions requiring leadership attention.

Week four manages implementation and communication. You finalize plans, assign accountability, establish tracking systems. You capture lessons learned and prepare for the next cycle.

This meeting rhythm needs to be complemented by Operational Agile Response mechanisms—daily and weekly processes that keep the organization aligned between formal IBP cycles. Daily tiered escalation meetings ensure frontline teams quickly surface issues that affect customer experience, operational performance, or supply continuity. These short, structured stand-ups move problems to the right level of the organization within hours, not weeks, enabling real-time corrective action. Weekly S&OE (sales and operations execution) meetings bridge the gap between daily firefighting and monthly planning. They review short-term demand signals, fulfillment performance, customer feedback, exceptions to plan, and market developments, ensuring the organization adjusts execution without rewriting the plan. Together, these agile response forums act as the operational nervous system of Value-Centric IBP—rapidly sensing, escalating, and resolving issues so that the monthly cycle can stay focused on learning, prioritization, and strategic decision-making rather than urgent operational noise.

Making Meetings Actually Work

Here's what kills most planning processes: meetings without discipline, wrong people attending, discussions that meander, no clear decisions.

Value-centric meetings start with customer voice: five minutes on segment updates featuring specific customer examples. This maintains external focus rather than drifting into internal concerns.

You use structured decision frameworks, prioritizing customer value impact. When functions disagree, you evaluate options based on customer value and competitive advantage potential, not just efficiency or cost.

You celebrate cross-functional successes in customer value delivery. Recognition reinforces collaborative behavior better than any organizational chart redesign.

The Maturity Question

Implementation lens: How to assess whether your organization is capable of executing Value-Centric IBP, not just designing it

Most organizations assume implementing processes automatically delivers results. It doesn't. Team maturity determines actual performance.

I assess teams across seven dimensions:

1. Meeting consistency and discipline: Do teams actually meet on schedule? Is attendance non-negotiable? Or do competing priorities constantly disrupt planning rhythm?

2. Participant composition: Do the right people with decision authority attend? Or do you get junior delegates who can't commit their functions?

3. Agenda quality: Are agendas distributed in advance with clear decision points? Or do meetings wander through poorly structured discussions?

4. Discussion focus: Do discussions stay on agenda, generating insights? Or do tangents consume time without advancing decisions?

5. Decision-making effectiveness: Do meetings produce clear, implementable decisions with ownership and timelines? Or do they end ambiguously?

6. KPI impact: Can teams demonstrate correlation between planning decisions and KPI improvements? Or is planning disconnected from business results?

7. Feedback loop closure: Do teams systematically review planning effectiveness and continuously improve? Or do they repeat the same problems?

Most teams operate at basic or developing maturity levels. Getting to competent requires deliberate capability building. Reaching advanced or mastery levels demands sustained effort and executive commitment.

The good news: Maturity is learnable. Teams improve through facilitation skill development, decision-making framework adoption, KPI tracking systems connecting planning to performance, and continuous improvement processes.

Implementation: What Actually Works

This Section's Executive Takeaway (60 Seconds)

Value-Centric IBP succeeds through staged capability building, not big-bang transformation. Leaders must fund the journey, protect focus, and resist technology-first shortcuts that bypass process and people readiness.

For Implementation Teams

The following phases provide a practical rollout model: sequencing capability development, pilots, scaling, governance, and analytics maturity over 12 to 18 months.

I've seen two Value-Centric IBP implementation approaches: the "big bang" full transformation and the gradual capability building. The big bang almost always fails. Gradual building almost always succeeds.

Phase 1: Foundation Building (Months 1 to 3)

Start by implementing customer value measurement systems and segmentation frameworks. Train teams on customer value analysis. You can't plan around customer value without the ability to measure it.

Build competitive intelligence capabilities and benchmarking processes. Develop competitive capability assessment frameworks. You need external perspective on market realities and competitive dynamics.

Assess current planning maturity using the seven dimensions. Design enhanced processes integrating customer value considerations. Develop facilitation capabilities supporting cross-functional collaboration.

Don't try changing everything at once. Build foundations first.

Phase 2: Pilot Implementation (Months 4 to 6)

Select pilot teams representing major business units or regions. Provide intensive training on Value-Centric IBP processes. Establish mentoring and support.

Let pilots test and refine processes. Monitor performance and gather feedback. Adjust based on learning.

Document early wins and improvements. Communicate success stories across the organization. Use pilot success to build momentum for broader implementation.

Phase 3: Scaled Implementation (Months 7 to 12)

Expand to all planning teams systematically. Implement supporting technology and analytical capabilities. Establish governance structures and accountability systems.

Implement comprehensive KPI measurement and reporting. Establish regular performance reviews and optimization cycles. Build continuous improvement capabilities.

Integrate capability development planning with operational planning. Establish long-term capability roadmaps and investment plans. Build organizational learning systems, capturing and sharing best practices.

Phase 4: Maturity and Beyond (Months 13-Plus)

Implement advanced analytics for customer value prediction and optimization. Automate routine planning processes, freeing time for strategic decision-making. Develop AI-powered insights for competitive intelligence.

Extend Value-Centric IBP to supplier and partner ecosystems. Develop collaborative planning with key stakeholders. Build integrated value delivery networks spanning organizational boundaries.

Establish innovation planning processes anticipating future customer value evolution. Build scenario planning capabilities for market disruption and competitive response. Develop dynamic capability adjustment processes adapting to changing conditions.

The Technology Trap

This Section's Executive Caution

Technology accelerates strategy only after process and capability are in place.

Implementation Reality

Sequence process → skills → systems, or adoption will fail.

Here's where most transformations fail: Organizations fall in love with sophisticated technology solutions, invest heavily in platforms and systems, then struggle with poor adoption and limited business impact. The pattern is predictable: Become enchanted with advanced capabilities, assume technology will drive process improvement and behavioral change, discover reality doesn't work that way.

Value-Centric IBP transformation succeeds when you reverse this sequence. Start with process design. Build human capabilities. Then deploy technology to scale proven approaches. This process-people-technology sequence recognizes that sustainable transformation requires changing how work gets done and building organizational capabilities before technology provides meaningful leverage.

Business processes and human capabilities generate the majority of transformation benefits. Technology amplifies and scales. Organizations mastering customer value-focused planning with basic tools achieve significant improvements. They can then leverage advanced technology to accelerate and automate.

Conversely, organizations deploying sophisticated technology without effective processes and capable people achieve disappointing results. Technology can't compensate for poorly designed processes, inadequate skills, or resistance to customer-focused decision-making.

Start simple. Master the basics. Add sophistication gradually as capabilities mature. Focus on actionable insights rather than comprehensive analysis. Prioritize decision-making speed over analytical perfection.

The Honest Reality Check

I will confess that Value-Centric IBP can be complex and demanding. If you're looking for a magic pill to fix everything overnight, Value-Centric IBP isn't it. We don't do miracle cures. But if you're up for a new workout routine that builds stamina, strength, and maybe even a six-pack of competitive advantage, you're in the right place. Best of all, this "exercise" program not only makes you happier; it also makes your partner, the customer, happier too. And let's be honest: Nothing beats being in a healthy, loving relationship, especially one that doesn't require couples therapy or divorce lawyers.

You're asking planning teams to simultaneously optimize customer value by segment, business value, competitive positioning, capability development, and operational efficiency. That's substantial cognitive load.

The monthly cycle requires extensive coordination, analysis, and decision-making. Most organizations already struggle with traditional IBP's five-step process. Adding customer value matrix analysis, capability road mapping, and competitive intelligence synthesis significantly increases planning burden.

On top of that, the framework assumes you've already implemented robust customer value measurement, established reliable segmentation, and built analytical capabilities. These are substantial prerequisites requiring significant development.

Resource requirements are real. Value-Centric IBP demands investment in customer analytics, competitive intelligence, capability development planning, and expanded coordination—all before demonstrating clear ROI.

You'll face organizational politics: power redistribution, functional resistance, career incentive misalignment. Cross-functional segment teams may conflict with functional hierarchies. Resource allocation based on customer value may threaten established power structures.

Many organizations are already pursuing multiple transformations: digital, agile, customer experience, AI integration. Adding Value-Centric IBP risks change saturation where initiatives compete rather than reinforce.

So let me ask the question this chapter doesn't fully answer: Under what conditions does Value-Centric IBP's additional complexity and investment generate returns justifying its costs?

For organizations with highly differentiated customer segments, long customer lifecycles, and competitive dynamics where relationships drive advantage—it's absolutely worth it.

For companies competing primarily on operational efficiency, with commoditized offerings, or in markets where customer preferences do not change rapidly—maybe simpler customer-focused enhancements to traditional IBP would suffice.

The stakes matter because competitive gaps compound over time. But honest assessment of your context matters more than framework enthusiasm.

The Real Point

Value-Centric IBP isn't just better planning. It's fundamentally different competition. Organizations mastering this integration don't just plan better. They compete more effectively by aligning every operational decision with customer value creation and competitive advantage development.

The transformation is hard. It takes time. It requires genuine commitment to change how you work. But the alternative is optimizing your way to irrelevance while competitors who understand customer value eat your lunch.

The question isn't whether customer value matters in planning. The question is whether you'll build these capabilities before your competitors do. Because in the end, plans really are worthless. But planning that integrates customer understanding, competitive positioning, and capability development into operational decision-making? That's everything!

Traditional IBP gives you the discipline to align functions and execute a plan. Value-Centric IBP asks a harder question: What is this plan doing to customer value, and are we building the capabilities to keep winning tomorrow, not just performing today? But here's the twist: You can redesign the process, upgrade the metrics, and even get the governance right, and still watch the whole thing collapse under real-world pressure if the culture keeps rewarding the old game. That's why the next chapter matters. Because in the end, Value-Centric IBP isn't installed. It's lived.

CHAPTER 11

Building a Customer-Centric Culture for Value-Driven IBP

Culture eats strategy for breakfast.
—Peter Drucker

When Perfect Processes Meet Reality

Let me tell you about two companies I watched implement nearly identical customer segmentation strategies.

Company A had everything right on paper. Elegant frameworks. Detailed processes. Sophisticated analytics. They spent months developing their approach and even more months training people on it.

It failed spectacularly.

Company B started with messier processes and less sophisticated tools. But they achieved remarkable results almost immediately.

The difference wasn't the strategy. It was the culture.

At Company A, the culture rewarded individual functional excellence over collaborative customer outcomes. Sales teams optimized for transaction volume because that's what got them promoted. Product teams prioritized technical elegance over user needs because that's what their peers respected. Operations focused on cost reduction because that's what executives praised in meetings.

Everyone knew the new customer-centric strategy was important. They'd all sat through the presentations. But when it came to actual decisions—the thousand small choices people make every day—they defaulted to what their culture actually rewarded. And their culture rewarded everything except customer value creation.

Company B's culture instinctively aligned around customer success. Employees naturally considered customer impact in daily decisions. Cross-functional collaboration emerged organically around customer value creation because that's just how things worked there. The processes were almost beside the point because the culture did most of the work.

This is the uncomfortable truth about Value-Centric IBP: The most sophisticated processes will fail without a corporate culture that genuinely prioritizes customer value creation over internal convenience, functional optimization, or short-term financial metrics.

What Culture Actually Is
(And Why It's So Hard to Change)

Corporate culture isn't what's written on your office walls or in your employee handbook. It's the shared beliefs, values, and behavioral norms that guide how employees think about their work and make decisions when no one is watching. Culture manifests in countless daily micro-decisions that collectively determine whether Value-Centric IBP becomes genuine organizational capability or remains superficial process compliance that fails to drive real improvement.

Here's why culture change is so damn difficult: Traditional organizational cultures often develop around functional excellence, operational efficiency, and internal metrics that directly conflict with customer-centric decision-making.

Sales cultures reward transaction volume over customer value, undermining long-term relationship building with Value Partners. Engineering cultures prioritize technical elegance over user experience, creating products that fail to address real customer needs. Operations cultures focused on cost reduction optimize processes in ways that create customer friction or reduce value delivery.

The misalignment becomes particularly problematic when implementing Value-Centric IBP because the process requires employees to balance multiple considerations simultaneously: customer value creation, competitive positioning, operational efficiency, and financial performance.

Without cultural support, employees default to optimizing for the metrics and behaviors their organizational culture actually rewards, regardless of what formal processes tell them to prioritize. They're not being difficult or resistant. They're being rational. Culture is the water they swim in, and it shapes their behavior far more powerfully than any process document ever could.

The Cultural Barriers You'll Face

Several common cultural patterns actively undermine customer-centric behavior. You need to recognize them before you can address them.

Risk-averse cultures that punish failure prevent the experimentation and learning required to understand evolving customer needs. If employees get punished for trying new approaches that don't work, they'll stick with safe, established approaches even when those approaches no longer serve customers well.

Hierarchical cultures that centralize decision-making prevent front-line employees from responding quickly to customer feedback or market changes. By the time a customer issue gets escalated through three management levels for approval, the customer has already left for a competitor.

Siloed cultures that optimize individual functional performance create internal competition, undermining collaborative customer value creation. When marketing is measured on lead generation, sales on transaction closure, and customer success on renewal rates, these functions optimize their individual metrics in ways that reduce overall customer value and lifetime profitability.

I've watched this play out: Marketing generates leads that sales can't convert because marketing optimized for volume over quality. Sales closes deals with customers who aren't good fits because they're optimizing for transaction count. Customer success inherits these mismatched relationships and gets blamed for poor retention rates they had no role in creating.

Short-term performance cultures prioritizing quarterly results undermine long-term customer relationship building. Value Partner relationships require sustained investment and patience that may not generate immediate financial returns. These relationships become vulnerable to abandonment during financial pressure unless cultural values support long-term thinking.

Internal focus cultures prioritizing operational metrics miss opportunities for value creation and innovation. These cultures excel at efficiency but struggle to understand why customers choose alternatives or how to create distinctive value propositions commanding premium pricing.

Why Culture Actually Matters Competitively

Organizations with strong customer-centric cultures create sustainable competitive advantages because culture is much more difficult for competitors to replicate than processes, technologies, or strategies. Competitors can copy your Value-Centric IBP frameworks and tools. They can hire away your people and reverse-engineer your processes. But they cannot easily replicate the cultural foundation that makes these processes effective.

Southwest Airlines' culture of putting employees first and customers second (knowing that happy employees create happy customers) has enabled them to maintain superior customer satisfaction and operational performance for decades. Their culture drives behaviors that competitors can observe but struggle to replicate because the behaviors emerge from deep cultural beliefs rather than management mandates. United can study Southwest's processes all they want. They can't copy the culture that makes those processes work.

Zappos built their entire competitive strategy around a customer service culture treating every customer interaction as an opportunity to create emotional connections rather than just transaction processing. This cultural foundation enabled customer service experiences generating massive word-of-mouth marketing and customer loyalty that competitors couldn't match through operational improvements alone.

The competitive advantage of customer-centric culture becomes self-reinforcing: It attracts employees who value customer success, customers who appreciate genuine care and attention, and partners who want to work with organizations known for integrity and customer focus. This positive reinforcement cycle creates momentum increasingly difficult for competitors to disrupt.

Netflix demonstrates powerful culture-strategy alignment through their "freedom and responsibility" culture empowering employees to make customer-focused decisions without extensive approval processes. This cultural foundation enables their recommendation algorithms, content development, and product features to evolve rapidly in response to customer preferences rather than being constrained by bureaucratic processes or internal politics.

Building Blocks: The Foundational Elements

Building customer-centric culture requires systematic attention to fundamental elements shaping how employees think about their work and make decisions.

Values and Beliefs That Actually Mean Something

The foundation lies in shared organizational beliefs about the purpose of business and the source of sustainable success. These beliefs must go beyond marketing slogans to become genuine convictions guiding difficult decisions and resource allocation choices.

Amazon's principle of "customer obsession" represents a genuine belief system, not just marketing. This belief manifests in decisions like their willingness to lose money on fast delivery to improve customer experience, their practice of reading customer emails in executive meetings, and their long-term investment in customer convenience features that may not generate immediate profits.

The beliefs must address how employees should handle conflicts between customer interests and short-term business metrics. Customer-centric organizations develop beliefs that long-term customer value creation generates superior business results even when it requires short-term sacrifice of efficiency or profitability.

But here's the critical part: These beliefs must feel authentic. Employees can smell bullshit from miles away. If leadership says "customers first" but actually rewards quarterly numbers above all else, the stated values become worse than meaningless. They become evidence of hypocrisy that actively undermines trust.

Salesforce's belief in "equality as a core value" extends to customer relationships, driving behaviors ensuring all customers receive respect and attention regardless of size or immediate profitability. This belief system guides decisions about resource allocation, product development, and customer service reinforcing their customer-centric positioning.

Behavioral Norms: What People Actually Do

Values are abstract. Behavioral norms are concrete. They define specifically how employees should interact with customers, collaborate across functions, and make decisions affecting customer value. These norms must be explicitly defined, consistently modeled, and systematically reinforced through daily organizational practices.

Customer interaction norms should emphasize listening, empathy, and solution-oriented thinking rather than just policy enforcement or efficient transaction processing. Employees should be expected to understand customer context, ask questions revealing underlying needs, and take ownership of customer outcomes rather than just completing assigned tasks.

Zappos' cultural norm of empowering customer service representatives to spend whatever time necessary to resolve customer issues, including authorization to send flowers or gifts to customers experiencing personal difficulties, demonstrates behavioral expectations prioritizing customer relationships over operational efficiency. Their famous story of the customer service rep who stayed on the phone for 10-plus hours helping a customer isn't an aberration. It's a demonstration of cultural norms in action.

Cross-functional collaboration norms should expect employees to consider customer impact when making decisions affecting other departments, share information helping colleagues serve customers better, and prioritize overall customer value over individual functional optimization.

HubSpot's cultural norm of "solve for the customer" requires employees to consider customer impact in decisions ranging from product feature prioritization to pricing changes to internal process improvements. This norm creates organizational reflexes naturally aligning with Value-Centric IBP principles.

Measurement and Rewards: What You Actually Incentivize

This Section's Executive Takeaway

Culture follows incentives, not intentions. If performance systems reward short-term volume, cost efficiency, or functional optimization in isolation, employees will rationally sacrifice customer value, even while repeating "customer first" in meetings. A Value-Centric IBP culture only becomes real when promotion, compensation, and recognition systems make long-term customer impact and cross-functional outcomes as visible and career-relevant as financial results.

For Implementation Teams

This section translates this principle into operating mechanisms: how to redesign scorecards, performance reviews, team metrics, and reward structures so customer value creation, collaboration, and long-term relationship health are reinforced consistently across roles, functions, and levels, rather than undermined by legacy KPIs and conflicting incentives.

Here's a blunt truth: Culture transformation requires measurement and reward systems reinforcing customer-centric behaviors rather than undermining them through conflicting incentives.

Traditional measurement systems often create internal competition and short-term optimization conflicting with customer value creation. You cannot build customer-centric culture while maintaining measurement systems rewarding anti-customer behavior.

Individual performance measurement should include customer impact metrics alongside traditional functional measures. Sales representatives might be measured on customer satisfaction and retention alongside revenue generation. Product managers could be evaluated on user adoption and customer outcome achievement rather than just feature delivery.

Team performance measurement should emphasize collaborative customer outcomes rather than just individual functional excellence. Cross-functional teams working on customer initiatives should be measured and rewarded based on customer success metrics requiring coordinated effort across multiple departments.

Netflix measures content team performance based on viewer engagement and satisfaction rather than just content production volume or cost efficiency. This measurement approach drives behaviors prioritizing customer value over operational convenience.

Reward systems should recognize and celebrate customer-centric behaviors through both formal recognition programs and informal cultural practices. Tell stories about employees who made exceptional customer-focused decisions. Provide career advancement opportunities for customer-centric leaders. Ensure compensation systems reward long-term customer value creation.

The alignment must be systematic and comprehensive, not superficial additions to existing systems. Employees quickly recognize when customer-centric rhetoric conflicts with actual measurement and reward practices. If you say customers matter but only promote people who hit short-term numbers regardless of customer impact, everyone learns what you actually value.

Communication: Keeping Customers Visible

Customer-centric culture requires communication patterns keeping customer perspectives visible and relevant in organizational decision-making. Regular customer voice integration ensures customer perspectives influence organizational discussions and decisions rather than being relegated to customer service departments. Share customer feedback in team meetings. Include customer success stories in company communications. Provide forums for employees to hear directly from customers about their experiences and needs.

Slack's practice of sharing customer success stories across the organization helps employees understand how their work contributes to customer outcomes, while regular customer feedback sessions provide insights informing product development and operational improvements.

At Medtronic every meeting begins not with numbers or forecasts, but with a patient story. It's a ritual that reconnects everyone—from engineers to executives—to the human purpose behind the company's work: "alleviating pain, restoring health, and extending life."

This practice traces back to founder Earl Bakken, who started a tradition in the 1960s of inviting patients to Medtronic's headquarters each Christmas. He wanted employees to hear firsthand how their devices had changed lives. The event became known as the Medtronic Holiday Party, where patients shared personal stories with employees, families, and board members. The experience often left the room in tears and in renewed alignment with the company's mission.

Decades later, the tradition continues. At every major meeting, Medtronic teams still open with a patient story, a living reminder that business success is inseparable from human impact.

Cross-functional information sharing should ensure customer insights reach all relevant departments rather than remaining siloed within customer-facing functions. Marketing insights about customer preferences should inform product development. Sales feedback about customer objections should influence pricing and positioning. Customer success insights about usage patterns should guide feature prioritization.

The communication patterns should create emotional connection with customers rather than just intellectual understanding. Employees who understand how their work impacts real people are more likely to make customer-centric decisions than those who only see customers as abstract metrics or transaction sources.

Two-way communication should provide forums for employee feedback, questions, and suggestions about customer-centricity implementation. Employees should have opportunities to influence changes in direction and share insights about barriers or opportunities for customer focus improvement.

Storytelling should use specific examples of customer impact to make abstract concepts concrete and emotionally resonant. Stories about how employee actions improved customer outcomes create more powerful motivation than general statements about customer importance.

Leadership's Make-or-Break Role

Leadership behavior represents the most powerful force for culture transformation because employees observe how leaders actually behave rather than just listening to what they say.

Let me be direct: If your executives don't genuinely model customer focus, culture transformation will fail. Period.

Executive Modeling Has to Be Authentic

Culture transformation begins with executive leaders who genuinely believe in customer-centricity and demonstrate that belief through their decisions, time allocation, and personal behaviors. Employees quickly recognize whether leadership commitment to customer focus is authentic or merely rhetorical. Fake it and you won't just fail to build customer-centric culture; you'll actively undermine trust and credibility.

Leadership modeling includes spending significant time with customers, making decisions prioritizing customer value over short-term financial metrics, and taking personal responsibility for customer outcomes rather than delegating customer focus to lower organizational levels. When CEOs personally respond to customer complaints, participate in customer success reviews, and make customer satisfaction a regular topic in executive meetings, they signal that customer focus represents genuine organizational priority.

Marc Benioff's personal involvement in customer success at Salesforce, including his practice of personally responding to customer tweets and emails, demonstrates authentic leadership commitment influencing organizational culture throughout the company. His willingness to publicly acknowledge customer complaints and take personal responsibility for resolution creates cultural expectations that customer issues receive immediate attention at all organizational levels.

Leadership authenticity requires making difficult decisions prioritizing customer value even when they conflict with short-term financial optimization or operational convenience. These decisions create cultural precedents guiding employee behavior during challenging situations where customer interests might conflict with other organizational pressures.

The modeling must be consistent and sustained, not episodic. Employees test leadership commitment through observation of behavior during stressful periods when maintaining customer focus requires sacrifice of other objectives. Leaders who abandon customer focus during financial pressure or competitive threats signal that customer-centricity represents a fair-weather priority rather than fundamental organizational commitment.

Decision-Making Frameworks That Embed Customer Focus

Customer-centric culture requires decision-making frameworks systematically considering customer impact and prioritizing customer value creation. These frameworks must be embedded in organizational processes rather than remaining abstract principles leaders invoke occasionally. Customer impact assessment should become standard practice for significant organizational decisions, with systematic evaluation of how changes affect different customer segments and overall customer value creation.

Amazon's customer-centric decision-making process requires teams to write detailed documents explaining how proposed initiatives will benefit customers, with customer impact serving as primary evaluation criteria for project approval and resource allocation decisions. This isn't bureaucracy for bureaucracy's sake. It forces people to actually think through customer impact rather than just asserting that something will be good for customers because it serves internal interests.

Priority-setting processes should incorporate customer value as primary criteria for evaluating competing initiatives and opportunities. Develop systematic approaches for comparing the customer value impact of different investment options, ensuring customer considerations influence strategic choices rather than being afterthoughts in business planning.

Organizational Structure: Enabling Customer Focus

Customer-centric culture often requires organizational structure changes eliminating barriers to customer focus and creating clear accountability for customer outcomes.

Traditional functional silos prevent the cross-departmental collaboration required for excellent customer experiences. If creating great customer experiences requires navigating a maze of departmental boundaries and competing priorities, those experiences won't get created consistently.

Customer-focused organizational design might include cross-functional teams responsible for specific customer segments or customer journey stages, with clear authority to make decisions optimizing customer value rather than just functional efficiency.

Spotify's squad-based organizational structure empowers small, cross-functional teams to make decisions optimizing user experience without requiring extensive approval processes or cross-departmental negotiations. This structure enables rapid response to customer feedback and market changes while maintaining organizational coordination around customer value creation.

Authority delegation should empower front-line employees to make customer-focused decisions without extensive approval processes creating delays and frustration. Customer service representatives, sales professionals, and customer success managers should have authority to resolve customer issues and implement solutions creating customer value within defined guidelines. The organizational structure should eliminate or minimize handoffs creating customer friction or confusion. Customers should experience seamless interactions with the organization rather than being passed between departments, optimizing for their own efficiency rather than customer experience.

Hiring and Development: Getting the Right People

This Section's Executive Takeaway

Culture doesn't scale through posters or speeches. It scales through who you hire, what you tolerate, and what you promote. If you want Value-Centric IBP to survive real pressure, you must treat customer orientation as a selection and leadership criterion, not a nice-to-have. The fastest way to kill a customer-centric strategy is to staff it with people who only know how to win internally.

For Implementation Teams

This section goes deeper into practical talent mechanisms: customer-oriented hiring signals, interview methods, onboarding immersion, and ongoing development programs that build customer reflexes across the organization, not just in customer-facing roles.

Building customer-centric culture requires systematic attention to talent acquisition and development prioritizing customer focus alongside technical skills and functional expertise.

Hiring for Customer Orientation

Customer-centric hiring requires recruitment processes assessing candidate attitudes toward customer service, collaborative problem-solving, and long-term relationship building rather than just technical competence and individual achievement.

Traditional hiring practices often prioritize functional expertise while neglecting the customer orientation needed for Value-Centric IBP success. You end up with brilliant people who are terrible at customer focus.

Behavioral interviewing should include scenarios revealing how candidates think about customer needs, handle customer conflicts, and balance customer interests with organizational constraints. Candidates should demonstrate natural empathy for customer perspectives and instinctive consideration of customer impact in decision-making.

Southwest Airlines' hiring process famously prioritizes attitude over aptitude, with extensive evaluation of candidate alignment with their customer service culture. They recognize that technical skills can be taught more easily than customer-focused attitudes, making cultural fit the primary selection criterion.

Values-based assessment should evaluate candidate alignment with customer-centric organizational values through both interview discussions and reference checking exploring how candidates have actually behaved in customer-facing situations. Previous customer advocacy, service excellence, or collaborative problem-solving provides better prediction of future customer focus than just stated beliefs about customer importance.

The recruitment process itself should demonstrate organizational customer focus through respectful, responsive, and transparent communication with candidates. The recruitment experience often provides candidates' first impression of organizational culture, making it important that recruitment practices reflect the customer-centric values the organization wants to reinforce.

Onboarding: Immersing People in Customer Perspective

Customer-centric onboarding should immerse new employees in customer perspectives, organizational customer success stories, and the connection between their role and customer value creation.

Traditional onboarding often focuses on policies, procedures, and functional training while neglecting the cultural foundation needed for customer focus. People learn the mechanics of their job without understanding why it matters to customers.

Customer exposure should be integrated into onboarding for all employees, not just those in customer-facing roles. New hires should hear directly from customers about their experiences, challenges, and goals, creating personal connection with the customer perspectives that should guide their decision-making.

Zappos' extensive cultural onboarding includes intensive exposure to customer service principles and direct customer interaction for all employees regardless of functional roles. This approach creates organization-wide understanding of customer impact and shared commitment to customer success.

Success story integration should expose new employees to organizational examples of exceptional customer focus, including both formal case studies and informal stories illustrating how customer-centric behavior creates positive outcomes for customers, employees, and the organization.

The onboarding process should explicitly connect individual roles to customer value creation, helping employees understand how their work contributes to customer success rather than just organizational operational efficiency. This connection creates meaning and engagement supporting sustained customer focus throughout employment.

Continuous Development: Building Capability over Time

Customer-centric culture requires ongoing development strengthening employee capabilities for understanding customer needs, collaborating across functions, and making decisions optimizing customer value. This development must be systematic and sustained, not episodic training quickly losing impact.

Customer insight development should build employee capabilities for gathering, interpreting, and acting on customer feedback and market intelligence. Employees throughout the organization should understand how to identify customer needs, evaluate customer satisfaction, and translate customer insights into operational improvements.

Cross-functional collaboration skills development should strengthen employee capabilities for working effectively across organizational boundaries to create customer value. This includes communication skills, conflict resolution, project management, and systems thinking enabling complex customer initiatives requiring multiple departments.

HubSpot's extensive internal academy provides ongoing education in customer success principles, inbound marketing philosophy, and collaborative problem-solving reinforcing their customer-centric culture while building practical capabilities for customer value creation.

The development programs should be directly connected to career advancement opportunities, ensuring customer-centric capabilities receive the same attention and investment as technical expertise. Employees should understand that customer focus represents a career advantage rather than just an additional expectation.

Overcoming Resistance:
The Change Management Reality

This Section's Executive Takeaway

Most "resistance" isn't rebellion. It's ambiguity, overload, and fear of being punished by old incentives while being asked to behave in new ways. Culture change sticks when leaders remove friction, clarify trade-offs, and realign systems so customer-centric behavior is safe, supported, and rewarded. If the organization feels squeezed, it will revert to the old playbook, no matter how inspiring the new one sounds.

For Implementation Teams

This section breaks down the common sources of resistance (role clarity, workload, skills, incentives) and offers concrete change-management moves—communications, enablement, process simplification, and reinforcement tactics—to reduce reversion and build durable adoption.

Culture transformation faces significant resistance because existing cultural patterns feel natural and comfortable while new behaviors initially feel awkward and unfamiliar. From my experience cultural resistance often emerges from legitimate concerns about workload, role clarity, and performance expectations rather than just stubborn opposition to change. Understanding these concerns enables development of change strategies addressing underlying issues rather than just mandating behavioral change.

The Real Sources of Resistance

Role clarity concerns arise when employees worry that customer focus will conflict with their functional responsibilities or create unrealistic performance expectations. Clear communication about how customer-centric behavior supports rather than undermines functional excellence helps address these concerns through education rather than just reassurance.

Workload concerns reflect employee worry that customer focus will create additional responsibilities without reducing other expectations. Change management should identify process improvements and efficiency gains creating capacity for customer focus rather than just adding requirements to existing workloads.

Microsoft's transition to customer-focused culture included systematic elimination of bureaucratic processes and redundant activities creating capacity for enhanced customer attention without increasing overall workload expectations.

Skill development concerns arise when employees feel unprepared for customer-focused responsibilities or worry about their ability to succeed with new performance expectations. Comprehensive training and support programs should build confidence alongside capability, ensuring employees feel equipped for customer-centric success.

Reward system concerns reflect employee recognition that existing measurement and compensation systems may not support customer-focused behavior. Transparent communication about performance management changes and timeline for implementation helps reduce anxiety about conflicting expectations.

Measuring Cultural Change: Are You Actually Making Progress?

This Section's Executive Takeaway

If you can't measure culture shift, you can't manage it, and you'll confuse activity for progress. Customer-centric culture shows up as behavior: faster decisions that protect customer value, fewer silo handoffs, better problem ownership, and clearer alignment between what you say and what you reward. Measurement isn't about turning culture into a dashboard; it's about proving the direction is real and correcting early when it isn't.

For Implementation Teams

This section goes deeper into how to instrument culture change using a practical mix of employee signals, behavioral observation, customer feedback, and performance metrics, so you can track adoption, spot friction points, and tie cultural shifts to customer and business outcomes.

Culture transformation requires systematic measurement tracking both behavioral changes and underlying attitude shifts supporting sustained customer focus.

Cultural assessment surveys should measure employee attitudes toward customer focus, perceived organizational support for customer-centric behavior, and confidence in ability to contribute to customer success. Regular assessment enables tracking of culture transformation progress and identification of areas needing additional attention.

Behavioral observation should track actual changes in customer-focused decision-making, cross-functional collaboration, and customer interaction quality rather than just stated intentions or policy compliance. Behavioral evidence provides more reliable indication of culture transformation success than survey responses alone.

Customer feedback should include evaluation of employee behavior and organizational responsiveness, providing external validation of culture transformation progress. Customer perspectives on service quality, responsiveness, and problem-solving effectiveness indicate whether cultural changes are creating meaningful customer experience improvements.

Zappos uses customer feedback about employee interactions to assess culture transformation progress and identify opportunities for further development of customer-focused behavior throughout the organization.

Performance metric integration should track customer-focused behaviors alongside traditional operational measures, providing comprehensive evaluation of how culture change affects overall organizational performance. Metrics should demonstrate clear connections between cultural transformation and business results.

The Hard Truth About Cultural Change

Let me close with something important: Building customer-centric culture represents one of the most powerful investments organizations can make in sustainable competitive advantage. But it's also one of the hardest.

Culture transformation requires sustained leadership commitment, systematic attention to organizational systems, and patience with the time required for deep behavioral change. We're not talking about a six-month project. We're talking about multi-year transformation touching every aspect of how the organization operates.

Many organizations start strong and fade. Leadership commits initially but loses focus when results don't appear immediately. Employees embrace new behaviors briefly but revert to old patterns when pressure hits. Systems get partially changed but leave enough conflicts that people become confused about what's actually expected.

I love hiking. On one guided trip, the instructor shared a method for climbing steep hills: Pick a pace you can actually sustain and keep going, one steady step at a time. No rushing, no flopping on a rock halfway up. Just deliberate consistency.

Changing corporate culture is no different. Take it one step at a time. Move at a speed your organization can handle—fast enough to make progress, slow enough to avoid cardiac arrest—but always with purpose.

That's how I eventually found myself standing on top of a mountain in the Canadian Rockies, sweaty but smiling. And that's how you'll one day look back and realize you've climbed the steep slope of culture change. Believe me, the view from the top makes every step worth it.

The organizations that succeed recognize that culture transformation is ultimately about creating organizational environments where customer-focused behavior feels natural and rewarding rather than forced or uncomfortable. When employees genuinely care about customer success and understand how their work contributes to customer value, they make thousands of daily decisions that collectively create superior customer experiences and competitive advantages.

The integration of customer-centric culture with Value-Centric IBP creates organizational capabilities enabling sustained competitive leadership through superior customer value creation. Culture provides the foundation making sophisticated processes effective, while processes provide the structure channeling cultural energy toward systematic competitive advantage creation.

Without the culture, your processes are just documents. With the culture, your processes become powerful tools for creating sustainable competitive advantage. That's why culture doesn't just support Value-Centric IBP. It makes or breaks it.

Once culture and planning are aligned, the question shifts from *whether* you can create customer value consistently to *how* you sustain and scale it over time. The next chapter turns to the role of technology, not as a silver bullet, but as an enabler that helps Value-Centric IBP evolve, adapt, and compound its impact as markets, customers, and capabilities continue to change.

CHAPTER 12

Evolutionary Technology Migration to Value Centric IBP

The real question is not whether machines
think but whether men do.
—B.F. Skinner

The Unauthorized Analysis That Stopped a $75M Transformation

The executive team gathered for the steering committee meeting on the new planning system implementation. Eighteen months into a three-year, $75 million transformation program, the program director presented impressive progress metrics: 78% of planned functionality delivered, system performance exceeding specifications, training completion ahead of schedule.

Then the CEO asked the question that changed everything: "Show me one planning decision we're making better because of this new system."

The program director cycled through dashboards, reports, and analytics. Everything looked impressive. Nothing showed actual decision improvement.

"We can forecast demand 15% more accurately," he offered.

"Are we serving customers better?" the CEO pressed.

"We've reduced planning cycle time from five days to three days," the director countered.

"Are we making more profitable decisions about which customers to prioritize?" the CEO continued.

The program director couldn't answer. The metrics showed technical success but couldn't demonstrate strategic value.

Then a junior analyst in the back of the room, invited to the meeting only to provide technical support, quietly raised her hand. "Actually, I might be able to answer that question. But you're not going to like what I found."

She pulled up an unauthorized analysis she'd created over several weekends, combining customer satisfaction data with profitability metrics that the new planning system tracked separately but never correlated.

The results shocked the room.

The company's three largest customers, representing 35% of revenue and receiving premium capacity allocation from both the old and new planning systems, ranked in the bottom quartile for both satisfaction and profitability. They generated high revenue but required extensive customization, created constant support demands, negotiated aggressively on price, and showed declining satisfaction scores despite premium service levels.

Meanwhile, mid-sized customers that both planning systems systematically deprioritized showed the highest satisfaction scores, the best profit margins, strong growth trajectories, and generated valuable referrals. These customers loved the company's standard offerings, rarely required support, paid premium prices willingly, and expanded their relationships consistently.

"Our planning system, both the old one and the new one we're implementing, optimizes backwards," she explained carefully. "We're allocating our best capacity to customers who don't value it and don't make us money, while rationing service to customers who love us and drive our margins."

The silence in the room was deafening.

The CFO finally asked the obvious question: "Why doesn't our new $75 million planning platform show us this?"

The CIO provided the uncomfortable answer: "Because we implemented it, like the old system, to optimize operational coordination, not customer value creation, we can forecast more accurately and plan faster, but we're forecasting and planning for the wrong priorities."

The CEO looked at the program director, then at the junior analyst's unauthorized dashboard, then back at the executive team. "Stop the implementation. We're not spending another dollar on this transformation until someone can show me how it helps us serve our best customers better and stop wasting resources on customers who destroy value."

What happened next surprised everyone. The CEO didn't cancel the program. He redirected it. "We have good technology," he said. "We just pointed it at the wrong problem. The question isn't whether we need better planning systems. The question is whether those systems help us understand which customers create value and how to serve them strategically."

This particular conversation did not unfold exactly as depicted, yet I have witnessed versions of it countless times in executive meetings, steering committees, and transformation workshops across industries. The script is familiar, even predictable. The names change. The systems change. But the underlying dynamic remains the same.

Have you experienced a similar moment in your career?

The purpose of implementing a new system is not to have a new system. Technology does not create value on its own. It is merely a conduit through which value can be enabled, amplified, or lost. The purpose is to create business value. What is often overlooked, or assumed without being defined, is *how* that value will actually be realized. Not the theoretical value promised in vendor presentations, but the tangible value that flows from better strategic choices, improved customer experiences, and differentiated capabilities.

The junior analyst's unauthorized analysis did what $75M of technology couldn't: It revealed which customers actually created mutual value worth investing in. The technology enabled the analysis but only when someone asked the strategic question the system wasn't designed to answer.

This chapter shows you how to evolve existing planning investments toward customer and business value optimization without replacing the operational excellence you've already built. More importantly, it shows you how to ask the right strategic questions before investing in technology capabilities, questions about customer value creation, not just operational coordination. Because in the end, the most sophisticated planning system in the world is worthless if it optimizes for the wrong things.

What Large System Implementations Actually Taught Me

Most organizations contemplating Value-Centric IBP transformation face a common challenge: They have substantial investments in ERP systems, supply chain planning platforms, customer relationship management systems, and business intelligence infrastructure that serve as the operational backbone of their business. The prospect of replacing these systems to enable customer value optimization seems both financially prohibitive and operationally risky.

I've heard this concern dozens of times across boardrooms and strategy sessions. As someone who lived through the dot-com boom working at i2 Technologies where we implemented some of the largest and most complex supply chain planning systems in the world, I learned something that most people miss about technology transformation: The reason for implementing systems is not the new system. It's the business value realization.

During those years, I watched companies spend hundreds of millions replacing perfectly functional systems because they believed the new technology would solve their problems. Some succeeded spectacularly. Others failed despite flawless technical implementations. The difference wasn't the quality of the new systems. It was whether the implementation focused on business value or technical perfection.

The successful implementations had a common pattern: They realized maximum value with the smallest amount of change. They enhanced what worked, fixed what didn't, and avoided disrupting operations that were already delivering results.

The failures? They ripped out everything and started over, believing that new technology automatically delivers new value. It doesn't. Technology enables value creation, but organizational disruption destroys it faster than new systems can build it.

The Technology Paradox: Why More Change Often Delivers Less Value

Here's the paradox I've observed across dozens of implementations: The more ambitious the technology transformation, the less likely it is to deliver business value.

It's not that ambitious transformations can't work. It's that they fail for organizational reasons, not technical ones. When you ask users to change everything simultaneously—new systems, new processes, new workflows, new metrics—the cognitive load becomes overwhelming. Resistance builds. Adoption stalls. Value realization gets delayed indefinitely. Meanwhile, competitors making smaller, focused enhancements are actually realizing value while you're still training people on the new system.

I watched this pattern repeat at company after company during my career. The implementations that tried to transform everything at once—replacing systems, redesigning processes, retraining entire organizations—looked impressive in project plans. But six months in, they'd hit organizational resistance that no amount of technical excellence could overcome.

The implementations that succeeded took a different path. They identified one or two high-impact enhancements, implemented them quickly, demonstrated value, then built momentum for the next enhancement. Each success made the next change easier because users experienced benefits rather than just disruption. This is why the evolutionary approach isn't just pragmatic. It's strategically superior.

Why Maximum Value with Minimum Change Works

The principle of maximum value with minimum change isn't about avoiding transformation. It's about ensuring transformation succeeds. Every change carries cost: user retraining, process disruption, data migration risk, integration complexity, and organizational resistance. These costs compound quickly in large implementations.

The evolutionary approach minimizes these costs while systematically building the capabilities that create value. Each enhancement delivers measurable business benefit while preserving organizational effectiveness. This creates a virtuous cycle: Early wins build confidence and momentum, users adopt enhancements because they make work easier rather than harder, and each capability layer provides the foundation for more sophisticated optimization.

Compare this to the big-bang approach where all changes happen simultaneously: massive user disruption, complex integration challenges, high implementation risk, and delayed value realization until everything works together.

I've led both types of implementations. The evolutionary approach delivers better business results with lower risk and higher user adoption. That's not opinion. That's track record across multiple industries and organizational contexts.

The same applies to AI applications in business operations and planning. What I'm seeing is revolutionary: AI and AI agents are evolving rapidly, creating capabilities we couldn't have imagined even a year ago. But here's what hasn't changed: The implementations that succeed focus relentlessly on business value while minimizing organizational disruption. The ones that chase technological sophistication for its own sake struggle regardless of how advanced their AI capabilities become.

The most successful AI implementations enhance existing planning processes rather than replacing them. They complement human judgment rather than attempting to eliminate it.

As someone who continues learning and adopting new AI capabilities, I can tell you: The technology is advancing faster than most organizations can absorb it. The evolutionary approach isn't just pragmatic. It's the only realistic path forward. Organizations that try to leap directly to cutting-edge AI capabilities often stumble not because the technology fails, but because the organization cannot absorb the change fast enough to realize value before momentum is lost.

The Four-Layer Architecture That Actually Works

This Section's Executive Takeaway

You do not need to rip and replace your planning stack to become value-centric. What you need is a layered architecture that adds customer value intelligence on top of existing ERP/IBP platforms, so planning decisions shift from "operationally correct" to "strategically right." The goal is business value with minimal disruption: faster learning, earlier wins, and a foundation that can scale into advanced AI without breaking operations.

For Implementation Teams

This section goes deeper into methods, data, and rollout, specifically the four layers (data foundation, semantic/knowledge graph, agentic AI, orchestration), what each layer does, and how to implement them incrementally while preserving existing workflows and vendor platforms.

The evolutionary transformation to Value-Centric IBP requires a pragmatic technology architecture that enables enhancement rather than replacement. The architecture consists of four distinct but interconnected layers that work together to augment existing enterprise systems: the Data Foundation Layer, the Semantic and Knowledge Graph Layer, the Agentic AI Layer, and the Integration and Orchestration Layer. Each layer serves a specific purpose while integrating seamlessly with existing enterprise systems to create a comprehensive Value-Centric IBP platform. Let's look at those four layers.

1. Data Foundation Layer: Building on What You Have

The data foundation layer serves as the unified repository that captures, harmonizes, and manages all information required for Value-Centric Integrated Business Planning while preserving and leveraging existing ERP and supply chain data structures. This is where most implementations either succeed or fail. The secret lies not in replacing what already works, but in extending it.

The data layer retains your existing systems for ERP transaction processing, CRM relationship management, master data governance, and operational reporting, while layering on customer value measurement data streams. Your established processes remain intact. What changes is the addition of a new lens that reveals how each transaction, forecast, and plan contributes to both customer and business value.

ERP workflows, CRM sales processes, and analytics platforms continue operating without disruption. Users maintain access to familiar reports and dashboards—now enriched with customer value context and competitive intelligence that elevate every discussion from operational efficiency to strategic relevance.

Through standardized APIs and integration protocols, the data foundation layer connects customer value measurement systems, competitive intelligence platforms, market research databases, and external data sources with core ERP, CRM, and planning systems. This enables seamless data flow: real-time streaming from customer touchpoints, batch synchronization from enterprise systems, and curated feeds from external sources. Data synchronization ensures alignment across all systems, maintaining consistency between transactional, relational, and value-based data.

Finally, the enhanced governance framework extends existing ERP standards to cover customer value and market intelligence data, ensuring accuracy, privacy compliance, and operational reliability. By treating customer value metrics with the same rigor as financial data, organizations build trust in insights that drive both strategic decisions and cultural change.

2. Semantic and Knowledge Graph Layer: Making Connections That Matter

The semantic layer transforms raw data from existing ERP and planning systems into contextual intelligence by mapping complex relationships between customers, products, capabilities, network flows, competitive factors, market dynamics, and more. This is where things get interesting. Traditional ERP relational databases excel at transactions but struggle with relationships. Knowledge graphs capture what your existing systems miss.

Enterprise relationship modeling creates knowledge graphs that map relationships between ERP customer records, CRM relationship data, product hierarchies, organizational capabilities, and market dynamics. Think of it this way: Your ERP knows that Customer A bought Product X. But does it know that Customer A values Product X for different reasons than Customer B, that those value perceptions are changing based on Competitor C's new offering, and that your capability investments should shift accordingly? That's what the semantic layer provides.

Customer value relationship networks map connections between customer characteristics, value realization patterns, product usage behaviors, relationship history from CRM systems, and business outcomes using data from existing ERP, CRM, and customer management systems. These networks enable sophisticated analysis of customer similarity, value migration patterns, and intervention effectiveness across different customer types and relationship stages. Customer relationship networks enhance existing CRM and ERP customer management capabilities by providing deeper understanding of what drives customer value realization and how different customers achieve success through various relationship approaches.

3. Agentic AI Layer: Intelligence That Enhances Human Judgment

The agentic AI layer provides intelligent automation and decision support that complements existing ERP and planning system processing while adding real-time monitoring, optimization, and strategic intelligence capabilities.

Let me emphasize something critical: AI agents enhance rather than replace existing batch processing systems by providing continuous intelligence and automated optimization between formal planning cycles.

I've watched the AI landscape evolve from simple automation to sophisticated agents that can handle complex decision-making. But the implementations that succeed maintain human judgment at the center while using AI to enhance rather than eliminate human decision-making.

The Hybrid Approach That Actually Works

Traditional IBP relies on batch processing cycles that aggregate data over specific time periods, perform optimization calculations, and generate planning recommendations on monthly or weekly schedules. This approach works well for stable demand patterns and predictable operational requirements but lacks the responsiveness required for dynamic customer value optimization and competitive response.

AI agents complement existing batch processing by providing continuous monitoring, real-time optimization, and intelligent decision support between formal planning cycles.

As someone who's implemented both traditional batch systems and modern AI-enhanced platforms, I can tell you: The hybrid approach delivers the best of both worlds. Your planning cycles continue providing operational discipline and cross-functional coordination. But between those cycles, AI agents monitor for changes that require immediate attention and provide optimization recommendations that keep your plans current.

The AI Agent Portfolio: What They Do and How They Work Together

Rather than describe each agent type exhaustively, let me show you the pattern once in detail, then illustrate how it applies across different agent types.

Customer value monitoring agents continuously analyze customer behavior patterns, satisfaction indicators, and value realization metrics from existing ERP transaction data, CRM interaction history, and external customer feedback systems.

These agents identify customers requiring intervention or optimization attention while existing ERP and CRM customer management processes continue normal operations. The key is that your existing processes keep running. The AI agents provide additional intelligence that makes those processes more effective.

Value pattern recognition agents monitor customer product usage, support interactions, and engagement levels to identify customers experiencing value delivery challenges before traditional metrics indicate problems. These agents analyze streaming data from customer touchpoints while existing IBP systems continue monthly planning cycles with aggregated historical data.

Think about it this way: Your monthly IBP process identifies trends and creates strategic plans. But what happens when a major customer starts showing signs of dissatisfaction in week two? Do you wait until next month's planning cycle to respond?

AI agents bridge that gap by providing continuous monitoring and immediate alerts when action is needed.

Predictive intervention alerts agents use machine learning models to identify customers likely to migrate to lower value matrix quadrants and automatically recommend specific intervention strategies. Predictive agents operate continuously while batch planning systems generate monthly intervention plans and resource allocation decisions.

Customer health score updates agents continuously update customer health assessments based on real-time behavior data, interaction sentiment, and value realization indicators. Health scoring agents provide immediate updates while batch systems generate comprehensive quarterly customer reviews and strategic assessments.

Competitive intelligence agents follow similar patterns: continuously monitoring competitor announcements, pricing changes, and customer perception shifts through social media analysis, news monitoring, and public information tracking while enriching quarterly strategic planning with immediate tactical intelligence.

Through my advisory work with AI-driven planning companies, I'm seeing competitive intelligence capabilities that would have seemed like science fiction during my i2 Technologies days. AI agents can now monitor thousands of competitive signals simultaneously and identify meaningful patterns that human analysts would miss. But they work best when they alert human strategists to make the final competitive response decisions.

Planning optimization agents apply the same hybrid model to resource allocation and capacity management: continuously evaluating utilization across customer value matrix quadrants, recommending immediate reallocation opportunities, and identifying investment acceleration or modification needs based on customer value impact assessment.

The key insight across all agent types: They don't replace your planning discipline. They fill the gaps between planning cycles, providing continuous intelligence that keeps your plans relevant and responsive while maintaining the coordination and strategic thinking that formal planning cycles provide.

Agent Type	Continuous Monitoring	Batch Process Enhancement	Key Value Delivered
Customer Value Monitoring	Real-time behavior patterns, satisfaction signals, usage trends	Enriches monthly customer reviews with leading indicators	Early intervention before churn appears in metrics
Competitive Intelligence	Social media, pricing changes, announcements	Informs quarterly competitive strategy	Tactical response speed with strategic context
Planning Optimization	Capacity utilization by value quadrant, immediate reallocation opportunities	Systematic capacity planning and investment decisions	Dynamic optimization between formal planning cycles

Integration and Orchestration Layer: Making It All Work Together

The integration and orchestration layer coordinates all technology components and enables seamless information flow between existing ERP systems, CRM platforms, supply chain planning systems, and enhanced customer value measurement capabilities. This is the unglamorous work that determines whether your implementation succeeds or becomes another expensive failure.

Let me tell you a story that illustrates why this layer matters so much.

When Agents Attack: The Orchestration Failure

As AI technology evolves, we're witnessing an inflation of AI agents across every corner of the planning process: customer monitoring, demand forecasting, capacity optimization, inventory management, competitive intelligence, supplier risk, and logistics optimization. Every company now seems to have more AI agents than actual planners. Each one proudly reports its insight with algorithmic confidence.

The problem? They don't talk to each other, at least not in human language. The result is a daily digital shouting match:

- The **demand agent** insists on more inventory ("Trust me, demand is about to spike!").

- The **capacity agent** screams, "Not a chance. We're already maxed out!"

- The **cost agent** lectures everyone about working capital and budget discipline.

- Meanwhile, the poor planner sits in the middle, trying to negotiate peace among machine personalities.

By 9:00 a.m., 30 perfectly intelligent agents have produced one perfectly exhausted human.

The irony is painful: The AI agents were technically perfect. The orchestration was nonexistent. Value realization collapsed under the weight of what can only be described as well-informed confusion.

This is why the orchestration layer isn't optional. It's not just the conductor of the symphony; it's the one keeping the brass section from attacking the strings. Without it, you don't get AI-enabled planning. You get AI-generated chaos between insight that empowers and intelligence that overwhelms.

Workflow Orchestration and Process Automation

Workflow orchestration and process automation automates planning processes and ensures customer value insights influence operational decisions across existing ERP, CRM, and planning systems without disrupting established workflows.

The workflow orchestration I've implemented in successful transformations follows a simple principle: Enhance, don't replace. Your planners continue working the way they always have, but now they have better information feeding their decisions.

Orchestration enhances existing business processes while maintaining operational continuity and user productivity across all customer-facing platforms. Workflow orchestration preserves existing ERP, CRM, and planning system processes while adding customer value optimization capabilities. Traditional workflows continue operating while enhanced orchestration provides customer value intelligence, relationship coordination, and strategic optimization across sales, service, and operational activities.

Agent Coordination and Trade-Off Management

Here's where the architecture gets sophisticated: As multiple AI agents operate simultaneously—monitoring customer value, tracking competitive intelligence, optimizing resources—they sometimes generate conflicting recommendations.

Consider a common scenario: Your customer value monitoring agent identifies a Margin Diluter customer showing strong engagement and recommends capacity prioritization. Simultaneously, your planning optimization agent flags that Value Partner customers are experiencing longer lead times due to capacity constraints. Your competitive intelligence agent reports a competitor targeting your Value Partners with improved delivery promises.

Without orchestration, you have three legitimate recommendations pointing in different directions. With orchestration, you get a structured decision framework:

Impact Analysis: Serving Margin Diluter customer delays Value Partner orders by five days on average

Value Quantification: Margin Diluter customer conversion worth $2 million over three years; Value Partner risk exposure $8 million annually

Competitive Context: Competitor delivery promise directly targets Value Partners, making timing critical

Risk Assessment: Margin Diluter customer can wait two weeks without churn risk based on engagement scores

Recommendation: Prioritize Value Partner capacity, proactively communicate with Margin Diluter customer, accelerate capacity expansion planning

The orchestration layer doesn't make the decision. It structures the trade-offs, so humans can make informed choices quickly.

Multi-agent coordination orchestrator agents manage these conflicts by implementing intelligent trade-off decision-making across agent recommendations. These orchestration agents don't make final decisions. They structure trade-off analysis for human decision-makers by aggregating agent recommendations, identifying conflicts and synergies, quantifying trade-off implications, and presenting decision options with clear business impact assessments.

Think of it as having an executive assistant who synthesizes recommendations from multiple advisors, highlights where they disagree, quantifies the implications of each path, and presents you with structured decision options rather than overwhelming you with conflicting advice.

The orchestration layer evaluates trade-offs across multiple dimensions:

Customer Value Impact: How does each option affect different customer segments? Does prioritizing one segment create risks or opportunities with others?

Financial Performance: What are the margin implications? Revenue impacts? Investment requirements?

Competitive Positioning: How does each option affect competitive dynamics? Does it strengthen or weaken strategic position?

Operational Feasibility: Can the organization actually execute the recommendation? What resource constraints apply?

Risk Assessment: What are the downside scenarios if the decision proves wrong? What's reversible versus irreversible?

The orchestration agents present these trade-offs through decision dashboards that show the multi-dimensional implications of each option. Human decision-makers see not just what agents recommend, but why they recommend it and what you're trading off by choosing one path over another.

This becomes critical as AI capabilities mature. Early implementations might have three or four agents generating occasional recommendations. Mature implementations might have dozens of specialized agents continuously optimizing different aspects of customer value delivery.

Without intelligent orchestration, this creates decision paralysis. With orchestration, it creates decision clarity.

The orchestration layer also manages agent learning and improvement. When human decision-makers override agent recommendations, the orchestration layer captures the reasoning and feeds it back to improve future recommendations. Over time, the agents learn organizational priorities and decision patterns, making their recommendations increasingly aligned with strategic intent.

Cross-System Analytics and Reporting Integration

Cross-system analytics and reporting integration combines customer value measurement with existing ERP, CRM, and planning system reporting through integrated dashboards and analytical platforms. Reporting integration preserves existing management reporting while adding customer value insights and strategic intelligence that spans transactional, relationship, and operational perspectives. Reporting integration maintains existing ERP, CRM, and planning system reporting while adding customer value analytics and competitive intelligence. Traditional reports continue serving established needs while enhanced analytics provide strategic customer value insights that combine transactional data, relationship intelligence, and operational optimization recommendations.

The orchestration layer ultimately determines whether your Value-Centric IBP transformation delivers coherent business value or becomes a collection of disconnected AI agents generating noise.

Critical Design Decisions: Getting the Economics Right

This Section's Executive Takeaway

The biggest hidden cost in planning modernization is not software. It's overbuilding data velocity and complexity that the organization can't translate into better decisions. "Real-time" only matters when it matches decision cadence, and architecture choices should be made to maximize value per unit of change, not technical sophistication. These design decisions set the economics of the whole journey.

For Implementation Teams

This section goes deeper into methods, data, and rollout: how to define "decision-time" refresh rates, tier data timeliness, right-size pipelines, and scale data velocity only as adoption and agent capabilities can actually use it.

Before diving into implementation phases, let's address three critical design decisions that determine both the cost and effectiveness of your Value-Centric IBP architecture.

The Economics of Data Freshness: A Reality Check

In the rush toward real-time analytics and instant decision-making, organizations often overlook a fundamental truth that I learned the hard way through multiple implementations: Real-time data refresh is both expensive and frequently impractical.

I've seen organizations spend millions building real-time data pipelines that feed dashboards nobody has time to monitor. The data arrives instantly, but decisions still happen weekly because that's when the planning team meets.

The key insight is that data refresh frequency should be strategically aligned with the organization's ability to make decisions and execute actions that create measurable results.

Redefining "Real-Time" Data

In planning, "real-time" is one of the most misunderstood terms. Many assume it means instantaneous data updates every second. But in reality, "real-time" should be understood as "decision-time." Data is only "real-time" if it arrives quickly enough to support the decisions being made. The right refresh rate depends not on technology's maximum speed, but on the velocity of decisions in the business.

Take a retail organization's inventory management system:

- Store managers might need hourly updates for daily operations

- Planners may only need daily updates to adjust weekly promotions

- Executives making quarterly product mix decisions often find weekly summaries sufficient

In each case, the data is "real-time" not because it streams every millisecond, but because it arrives in time to support the decision at hand. This redefinition shifts the focus from chasing speed for its own sake to matching data cadence with decision cadence.

Strategic Timeliness Categories

Organizations can classify their data needs into four strategic timeliness categories:

Mission-Critical Timeliness (Milliseconds to Seconds): Reserved for systems where immediate response prevents significant loss or captures fleeting opportunities. These systems justify the highest infrastructure costs because delays directly translate to material business impact.

Operational Timeliness (Minutes to Hours): Supports day-to-day business operations where rapid response creates competitive advantage or prevents service degradation. The refresh frequency balances responsiveness with cost efficiency.

Tactical Timeliness (Daily to Weekly): Enables informed management decisions and performance optimization. The focus shifts from immediate response to informed analysis and planning.

Strategic Timeliness (Weekly to Quarterly): Supports long-term planning and strategic decision-making. The emphasis is on comprehensive analysis rather than immediate action.

A manufacturing company might implement real-time monitoring for production line safety systems while updating financial reporting data daily and refreshing market analysis weekly.

This tiered approach can reduce infrastructure costs by 60% to 80% compared to uniform real-time strategies while maintaining appropriate responsiveness for each business function.

Evolution with Agentic AI Capabilities

As artificial intelligence agents become more sophisticated in autonomous decision-making and action execution, the value equation for frequent data refresh will evolve significantly.

This is where my advisory work with companies like FourKites, Emerix and RelationalAI becomes relevant. We're seeing AI agents that can independently process complex information and execute sophisticated workflows far faster than human-driven processes.

However, even in an AI-driven future, the principle of strategic timeliness remains paramount. Advanced AI agents will still operate within the constraints of organizational decision cycles, implementation timelines, and value creation opportunities. This evolution creates a natural growth path where data refresh investments scale alongside AI sophistication. Organizations can start with human-optimized refresh frequencies and gradually increase data velocity as their AI agents demonstrate the ability to extract additional value from more frequent updates.

The goal is creating a data ecosystem that serves the organization's actual needs rather than pursuing technological perfection.

Leveraging Existing IBP Platforms: Building on Proven Foundations

This Section's Executive Takeaway

Most companies already own powerful IBP capabilities. They're just not pointed at customer value. The win is to extend platforms (o9, Kinaxis, SAP IBP, Oracle, Blue Yonder, etc.) so customer value becomes a planning input, not an afterthought. This protects prior investment, reduces risk, and accelerates time-to-value.

For Implementation Teams

This section goes deeper into methods, data, and rollout. It offers three practical enhancement paths (configuration, integration extension, hybrid architecture), plus how to sequence "make value visible → make it useful → make it influential" without breaking upgrade paths or user adoption.

The four-layer architecture I've described might sound like building from scratch. It's not. Most organizations already have substantial planning infrastructure from vendors like o9 Solutions, Kinaxis RapidResponse, Blue Yonder, Oracle Advanced Supply Chain Planning, or SAP Integrated Business Planning. The question executives always ask: "Do we need to replace our existing platform to implement Value-Centric IBP?"

The short answer: No. The longer answer reveals something important about how modern planning platforms actually work and how they can evolve toward customer value optimization. Having implemented many of these platforms during my career, I believe they can be powerful foundations. The mistake is thinking you need to rip them out to add customer value capabilities.

Modern IBP platforms represent massive investments in planning sophistication. They manage complex demand forecasting, constraint-based optimization, scenario modeling, and cross-functional collaboration, capabilities that have taken decades to refine.

My hope is that the industry embraces the potential of Value-Centric IBP and weaves its principles into future product releases. After all, what good is a state-of-the-art planning engine if it forgets the most important gear in the system: the customer? Until that happens, the evolutionary approach offers a practical path forward: Leverage the strengths of today's platforms while layering on customer value optimization as an enhancement, not a replacement.

Three Enhancement Approaches

Configuration-based enhancement uses existing platform capabilities to add customer value considerations without custom development or system modification. Customer value matrix segmentation becomes additional planning hierarchies. Value-based constraints become optimization parameters. Competitive scenarios become standard scenario planning approaches. This preserves vendor support and upgrade paths while adding customer value capabilities through proven configuration methods.

Integration extension adds customer value measurement, competitive intelligence, and AI agent capabilities through standard platform extension interfaces. Customer value data becomes additional planning inputs. Competitive intelligence feeds scenario parameters. AI agents provide decision support enhancements. This maintains existing planning functionality while adding strategic capabilities through vendor-supported integration approaches.

Hybrid architecture combines existing platform capabilities with external customer value measurement and AI agent platforms through standard integration interfaces. Planning platforms continue providing operational excellence while external systems deliver customer value analytics and competitive intelligence that enhance planning effectiveness.

The Implementation Reality

Here's what I've learned from actually implementing these enhancements: The technology isn't the hard part. Modern IBP platforms provide the capabilities you need. The challenge is organizational: getting planners to incorporate customer value considerations into decisions they've made the same way for years, ensuring sales and operations align on customer value priorities, and maintaining enhancement momentum when initial changes require adjustment and learning.

Success requires starting with high-impact, low-complexity enhancements that demonstrate value quickly. Add customer value visibility to existing planning dashboards first. Let planners see how value matrix positioning correlates with planning challenges they already face. Then gradually introduce value-based constraints and optimization objectives as planners recognize the value of customer-centric planning.

Capability-Based Migration:
The Roadmap to Value-Centric IBP

This Section's Executive Takeaway

Transformation succeeds when it is staged as a capability journey, not a system launch. The goal is to move from visibility → prediction → integration → selective automation, with clear value proof at each milestone. This creates momentum, reduces political risk, and prevents spending on "better planning" that still optimizes the wrong customers.

For Implementation Teams

This section goes deeper into methods, data, and rollout, looking into milestones, timelines, readiness questions, success indicators, and what to implement in each phase so the organization earns the right to advance (instead of "big-bang" complexity).

The migration from traditional IBP to Value-Centric IBP follows a systematic evolution that builds capabilities incrementally while preserving operational continuity and maximizing return on existing technology investments.

Before diving into capability milestones, answer three questions that determine your migration path:

Customer data readiness: Can you currently measure customer value across all dimensions, or do you need foundational data infrastructure?

Organizational readiness: Will planners embrace customer-centric optimization, or do you need proof points before scaling?

Technology readiness: Do your existing systems have APIs and integration capabilities, or will integration be a heavy lift?

Your answers determine whether you move quickly through milestones or need extended foundation building.

Foundation Milestone: From Invisible to Visible

Goal: Make customer value visible in existing planning processes

Typical timeline: Three to six months for most organizations

Foundation enhancement establishes customer value measurement and basic AI agent capabilities using existing ERP and planning systems as the platform.

Start here. Don't try to boil the ocean in the foundation milestone.

Customer value data integration extends existing ERP customer master data with value measurement attributes and implements basic customer value surveys and feedback collection programs.

Customer value scores become additional attributes in existing customer records while traditional customer management processes continue unchanged.

Data integration preserves existing ERP functionality while adding customer value context to customer interactions, order processing, and account management. Users continue working with familiar ERP interfaces while receiving customer value insights that enhance decision-making effectiveness.

Basic AI agent deployment introduces customer value monitoring agents that track satisfaction indicators and usage patterns by tapping into existing ERP data and customer interaction records.

To unlock their potential, steer clear of the traditional corporate implementation cycle, you know, the one that involves endless approvals, committee reviews, and governance so risk-averse it could make a parachute jealous. AI thrives on iteration, not red tape.

That's why forward-thinking organizations are adopting a POD (product-oriented development) model. These small, cross-functional teams operate with clear mandates but minimal bureaucracy. Their mission: Move from concept to prototype in weeks, not quarters. They don't prove value with PowerPoint decks. They prove it with working solutions. The secret to POD success is setting clear boundaries and success metrics upfront, then giving the team the freedom to innovate inside those lines. The result is faster time-to-value and a culture of experimentation that AI needs to grow.

Best of all, monitoring agents don't overthrow existing systems. They run alongside your batch reporting cycles like an enthusiastic intern who never sleeps, providing real-time insights into customer value shifts, while the old reports keep doing their steady, traditional job.

Planning system customer value integration adds customer value matrix positioning to existing supply chain planning systems through customer hierarchy extensions and planning parameter enhancements. Planning systems continue generating operational plans while incorporating customer value considerations in optimization decisions. Planning integration preserves existing planning processes while adding customer value context to capacity allocation, service level management, and resource optimization. Planners continue using familiar planning interfaces while receiving customer value insights and recommendations.

Success Indicators for the Foundation Milestone:

- Customer value scores visible in CRM and ERP for 80%-plus of active customers

- At least one "aha moment" where customer value data revealed unexpected insights

- Planners referencing customer value matrix in planning discussions without prompting

- Basic AI agents providing weekly summaries that influence at least one planning decision

Intelligence Milestone: From Reactive to Predictive

Goal: Anticipate customer value changes before they appear in financial metrics

Typical timeline: Three to five months, overlapping with foundation milestone completion

Note the overlap with the foundation milestone. You don't wait for the foundation milestone to complete before starting the intelligence milestone. Successful implementations layer capabilities progressively.

Advanced AI agent capabilities deploy predictive analytics agents for customer value migration forecasting and competitive intelligence agents for market monitoring and competitive response recommendations.

Advanced agents operate continuously while existing batch planning systems continue monthly and quarterly planning cycles. Advanced agent capabilities enhance existing planning effectiveness by providing strategic intelligence and optimization recommendations between formal planning cycles. Batch planning incorporates agent insights while maintaining established planning discipline and coordination.

Competitive intelligence integration implements systematic competitive monitoring and analysis capabilities that integrate with existing planning systems and strategic planning processes.

Competitive intelligence enhances existing market analysis while maintaining established strategic planning cycles. Competitive intelligence integration preserves existing strategic planning processes while adding systematic competitive analysis and market intelligence. Strategic planning teams continue established planning approaches while receiving enhanced competitive insights and analysis.

Value matrix optimization enhances existing planning system optimization algorithms with customer value matrix objectives and constraints. Optimization algorithms balance operational efficiency with customer value delivery requirements through enhanced objective functions and constraint modeling. Optimization enhancement preserves existing planning effectiveness while adding customer value objectives and strategic considerations.

Planning systems continue optimizing operational performance while incorporating customer value requirements and competitive positioning needs.

Success Indicators for the Intelligence Milestone:

- Predictive models identifying 60%-plus of customer value migrations before they appear in retention metrics

- At least two planning decisions changed based on competitive intelligence insights

- Optimization runs producing measurably different outcomes when customer value objectives are included

- Cross-functional planning meetings regularly discussing customer value predictions

Integration Milestone: From Siloed to Unified

Goal: Coordinate customer value insights across all planning processes

Typical timeline: Four to six months, overlapping with the intelligence milestone completion

Advanced analytics phase implements sophisticated predictive modeling, automated optimization, and comprehensive integration across all enterprise systems while maintaining existing operational processes and user interfaces.

Predictive analytics implementation deploys machine learning models for customer value forecasting, competitive impact prediction, and market evolution analysis that enhance existing planning systems with strategic intelligence and optimization recommendations.

Predictive analytics enhances existing planning accuracy and strategic relevance while maintaining established planning processes and workflows. Planning teams continue established planning approaches while receiving enhanced forecasting accuracy and strategic intelligence.

Automated optimization deployment implements automated resource allocation optimization, capacity planning enhancement, and supply chain optimization that operate continuously alongside existing batch planning cycles. Automated optimization provides immediate recommendations while batch planning generates systematic strategies. Automated optimization enhances existing planning effectiveness while maintaining established planning coordination and discipline. Planning systems continue generating operational plans while receiving automated optimization recommendations and strategic enhancement.

Enterprise integration completion implements comprehensive integration across ERP, planning, and customer management systems that provides unified customer value visibility and coordinated optimization across all enterprise functions.

Enterprise integration preserves existing system functionality while providing unified customer value insights and coordinated optimization. Users continue working with familiar systems while receiving enhanced customer value context and strategic coordination.

Success Indicators for the Integration Milestone:

- Customer value data flowing seamlessly across all planning systems without manual intervention

- Sales, operations, and finance using consistent customer value definitions and metrics

- At least one quarter-over-quarter improvement in resource allocation efficiency attributed to value-based optimization

- Executive dashboards showing unified view of customer value across all business functions

Maturity Milestone: From Enhanced to Autonomous

Goal: Automate routine optimization, elevate humans to strategic decisions

Typical timeline: Three to five months for initial business unit, then scaling

Intelligent automation phase implements advanced AI agent capabilities that automate routine optimization decisions while providing strategic recommendations for complex planning scenarios.

This phase achieves full Value-Centric IBP capabilities while maintaining operational excellence.

Intelligent planning automation implements AI agents that automatically handle routine customer value optimization decisions while escalating strategic choices to human planners using existing planning systems and established approval processes.

Planning automation enhances existing planning efficiency while maintaining human oversight for strategic decisions. Planning teams focus on strategic analysis and decision-making while AI agents handle routine optimization and operational coordination.

Real-time market response implements AI agents that automatically adjust planning decisions based on competitive activities, market changes, and customer value feedback while maintaining coordination with existing planning cycles and approval processes.

Market response capabilities enhance existing planning responsiveness while maintaining planning discipline and coordination. Planning systems continue generating systematic strategies while AI agents provide immediate response to market changes and competitive activities.

Organizational scaling implementation extends Value-Centric IBP capabilities across multiple business units, geographic regions, and customer segments through enhanced system integration and AI agent coordination while preserving local operational processes and management structures. Organizational scaling preserves existing operational management while providing coordinated customer value optimization across organizational boundaries. Local teams continue established operations while receiving coordinated customer value insights and strategic coordination.

Success Indicators for the Maturity Milestone:

- 40%-plus of routine planning decisions automated with human validation rather than human initiation

- Measurable improvement in planning responsiveness to market changes (days to hours for tactical adjustments)

- Successful scaling to at least two additional business units or regions

- Documented business value: improved margins, better retention, or enhanced competitive positioning

Implementation Red Flags and Success Catalysts

Frameworks are easy to read about, but here's the hard truth: They don't prepare you for the messy reality of implementation. I've led transformations that soared and others that struggled and needed more intervention to be successful. The difference usually isn't the technology. It's the change management, organizational readiness, and the persistence to push through the inevitable bumps in the road.

Red Flags That Predict Implementation Failure

After decades of implementations, I can spot the warning signs within weeks:

Finance and sales can't agree on what "customer value" means. If these two functions are fighting over definitions in month two, you'll be fighting over resource allocation forever. Pause and get alignment before proceeding.

IT treats this as a technology project rather than business transformation. When the IT team talks about system architecture but never mentions customer outcomes, you're building sophisticated infrastructure that won't deliver business value.

Pilot results are declared successful without measurable business impact. "Users like the new dashboard" is not success. "We reallocated

$2 million in capacity from Value Destroyers to Value Partners and improved both satisfaction and margins" is success.

Planners view customer value metrics as "extra work" rather than decision enhancement. If planners are asking "When can we stop tracking this?" instead of "How can we use this better?" your change management has failed.

Executive sponsors change before phase two completes. New executives want to put their stamp on initiatives. If your sponsor leaves, expect at least a three-month delay while the new leader "evaluates" whether to continue.

If you see three or more of these, pause and fix organizational alignment before proceeding. Technical success without organizational readiness equals expensive failure.

Catalysts That Accelerate Success

Conversely, certain factors dramatically accelerate value realization:

A champion planner who "gets it" and influences peers. One respected planner who demonstrates value and shares success stories with colleagues is worth ten executive mandates. I've seen single planners transform entire organizations by showing—not telling— how customer value insights improve decisions. When their peers see them making better capacity allocation calls, predicting customer issues before they escalate, or optimizing resource deployment for measurably better outcomes, adoption spreads organically.

One undeniable success story from pilot implementation. Nothing builds momentum like a planner who reallocated capacity based on customer value insights and delivered measurably better results than the previous quarter. The story needs to be specific: "I shifted 15% of capacity from Customer X to Customer Y based on value matrix positioning. Customer Y expanded their relationship by 40%, Customer X didn't notice the service level change, and my region's margins improved 8%." That kind of concrete proof overcomes more skepticism than any executive presentation.

Executive who asks, "What does this mean for customer value?" in every planning review. When leaders consistently redirect conversations from operational metrics to customer value implications, the organization learns what matters. The question doesn't need to be confrontational. It can be genuinely curious: "These inventory numbers look good. Which customer segments does this inventory strategy serve best?" Over time, planners internalize the question and start answering it before being asked.

Finance partner who helps quantify value creation rather than just policing costs. When finance becomes an ally in measuring customer value rather than just an auditor of expenses, transformation accelerates dramatically. The finance person who says, "Let's figure out how to measure this" instead of "We can't track that," becomes a force multiplier for change.

Customer-facing teams hungry for better prioritization frameworks. Sales and customer success teams often intuitively understand which customers create value but lack data to support their instincts. When Value-Centric IBP validates their intuition with rigorous analysis, they become enthusiastic advocates. Their stories about customer relationships add qualitative context that makes quantitative analysis more credible.

These catalysts can compress 18-month transformations into nine-month successes. More importantly, they create sustainable change because adoption happens through demonstrated value rather than executive mandate.

The Reality of Implementation Success

This Section's Executive Takeaway

Technology migration fails when it's treated as an IT program with technical milestones instead of a value program with decision outcomes. Adoption depends on continuity: Keep workflows familiar, introduce value insights in-context, and evolve performance measures so teams feel the benefit rather than the burden. In practice, the "implementation" is a culture and operating-model shift disguised as a system enhancement.

For Implementation Teams

This section goes deeper into methods, data, and rollout, all change-management levers that actually move adoption: user experience continuity, process integration patterns, KPI evolution, red flags/catalysts, and how to embed value metrics into existing planning routines without creating reporting overhead.

Migrating to Value-Centric IBP successfully demands more than technical capability. It requires careful attention to organizational readiness, thoughtful change management, and technology integration that strengthens strategic capabilities while preserving operational continuity.

User Experience Continuity

Existing ERP and planning system users must continue working with familiar interfaces and processes while gradually adopting customer value insights and recommendations. User training should focus on enhancement rather than replacement of established skills and workflows.

User continuity preserves organizational productivity while building customer value capabilities. Training programs should emphasize how customer value insights enhance existing decision-making rather than requiring fundamental workflow changes.

Users adopt customer value approaches gradually through positive experience rather than forced compliance. When planners discover that customer value data helps them make better decisions more easily, adoption accelerates naturally. When they experience customer value tracking as additional reporting burden without clear benefit, resistance builds quickly.

The key is integration that feels invisible. Planners shouldn't need to log into separate systems or run special reports to access customer value insights. Those insights should appear contextually within the planning workflows they already use: a customer value score next to the customer name, a value matrix position indicator on the capacity allocation screen, a predictive alert within the daily planning dashboard.

Process Integration Approach

Value-Centric IBP should enhance existing business processes through optional features and decision support rather than mandatory process changes. Business processes should evolve naturally toward customer value optimization rather than requiring immediate fundamental changes.

Process integration preserves existing business effectiveness while gradually introducing customer value optimization. Enhancement features should become standard practice through demonstrated value rather than management mandate.

Start with making customer value visible, then move to making it useful, and only then make it influential in formal processes. Trying to mandate process changes before users see value creates resistance. Showing value first creates demand for process formalization.

For example, begin by displaying customer value matrix positioning in planning meetings without requiring it to influence decisions. Let planners reference it organically when it helps explain capacity constraints or prioritization choices. After several months of planners finding it useful informally, formalize it as a standard consideration in capacity allocation decisions. The formalization codifies behavior that's already proven valuable rather than imposing behavior that feels arbitrary.

Performance Measurement Evolution

Introduce customer value metrics alongside existing operational and financial KPIs rather than replacing established measurement systems. Performance management should evolve toward customer value focus while maintaining accountability for operational excellence and financial performance.

Performance evolution preserves existing management effectiveness while adding customer value accountability. Measurement systems should demonstrate customer value importance through enhanced insights rather than metric replacement.

Management focus expands to include customer value while maintaining operational and financial discipline. The goal isn't replacing "units shipped on time" with "Value Partner satisfaction scores." It's adding customer value context that explains why operational metrics matter and which operational priorities deserve greatest focus.

When planners see that improving customer value metrics correlates with better operational and financial outcomes, the metrics become self-reinforcing. When customer value metrics feel disconnected from the operational and financial results planners are accountable for, the metrics become ignored.

Building the Future on Proven Foundations

The evolutionary approach to Value-Centric IBP technology transformation recognizes that sustainable competitive advantage comes from enhancing existing organizational strengths rather than replacing established capabilities. This isn't just philosophy. It's based on what actually works in real implementations with real business results.

This evolutionary strategy minimizes implementation risk while maximizing return on existing technology investments. Organizations maintain operational excellence and user productivity while gradually building customer value optimization capabilities that enhance rather than replace established planning effectiveness.

AI agents complement existing batch processing systems while providing real-time monitoring and optimization that improve planning responsiveness and strategic intelligence. The hybrid approach delivers the best of both worlds: the discipline and coordination of formal planning cycles combined with the responsiveness and intelligence of continuous AI monitoring.

As AI continues evolving, and it's evolving faster than most organizations can absorb, the evolutionary approach becomes even more critical. Organizations that try to leap directly to the cutting edge often stumble not because the technology fails, but because organizational change capacity becomes the limiting factor. Those that build systematically on proven foundations achieve sustainable competitive advantages that compound over time.

The Path Forward: Transformation That Actually Succeeds

Despite decades of technological advancement, large-scale IT and digital transformation initiatives remain notoriously risky. According to McKinsey & Company, around 70% of complex digital transformations fail to meet their stated objectives, often due to inadequate change management, unclear value focus, and weak cross-functional alignment.

Similarly, the Standish Group's CHAOS Report shows that only about 29% of IT projects are delivered successfully—on time, on budget, and with full functionality—while the rest are either challenged or fail outright.

Complementary research from Gartner and Harvard Business Review confirms that more than 50% of enterprise technology implementations exceed budget or underdeliver on business value, revealing that technical success alone is not synonymous with transformation success.

The minority of programs that do succeed share a clear, consistent pattern: They focus relentlessly on value realization, not system deployment.

McKinsey's research shows that organizations with clearly defined value targets, empowered cross-functional teams, and visible executive sponsorship are three times more likely to succeed than those driven primarily by technical milestones.

Bain & Company's findings reinforce this view: High-performing organizations explicitly link transformation goals to measurable business KPIs and sustain momentum through early "quick wins" that demonstrate tangible progress.

In essence, the difference between failure and success lies not in the sophistication of the system, but in the clarity of value definition and disciplined alignment. Successful transformations connect technology, process, and culture around shared value outcomes, precisely the organizing principle of Value-Centric Integrated Business Planning (IBP). The ones that succeeded weren't the ones with the most sophisticated technology or the biggest budgets. They were the ones that kept asking: "Does this help us serve our best customers better?" That question still separates successful transformations from expensive failures.

Value-Centric IBP isn't about AI sophistication or architectural elegance. It's about systematically connecting every planning decision—capacity allocation, inventory positioning, capability investment, resource deployment—to the customers and relationships that create mutual value.

The technology enables that connection. The four-layer architecture provides the framework. The capability-based migration reduces risk. But the real transformation happens when your planners stop optimizing for volume and margin targets and start optimizing for the customer relationships that drive sustainable competitive advantage. That's when planning becomes strategy. That's when your ERP becomes a competitive weapon. That's when technology investment delivers business value.

The technology is there. The frameworks work. The implementation approaches have been proven across industries and organizational contexts. The question is whether your organization will take the evolutionary path that actually succeeds or chase the rip-and-replace approach that looks bold but rarely delivers.

I've seen both paths. I've led implementations down both roads. The evolutionary approach delivers better business results with lower risk and higher user adoption. That's not theory. That's experience across decades and industries.

The most successful Value-Centric IBP implementations preserve organizational stability while adding strategic capabilities that drive competitive advantage through superior customer value delivery. Technology evolution occurs through systematic enhancement rather than disruptive replacement, enabling organizations to achieve Value-Centric IBP benefits while maintaining operational excellence and user confidence.

Technology transformation success depends on recognizing that existing ERP and planning systems provide valuable foundations for Value-Centric IBP capabilities rather than barriers to customer value optimization. Organizations that leverage existing system strengths while systematically adding customer value capabilities achieve sustainable competitive advantages through enhanced planning effectiveness and strategic intelligence.

Through my advisory work and continued learning about AI capabilities, I'm convinced the future belongs to organizations that evolve existing technology investments toward Value-Centric IBP capabilities while maintaining operational excellence and user productivity. These organizations achieve superior customer value delivery through enhanced planning capabilities that build on proven foundations rather than disruptive replacements. Evolutionary technology migration enables sustainable competitive advantage through systematic capability building that preserves organizational strengths while adding strategic enhancement.

The Choice Is Yours

You have a choice to make.

You can continue optimizing your planning systems for operational coordination: forecasting more accurately, planning more efficiently, coordinating more effectively. Your systems will work perfectly by operational metrics while competitors systematically capture your highest-value customers.

Or you can evolve your planning systems toward customer value optimization: building on the operational excellence you've already achieved while adding the strategic intelligence that drives competitive advantage.

The first path is safer in the short term. The second path wins in the long term.

Start where you are. Build on what works. Add what's missing.

But never lose sight of why you're building it: to serve your best customers better than anyone else can, while systematically optimizing your portfolio toward relationships that create mutual value.

That's how real transformation happens.

That's how planning becomes competitive advantage.

That's how technology investments deliver business value that compounds over time.

The evolutionary path isn't just pragmatic. It's the path that actually succeeds.

Once technology and planning are aligned around value, the competitive arena expands beyond individual firms. The next chapter examines how advantage is increasingly won not company versus company, but value chain versus value chain, where ecosystems, partners, and platforms determine who creates, captures, and compounds customer value.

CHAPTER 13

Value Chain vs. Value Chain: Competing in the Ecosystem Era

*A company's success no longer depends on
its ability to compete, but on its ability
to orchestrate the right ecosystem.*
—Marco Iansiti and Roy Levien, *The Keystone Advantage*

When Individual Excellence Isn't Enough

The nature of business competition has fundamentally transformed. I've seen smart, well-run companies excel at everything they directly control: Their products are excellent, their operations efficient, their customer service solid. Yet they still lose market share. Why? Because competitors who aren't necessarily better at any one thing have learned to orchestrate superior ecosystems built around customer value creation. The game changed. Individual company capabilities no longer determine winners. Entire value chains compete against other value chains.

Apple's sustained advantage doesn't come from any single component. Many competitors use the same processors, screens, or batteries. What differentiates Apple is that it designed its entire value chain around an integrated user experience rather than around hardware production efficiency. From chip design (Apple Silicon) to proprietary operating systems (iOS, macOS), to tightly integrated hardware, services, and retail experiences, every element reinforces the same purpose: seamless user experience and ecosystem loyalty.

Traditional smartphone manufacturers, by contrast, still operate with fragmented ecosystems: outsourced hardware, open operating systems, carrier-dominated distribution, and third-party service dependencies. Even when they innovate at the product level, they struggle to replicate Apple's customer lock-in and cross-device synergy because their value chains were built for scale, not for experience integration.

Amazon's competitive power doesn't come from low prices alone. It stems from a value chain intentionally designed for customer obsession and data-driven adaptation. Every component—from Amazon Web Services infrastructure to logistics networks, recommendation algorithms, and Prime membership—feeds into a single value promise: convenience, reliability, and personalization.

Traditional retailers, meanwhile, still operate supply chains optimized for in-store transactions, seasonal merchandising, and fragmented customer data systems. Their e-commerce platforms often function as digital extensions of physical stores rather than integrated ecosystems.

Amazon's integration of logistics, data, and digital touchpoints allows it to anticipate needs rather than simply react to demand. Its ecosystem learns continuously, turning operational data into customer insight and then into faster, more relevant experiences.

This ecosystem-level competition has profound implications for Value-Centric IBP because planning processes must now extend beyond organizational boundaries to orchestrate value creation across multiple companies, technologies, and market participants.

Up to this point, Value-Centric IBP has focused on optimizing decisions inside the enterprise; this chapter extends that same logic to competition that now occurs between value chains and ecosystems rather than individual firms.

The challenge is no longer just aligning internal functions around customer value. It's coordinating entire ecosystems around superior customer outcomes while maintaining competitive differentiation and sustainable profitability.

How Value Chain Thinking Evolved (And Why Old Models Don't Work)

Traditional value chain concepts, developed when most value creation occurred within individual companies, inadequately describe modern competitive dynamics where value emerges from complex interactions between multiple organizations, platforms, and customer touchpoints.

From Linear Chains to Network Effects

Michael Porter's original value chain model conceptualized value creation as a linear sequence within individual companies: inbound logistics, operations, outbound logistics, marketing and sales, and service. This linear model worked well when most value creation occurred within company boundaries and competition focused on operational efficiency.

That's not how modern value creation works.

Amazon's value creation doesn't follow a linear chain. It emerges from complex interactions between their e-commerce platform, cloud computing services, logistics network, content creation, advertising platform, and third-party seller ecosystem. Each component enhances the others through data sharing, customer insights, and operational synergies that create value impossible for any individual component to generate alone.

Netflix demonstrates network value creation through the interaction between content licensing, original programming, recommendation algorithms, global distribution, and subscriber data. The value emerges not from any single capability but from integration across their entire ecosystem.

Linear models miss this completely. They can't capture how platform effects, network dynamics, and ecosystem collaboration create value that transcends what any individual company could deliver.

Reversing the Logic: Customer-Defined Value Chains

Traditional value chain thinking starts with company capabilities and works forward toward customer delivery. Customer-centric value chains reverse this logic, beginning with customer outcomes and working backward through all the capabilities, partnerships, and processes required to deliver those outcomes effectively.

This reversal fundamentally changes how you think about ecosystems. Instead of optimizing supplier relationships for cost and efficiency, you optimize for capabilities that enhance customer value creation. Instead of viewing distribution channels as cost centers, they become customer experience platforms influencing satisfaction and loyalty.

Apple's retail strategy exemplifies this. Rather than just distributing products through existing channels, Apple designed retail experiences supporting their customer value proposition around simplicity, design excellence, and integrated technology experiences. The retail stores aren't distribution points. They're integral components of their value chain enabling customer education, support, and relationship building. Traditional computer manufacturers viewed retail as someone else's problem. Apple recognized that retail experiences directly affected customer value perception and made it part of their orchestrated ecosystem.

Platform Dynamics Change Everything

Platform businesses demonstrate how value chains can become competitive moats through network effects, switching costs, and ecosystem development creating sustainable competitive advantages. Successful platforms don't just deliver products or services. They enable value creation by multiple participants while capturing value through their central coordination role.

Salesforce's platform strategy extends beyond traditional supplier-customer relationships to include third-party developers, system integrators, and complementary service providers who enhance customer value while strengthening Salesforce's competitive position. The platform creates value for customers through expanded functionality while creating switching costs through ecosystem integration and data lock-in.

Amazon Web Services illustrates platform dynamics through the interaction between infrastructure services, developer tools, marketplace applications, and customer solutions. Customers don't just buy computing capacity. They access entire innovation ecosystems enabling their own value creation and competitive positioning.

This is fundamentally different from traditional value chain competition. Platforms create reinforcing cycles where success attracts more participants, which creates more value, which attracts more participants. Individual companies competing against platforms often can't match the ecosystem value even when they offer superior individual products or services.

Understanding Modern Value Chains: What Actually Matters

Modern value chains extend far beyond traditional company boundaries to include all the capabilities, relationships, and processes contributing to customer value creation.

The End-to-End Customer Experience Chain

Customer-centric value chains begin with customer outcomes and encompass all the touchpoints, processes, and capabilities influencing customer value perception. The lesson is clear, customer value often depends more on how well everything works together than on the brilliance of any single part.

Think of modern e-commerce like a symphony. You've got website design on strings, payment processing on percussion, inventory and fulfillment on brass, delivery tracking on woodwinds, and customer service belting out vocals. If one player is off-key, say, a failed payment or a delayed shipment, the whole performance falls apart. But when the orchestra plays in harmony, the experience becomes unforgettable, and competitors can't easily copy the music.

The customer experience chain includes both digital and physical touchpoints that must be coordinated to create seamless experiences. Mobile apps, websites, physical stores, customer service centers, delivery partners, and payment processors all contribute to overall customer satisfaction and must be aligned around consistent value propositions rather than optimized independently.

Digital Infrastructure: The Hidden Competitive Layer

Modern value chains increasingly depend on digital infrastructure and data flows connecting physical processes with customer insights, predictive analytics, and automated optimization. These digital layers often provide more competitive differentiation than physical capabilities because they enable personalization, efficiency, and responsiveness that traditional approaches cannot match.

Data integration across value chain partners enables real-time visibility into customer behavior, demand patterns, and operational performance supporting proactive decision-making rather than reactive problem-solving.

Retailers who share point-of-sale data with suppliers enable better demand forecasting and inventory optimization than those relying on traditional order-based communication. The data integration creates competitive advantages through reduced stockouts, lower inventory costs, and better product availability, benefits neither party could achieve independently.

Digital platforms connecting multiple value chain participants enable coordination and optimization that individual companies cannot achieve alone. Transportation and logistics platforms coordinate multiple carriers, routes, and delivery options to optimize cost and service levels across entire networks rather than just individual shipments.

Supplier Ecosystems: Deeper Than You Think

Modern competitive advantages often depend on supplier ecosystem capabilities and integration, not just direct supplier relationships. Tier 2, Tier 3, and raw material suppliers increasingly influence customer value through sustainability practices, innovation capabilities, risk management, and operational flexibility affecting final customer outcomes.

Apple's supplier ecosystem demonstrates deep integration extending beyond traditional procurement to include design collaboration, capacity planning, quality management, and sustainability initiatives supporting their brand positioning and customer value proposition. Their supplier audits and capability development programs ensure ecosystem capabilities align with customer expectations rather than just cost and quality requirements.

Automotive manufacturers increasingly compete based on their suppliers' capabilities in electric vehicle technology, autonomous driving systems, and software integration rather than just their own design and assembly capabilities. Tesla's vertical integration strategy reflects recognition that supplier ecosystem capabilities often determine competitive positioning more than individual company capabilities.

Strategic Partnerships: Expanding Capabilities Without Building Them

Strategic partnerships and alliances create value chain capabilities that individual companies cannot develop economically or quickly enough to maintain competitive positioning.

Microsoft's partnership ecosystem includes technology integrators, software developers, cloud service providers, and industry specialists who collectively enable customer solutions Microsoft cannot deliver independently. The partnership network creates customer value while enabling Microsoft to focus on platform capabilities rather than industry-specific solutions.

Starbucks' partnership with Spotify creates customer value through music discovery and personalization while enhancing the in-store experience and customer engagement. The partnership leverages both companies' capabilities to create customer value neither could deliver independently while strengthening customer relationships for both partners.

These partnerships aren't just vendor relationships. They're strategic capabilities that extend what you can deliver to customers without requiring internal development of every capability.

Strategic Implications: Playing a Different Game

Competing at the value chain level requires fundamentally different strategic thinking than traditional company-versus-company competition.

Somebody Has to Be the Orchestrator

Successful value chain competition requires someone to serve as the ecosystem orchestrator who aligns all participants around common customer value objectives. This orchestration role often provides sustainable competitive advantages because it creates switching costs and dependencies protecting market position even when individual products or services become commoditized.

Amazon's orchestration of their marketplace ecosystem demonstrates how platform leadership creates competitive advantages through network effects, data insights, and operational integration that individual sellers cannot replicate independently. Amazon provides infrastructure, customer access, and operational services while capturing value through platform fees and data insights informing their own competitive strategies.

The orchestration role requires capabilities for partner management, performance measurement, conflict resolution, and value sharing ensuring all ecosystem participants benefit from collaboration while maintaining alignment around customer value creation.

Here's what makes this tricky: Organizations excelling at orchestration often capture disproportionate value from ecosystem success while creating barriers to competitive ecosystem development. This creates tension with partners who provide essential capabilities but receive smaller value shares.

Ecosystem leadership requires balancing competition and collaboration because many value chain partners may also be competitors in adjacent markets. Apple competes with Google in mobile operating systems while partnering with them for search services and app distribution. Managing these complex relationships requires sophisticated strategic thinking.

Customer-Informed Supply Chain Design

Traditional supply chain optimization focuses on cost, efficiency, and reliability without systematic consideration of customer value implications.

Customer-informed supply chain design begins with customer value requirements and works backward through all the capabilities and processes needed to deliver those requirements effectively. This approach often reveals that cost optimization can undermine customer value creation when it reduces flexibility, responsiveness, or quality in ways affecting customer satisfaction.

Premium customers may value delivery speed and reliability more than cost efficiency, justifying different supply chain designs optimizing for customer outcomes rather than just operational metrics.

Amazon's supply chain design demonstrates customer-informed optimization through their investment in fulfillment centers, delivery capabilities, and inventory positioning enabling fast delivery for Prime customers while maintaining cost efficiency for standard customers. The supply chain design reflects customer value priorities rather than just cost minimization.

Customer segmentation should influence supply chain design decisions including service levels, inventory positioning, delivery options, and quality standards aligning with different customer value requirements and willingness to pay.

Multi-Tier Supplier Visibility and Collaboration

Modern value chain competition requires visibility and collaboration extending beyond direct suppliers to include Tier 2, Tier 3, and raw material suppliers who increasingly influence customer value. Supply chain disruptions often originate in lower-tier suppliers who provide components or materials affecting multiple direct suppliers simultaneously.

The 2011 earthquake and tsunami in Japan disrupted automotive production globally because many Tier 2 and Tier 3 suppliers were concentrated in affected regions. The disaster demonstrated how downstream risks can affect entire value chains regardless of direct supplier diversity.

Collaboration with multi-tier suppliers enables innovation, sustainability, and risk management capabilities that individual companies cannot achieve independently. Collaborative product development including supplier innovation capabilities often produces superior customer solutions while reducing development costs and time to market.

Sustainability and ethical sourcing increasingly influence customer value perceptions, making multi-tier supplier practices strategic considerations rather than just compliance requirements. Customers who value environmental and social responsibility evaluate entire value chain practices, not just direct company policies.

Technology Integration: The Digital Glue

Value chain competition increasingly depends on technology integration and digital transformation enabling real-time coordination, data sharing, and automated optimization across multiple organizations and processes. These digital capabilities often provide more sustainable competitive advantages than physical assets because they're harder to replicate and create network effects strengthening over time.

IoT sensors and connectivity enable real-time monitoring and optimization across entire value chains from raw material extraction through customer usage. This visibility supports proactive problem-solving, predictive maintenance, and customer service creating competitive advantages through superior reliability and responsiveness.

AI and machine learning enable optimization and personalization, improving customer value while reducing costs. Demand forecasting incorporating customer behavior patterns, market trends, and operational constraints can optimize inventory positioning and production scheduling across multiple suppliers simultaneously.

Blockchain and distributed ledger technologies enable transparency and traceability supporting sustainability, authenticity, and compliance requirements increasingly influencing customer value perceptions. Luxury goods customers valuing authenticity benefit from blockchain verification preventing counterfeiting while supporting premium pricing.

Orchestrating Value Chains
Through Value-Centric IBP

This Section's Executive Takeaway

Competitive advantage is no longer created inside the firm but across the ecosystem. Strategy now means deciding which role you play in the value chain, especially whether you are an orchestrator, and ensuring planning, investment, and performance management are aligned to customer outcomes across partners, not just internal functions. Value-Centric IBP becomes the mechanism that connects customer value, partner coordination, and financial discipline into a single strategic system.

For Implementation Teams

This section goes deeper into how Value-Centric IBP extends beyond the enterprise into ecosystem planning, covering product, demand, supply, and financial planning across partners, platforms, and value chain participants, and how to operationalize customer-value-based orchestration in day-to-day planning processes.

Value-Centric IBP provides the framework for orchestrating complex value chains around customer value creation while maintaining operational coordination and financial discipline across multiple organizations and stakeholders. This orchestration requires extending traditional IBP processes beyond organizational boundaries to include partner collaboration, ecosystem optimization, and customer value measurement.

Product Planning: Innovation Beyond Your Walls

Product planning in value chain competition must consider not just internal development capabilities but also partner innovations, supplier technologies, and ecosystem developments that could enhance or threaten customer value propositions.

Collaborative Innovation Planning

Innovation increasingly occurs through collaboration between multiple value chain participants rather than just internal R&D.

Apple's product innovation demonstrates collaborative planning including supplier technology development, manufacturing process innovation, and ecosystem capability enhancement collectively enabling product features and customer experiences competitors struggle to replicate.

Your suppliers may be developing technologies that could transform your products. Your partners may be building capabilities that could enhance your customer value proposition. Product planning needs to systematically evaluate these external innovations and integrate them into your roadmap.

Innovation planning should consider how emerging technologies from suppliers, partners, or adjacent industries might enhance customer value propositions while identifying threats from competitive ecosystem innovations that could disrupt existing value propositions.

Platform and Ecosystem Development

Product planning for platform businesses must consider how product features and capabilities influence ecosystem attractiveness, partner success, and network effects driving customer value and competitive positioning.

Salesforce's product planning includes platform capabilities enabling third-party development while considering how platform enhancements affect partner success and customer value creation. Platform features making partner development easier or more profitable strengthen the ecosystem while creating competitive advantages.

You're not just building products. You're building platforms that others build on. Every product decision affects your ecosystem's health and attractiveness.

Demand Planning: Ecosystem Intelligence Integration

Demand planning in value chain competition must incorporate insights from multiple ecosystem participants who interact with customers and markets in ways providing leading indicators of demand changes and customer value evolution.

Partner and Channel Intelligence

Distribution partners, retailers, and service providers often have customer insights that complement and enhance internal market intelligence. These partners see customer behavior patterns, competitive dynamics, and market trends your internal teams might miss or interpret differently.

Channel partner feedback about customer requests, competitive pressure, and market trends provides early warning indicators about demand changes and customer value evolution that traditional forecasting might not capture until changes appear in historical sales data.

Integration should include systematic processes for gathering, evaluating, and incorporating partner insights into demand planning while balancing different perspectives and potential biases.

Customer Journey Demand Intelligence

Value chain demand planning should consider how customer behavior across entire journeys affects demand patterns rather than just focusing on purchase decisions. Customer success metrics from implementation and usage provide leading indicators of expansion demand and retention risk that traditional forecasting approaches might miss. High customer satisfaction during implementation often predicts expansion opportunities while poor onboarding experiences predict churn risk regardless of product quality.

Ecosystem Network Effects

Platform and ecosystem businesses experience demand patterns influenced by network effects, user behavior, and partner success that differ significantly from traditional product demand. More users make platforms more valuable for all participants, creating positive feedback loops that can accelerate demand growth or create challenges during slowdowns.

Partner success on platforms influences customer demand because thriving partner ecosystems provide more value to customers while struggling partner ecosystems reduce platform attractiveness. Platform demand planning should consider partner health metrics alongside traditional customer demand indicators.

Supply Planning: Coordinating Across Boundaries

Supply planning for value chain competition must coordinate across multiple organizations, geographies, and capabilities while optimizing for customer value rather than just cost and efficiency.

Partner Capacity and Capability Planning

Supply planning must consider partner capacities, capabilities, and constraints affecting overall ecosystem ability to deliver customer value. Partner limitations often become system constraints affecting customer satisfaction regardless of internal operational excellence. Your perfect internal operations mean nothing if your key partner can't scale to meet demand.

Planning should include systematic assessment of partner capabilities, capacity utilization, and development needs affecting ecosystem performance and customer value delivery. Partner capability gaps might require internal investment, alternative partner development, or customer expectation management.

Service Level Differentiation Across Ecosystems

Different customer segments may require different ecosystem service levels affecting partner coordination, resource allocation, and cost structures.

Value Partners might justify premium ecosystem capabilities while Value Destroyers receive standard service levels optimizing efficiency across the ecosystem.

Service-level differentiation requires partner alignment and capability development supporting segment-specific customer value delivery. Premium service levels might require dedicated partner resources, enhanced communication, or specialized capabilities that standard service levels don't require.

Risk Management and Resilience

Value chain supply planning must consider risks and resilience requirements across entire ecosystems rather than just internal operations. Disruptions in any part of the value chain can affect customer value delivery regardless of internal operational excellence. Your operations might be perfect, but if your Tier 2 supplier in Malaysia has problems, your customers still suffer.

Risk assessment should include partner financial stability, geopolitical risks, technology dependencies, and concentration risks that could affect ecosystem performance and customer value delivery.

Resilience planning should include alternative partner development, backup capability identification, and rapid response protocols maintaining customer value delivery during disruptions while minimizing ecosystem impact.

Financial Planning: Ecosystem Economics

Financial planning for value chain competition must consider value creation and capture across entire ecosystems while optimizing for long-term competitive positioning rather than just short-term profitability.

Ecosystem Investment and Return Analysis

Financial planning should evaluate investments strengthening ecosystem capabilities and competitive positioning even when returns accrue primarily to partners or customers rather than directly to the investing organization.

Platform businesses often invest in partner success programs, developer tools, and ecosystem infrastructure generating returns through increased platform usage, customer satisfaction, and competitive positioning rather than direct revenue from the investments.

The analysis should consider option value and competitive protection benefits from ecosystem investments alongside traditional ROI calculations that might undervalue strategic benefits.

Value Sharing and Partner Economics

Financial planning must consider how value creation and capture is shared across ecosystem participants to ensure sustainable partner engagement while maintaining appropriate returns for ecosystem orchestration and investment.

Partner economics affect ecosystem health and competitive positioning because unsustainable partner models lead to ecosystem degradation while overly generous models reduce orchestrator returns and investment capability.

This is delicate: Squeeze partners too hard and they leave or underperform. Give them too much and you can't sustain the ecosystem investments needed for competitive positioning.

Total Ecosystem Optimization

Financial optimization should consider total ecosystem costs and value creation rather than just internal costs and margins. Investments increasing partner costs but creating superior customer value might generate higher overall ecosystem returns through pricing, retention, and expansion opportunities.

Customer lifetime value calculations should reflect ecosystem contributions to customer satisfaction, retention, and expansion rather than just internal activities and investments.

Digital Transformation: Enabling Ecosystem Integration

This Section's Executive Takeaway

Ecosystem leadership depends on digital integration, not just partnerships. Data sharing, predictive analytics, and coordinated decision-making across firms create switching costs, speed advantages, and learning loops that competitors struggle to replicate. Technology becomes the connective tissue that turns a loose network of partners into a value-creating system.

For Implementation Teams

This section goes deeper into the technology and data architecture required to enable ecosystem orchestration, covering cross-company data integration, analytics, AI-enabled optimization, visibility platforms, and the operational governance needed to make multi-party planning and execution work in practice.

Digital transformation enables value chain integration and optimization creating competitive advantages through real-time coordination, data sharing, and automated decision-making across multiple organizations.

Data Integration and Analytics Across Partners

Value chain competition increasingly depends on data integration and analytics capabilities providing insights and optimization opportunities across entire ecosystems rather than just individual organizations.

Visibility and Coordination

Digital platforms providing visibility into customer demand, inventory levels, production capacity, and delivery status enable proactive coordination improving customer value while reducing costs across entire value chains.

Walmart's supplier integration provides real-time point-of-sale data enabling suppliers to optimize production and inventory while improving product availability and reducing stockouts affecting customer satisfaction.

Integration should include standardized data formats, automated data sharing, and analytics capabilities enabling rapid decision-making and coordination across multiple partners and systems.

Predictive Analytics and Optimization

Machine learning and AI enable predictive analytics and optimization across value chains improving customer satisfaction while reducing costs through better demand forecasting, inventory optimization, and capacity planning.

Amazon's demand forecasting integrates customer behavior data, market trends, promotional plans, and supplier capacity to optimize inventory positioning and delivery speed while minimizing costs across their entire fulfillment network.

Predictive analytics should consider customer value implications alongside operational optimization to ensure efficiency improvements don't compromise customer satisfaction or competitive positioning.

Customer Insight Sharing

Customer insights gathered throughout value chains provide comprehensive understanding of customer behavior, preferences, and satisfaction that individual organizations cannot develop independently.

Customer feedback from retail partners, service providers, and other touchpoints provides insights into customer experience quality and improvement opportunities affecting future purchasing decisions and loyalty.

Sharing should include privacy protection and competitive sensitivity management while maximizing ecosystem learning and customer value improvement opportunities.

The Transition Reality of Ecosystem Competition

The transition from company-versus-company to value chain-versus-value chain competition represents a fundamental shift in competitive strategy requiring new capabilities, metrics, and organizational approaches. Success depends on developing ecosystem orchestration capabilities aligning multiple organizations around customer value creation while maintaining competitive differentiation and sustainable profitability.

But ecosystem competition also creates new risks and challenges requiring sophisticated management capabilities and strategic thinking. You must balance competition and collaboration. Many value chain partners are also competitors in adjacent markets. Managing these complex relationships requires strategic sophistication that many organizations lack.

You must optimize for long-term ecosystem health while maintaining short-term performance and profitability. Partners need sustainable economics or they leave. But giving away too much value undermines your ability to invest in ecosystem development.

You must coordinate across organizational boundaries without direct control. Traditional management approaches based on authority and hierarchy don't work when you're orchestrating partners rather than managing employees.

The complexity is real. Organizations that successfully navigate this complexity create sustainable competitive advantages through ecosystem capabilities difficult for competitors to replicate. These advantages compound over time as ecosystem relationships deepen, customer switching costs increase, and operational integration creates barriers to competitive entry.

But organizations that fail at ecosystem orchestration often find their superior individual capabilities irrelevant because competitors with better integrated ecosystems deliver superior customer value despite inferior individual components.

Moving Forward: Building Ecosystem Capabilities

Value-Centric IBP provides the framework for managing ecosystem complexity by extending traditional planning processes beyond organizational boundaries to include partner collaboration, ecosystem optimization, and customer value measurement. The integration of customer value considerations with ecosystem coordination enables competitive advantages that individual organizations cannot achieve independently.

The future belongs to organizations that can successfully orchestrate ecosystems around customer value creation while maintaining the agility and innovation needed to adapt as customer needs and competitive dynamics continue evolving. The combination of Value-Centric IBP processes with ecosystem thinking provides the foundation for building these capabilities and competitive advantages.

Organizations mastering value chain competition recognize that their boundaries extend far beyond their legal entities to encompass all the partners, suppliers, platforms, and relationships contributing to customer value creation. They design their planning processes, organizational structures, and management systems to orchestrate these extended value chains around customer outcomes rather than just optimizing internal operations. They invest in ecosystem capabilities, partner relationships, and integration technologies creating competitive advantages that individual companies cannot replicate regardless of their internal excellence.

This is the new competitive game. Playing it well requires thinking beyond your organizational boundaries to understand, orchestrate, and optimize entire value chains around customer value creation. Because in the end, customers don't care about your internal excellence. They care about the total value they receive. And that value increasingly depends on your entire ecosystem, not just your individual capabilities.

Competing at the level of ecosystems changes not only where value is created, but how quickly it shifts and how fragile today's advantages can become. When entire value chains are your competitive unit, stability disappears and tomorrow's differentiator can become today's table stakes almost overnight. That reality leads to the next question: How do you plan when customer value, partner dynamics, and competitive positions are all in motion at once? The answer is not a better forecast, but a different kind of readiness, one that prepares the organization for multiple futures rather than betting on a single one.

CHAPTER 14

Dynamic Scenario Planning for Value-Centric IBP

*The best way to predict the future is
to create it. The second best way is to
prepare for multiple versions of it.*
—Peter Drucker

When Today's Advantage Becomes Tomorrow's Expectation

As you've surely gathered by now, customer value is not a static concept. Too many times a company builds what they think is a sustainable competitive advantage. They invest heavily. Execute brilliantly. Customers love it. Then, seemingly overnight, it becomes table stakes that everyone must offer just to stay in the game.

Amazon's free two-day shipping wasn't just a nice perk. It fundamentally shifted customer expectations across all e-commerce. What started as Prime's killer feature became the baseline standard customers now demand from every online retailer. Companies that thought they were competing on product quality suddenly found themselves losing customers over shipping speed, regardless of how good their products were.

This is why treating customer value as a fixed target guarantees you'll miss it.

Netflix illustrates this perfectly. Their value proposition has transformed multiple times: from convenient DVD delivery (beating Blockbuster's limited selection and late fees) to streaming accessibility (redefining convenience entirely) to original content creation (competing with studios rather than just distributors). Each evolution came from anticipating how customer needs and competitive dynamics would shift, not just responding after the shift happened.

The companies that thrive aren't the ones that predict the future perfectly; nobody does that. They're the ones that prepare for multiple possible futures and build the agility to succeed regardless of which one materializes.

This chapter explores how to integrate dynamic scenario planning into Value-Centric IBP, transforming planning from "here's our forecast" into "here are the futures we're preparing for and how we'll win in each one." This chapter marks the shift from planning around a single expected future to building the capability to compete across multiple plausible futures as customer value and competitive dynamics evolve.

Why Static Planning Doesn't Work Anymore

Traditional scenario planning focuses primarily on operational and financial variables: What if revenue grows 10% versus 5%? What if costs increase 15%? What if we lose that major customer?

These are important questions, but they miss the more fundamental shifts that actually reshape markets: How might customer value perceptions evolve? Which of our current differentiators will become commoditized? What new value dimensions might emerge that we're not even considering today?

As already mentioned, digital transformation has compressed the time between competitive innovations and market adoption. A startup can launch a new approach on Monday, and by Friday your customers are asking why you don't offer the same thing. Social media amplifies both customer satisfaction and dissatisfaction instantly. What used to take years to shift now happens in months or weeks.

This acceleration means planning processes built for stable environments don't just underperform. They actively mislead. You optimize for conditions that have already changed by the time your plan is implemented.

Value-centric scenario planning recognizes that customer value operates as a complex, multi-dimensional concept changing continuously in response to internal and external forces. The goal isn't predicting the future with certainty. It's developing organizational agility and response capabilities that enable success regardless of which scenario materializes.

How Customer Value Actually Changes

Let me walk you through the patterns I've observed in how customer value evolves. Understanding these dynamics is essential for developing scenarios that capture realistic possibilities rather than just linear extrapolations.

The Expectations Escalation Cycle

Innovations that initially create competitive advantages become customer expectations that all suppliers must meet. This isn't gradual. It happens in waves that can catch you completely off-guard if you're not watching.

Remember when having a mobile app was innovative? Now customers expect every business to have one, and having a *bad* mobile experience is worse than having none at all. The innovation that once differentiated you becomes the baseline that gets you into the game.

This escalation pattern matters for Value-Centric IBP because capabilities that currently differentiate your organization may become competitive necessities rather than advantages. You need scenarios that anticipate when current value drivers might become commoditized and identify the next generation of value creation opportunities.

Tesla's Autopilot feature initially provided massive differentiation. Now every major automaker is racing to offer similar capabilities because customers increasingly expect them. Tesla's continued advantage comes from anticipating this commoditization and already developing the next generation of autonomous capabilities while others are still catching up to their current features.

Value Dimension Emergence

Sometimes entirely new ways of delivering value emerge that didn't exist or matter before. The rise of sustainable and ethical consumption created value dimensions around environmental impact and social responsibility that weren't significant factors in many industries a decade ago.

Patagonia built their brand partly by recognizing that environmental consciousness would become a significant value dimension for outdoor apparel customers. They didn't just respond to demand for sustainable products. They helped create that demand by making it a central part of their value proposition before most customers even knew they cared about it.

These emergence patterns create scenarios where your current value proposition might be delivering brilliantly on dimensions customers care about today while completely missing dimensions that will matter tomorrow.

Segment Migration Patterns

Different customer segments experience value evolution at different rates and in different directions, which creates fascinating complexity for planning.

Early adopters often value innovation and cutting-edge capabilities even when they're imperfect. They'll tolerate bugs and rough edges to get access to new functionality. Mainstream customers prioritize reliability and ease of use over novelty. Enterprise customers might focus on integration and compliance capabilities that small businesses barely consider. These differential evolution patterns create scenarios where segment value priorities diverge over time, requiring fundamentally different strategies for maintaining relevance across your customer portfolio.

I've watched this play out in software: Some segments migrate toward premium value propositions with more features and sophistication, while others become more price-sensitive and want simpler, more affordable options. Trying to serve both with a single offering often means disappointing everyone.

The segment lifecycle pattern is particularly important: Startup customers initially focused on rapid growth might become more interested in operational efficiency and risk management as they mature. Your current Growth Potential customers might evolve into Value Partners, but their value priorities will shift as their businesses develop, requiring you to evolve what you deliver.

Competitive Value Disruption

The disruptions that really hurt don't come from competitors doing what you do but better. They come from competitors redefining what value means.

Uber didn't provide better taxi service. They redefined transportation value around convenience, transparency, and digital experience. Traditional taxi companies could improve dispatch times and driver training all they wanted, but they were optimizing for a value proposition customers were moving away from.

Airbnb didn't just offer cheaper accommodations. They created new value around authentic local experiences and community connection. Hotels could lower their prices, but that wouldn't address the fundamentally different value proposition Airbnb offered.

These disruption patterns create scenarios where your established value proposition becomes insufficient even when you're delivering it excellently. You're solving yesterday's problem really well while customers are moving toward tomorrow's needs.

Technology-Driven Value Transformation

Technological change creates new possibilities for value delivery while potentially making existing value propositions obsolete, often simultaneously.

Cloud computing transformed enterprise software value from ownership and control to accessibility and scalability. Companies that built their value proposition around powerful on-premise solutions suddenly found customers cared more about accessing software from anywhere than about having the most feature-rich local installation.

AI and automation can enhance customer experiences while reducing costs, but they can also eliminate jobs and create anxiety about human relevance that affects value perceptions. The same technology that makes your product more valuable to some customers might make it threatening or undesirable to others.

Mobile technology shifted consumer value from content consumption to content creation and sharing. Companies focused on delivering content efficiently missed the bigger shift toward enabling customers to create and share their own content.

Each technological wave creates scenarios where value landscapes transform rapidly. Organizations that just respond to changes after they occur are always playing catch-up. The winners anticipate transformations and position themselves to benefit from them rather than being disrupted by them.

Segment Movement Scenarios: Where Customers Might Go

One of the most critical aspects of scenario planning for Value-Centric IBP is understanding how customers might transition between different positions in your customer value matrix. These movements directly impact resource allocation, capability requirements, and revenue projections.

Let me walk through some common scenarios I've seen play out:

Economic Stress-Driven Priority Shifts

When economic pressure hits, customers don't just buy less. They fundamentally reconsider what they value. Value Partners might migrate toward Retention Risks if your premium offerings suddenly feel like luxuries rather than necessities. Retention Risk customers might shift toward Value Destroyers when growth budgets get slashed and every expense faces scrutiny.

The 2008 financial crisis created exactly this pattern: Enterprise customers who valued cutting-edge capabilities suddenly cared much more about cost predictability and risk reduction. SaaS companies that anticipated this shift and prepared appropriate offerings maintained relationships. Those that kept pushing premium innovation lost customers to competitors offering "good enough" solutions at lower prices.

But here's what makes this interesting: Not all customers respond the same way to economic stress. Some double down on strategic investments, seeing downturns as opportunities to build competitive advantages while others are cutting back. Your scenario planning needs to predict not just that economic stress will happen, but which of your customers will respond in which ways.

Technology-Driven Job Transformation

When new technologies automate tasks your customers currently perform, their value priorities shift dramatically. Junior employees who valued learning and skill development might suddenly worry about job security and resist rather than embrace your innovations.

I watched this happen with marketing automation: Individual contributors who initially loved efficiency tools became anxious when those tools got sophisticated enough to eliminate positions. The value proposition that worked when automation was an enhancement stopped working when it became a replacement.

This creates scenarios where your technical improvements actively harm your value delivery to certain segments. The better your product gets at automation, the more threatening it becomes to users who see their jobs disappearing.

Regulatory and Compliance Evolution

Regulatory changes can instantly transform segment value priorities. Customers who barely cared about compliance suddenly treat it as their top priority when new regulations create liability exposure or competitive requirements.

General Data Protection Regulation (GDPR) transformed how European customers valued data-handling capabilities. Features that were nice-to-haves became deal-breakers overnight. Companies that anticipated this regulatory shift and built compliance capabilities in advance gained significant competitive advantages. Those that treated it as a burden to be addressed at the last minute found themselves scrambling while customers explored alternatives.

The scenario planning challenge is that regulatory changes often happen suddenly but require long capability development timelines. You need to start building compliance capabilities before regulations are finalized, based on scenarios about which regulations might emerge and what they'll require.

Reputation and Trust Disruption

Social media has made reputation incredibly fragile. A single incident can shift how entire customer segments perceive your value delivery, even if your actual capabilities haven't changed at all.

United Airlines' forcible passenger removal incident didn't change their operational capabilities, but it fundamentally shifted how many customers perceived the value of flying United. Value Partners reconsidered relationships not because service quality declined, but because trust eroded.

These reputation scenarios create conditions where you might deliver exactly the same value you always have, but customers perceive it completely differently based on factors that may feel unfair or disconnected from your actual performance.

Integrating Scenarios Into Monthly Planning

This Section's Executive Takeaway

Scenario planning only creates advantage if it changes real decisions, not just strategic documents. Leaders must ensure that every core planning conversation—product, demand, supply, finance, and executive review—explicitly tests priorities, investments, and risks against multiple plausible futures, not a single forecast. This shifts IBP from optimizing for efficiency to building strategic resilience and optionality.

For Implementation Teams

This section details how to embed scenario thinking into each step of the monthly IBP cycle, including how to translate alternative futures into concrete product priorities, demand assumptions, capacity decisions, financial trade-offs, and executive choices.

The real test of scenario planning isn't whether your scenarios are clever. It's whether they actually influence operational decisions and resource allocation. Too often, scenario planning remains a separate strategic exercise that has minimal impact on what the organization actually does. Effective integration means every IBP process systematically considers multiple possible futures rather than optimizing for a single forecast.

Product Management Review: Planning for Multiple Value Futures

Traditional product planning assumes you know what customers will value next year. Value-centric scenario planning recognizes that customer needs and value priorities might evolve in fundamentally different directions.

Different scenarios often require different innovation approaches. Economic uncertainty might favor incremental improvements and cost reduction initiatives that deliver value with lower risk. Growth scenarios might justify breakthrough innovation investments that create new competitive advantages but require substantial resources and carry higher failure risk.

The challenge is prioritizing innovation investments based on which capabilities are most likely to remain relevant across multiple futures. Automation capabilities might provide value in both growth and contraction scenarios, enabling expansion during growth and efficiency during contraction. Premium experience enhancements might only generate returns in favorable economic conditions when customers have the budgets for non-essential improvements.

Here's what makes this hard: Organizational capabilities take years to develop. You can't wait until scenarios materialize to start building capabilities. You need to make long-term investment decisions based on which scenarios seem most likely or most impactful, knowing you might be wrong.

The capability development scenarios (from Chapter 9) should consider which investments provide the greatest option value across different possible futures while identifying capabilities that might become obsolete if specific scenarios materialize. Investing heavily in capabilities that only matter under one scenario is risky. Investing in capabilities that provide value across multiple scenarios is smart but harder to identify.

Netflix's content strategy demonstrates this approach: They invest in diverse content types and genres that provide value under different scenarios. If customer preferences shift toward documentary content, they're positioned. If scripted dramas dominate, they're ready. If international markets become crucial, they've already built multilingual content capabilities.

Demand Planning: Forecasting Multiple Customer Futures

Traditional demand planning extrapolates historical trends and adds sales team input. Scenario-based demand planning recognizes that customer behavior and purchasing patterns might change in ways that make historical patterns misleading.

Different customer segments often respond differently to the same external conditions. Value Partners might maintain spending during economic uncertainty, viewing your offerings as strategic necessities they can't cut. Retention Risk customers might slash budgets immediately, treating your offerings as discretionary expenses. This differential response creates demand scenarios where total volume might decrease, but mix shifts dramatically toward certain segments. Your forecast might show declining overall revenue but increasing revenue from Value Partners, requiring different resource allocations than a simple volume decline would suggest.

Customer behavior patterns can change rapidly in response to external conditions or competitive innovations. Usage-based business models need scenarios considering how customer behavior might evolve. Economic pressure might drive customers toward more intensive usage of cost-saving features while reducing usage of premium capabilities. Competitive innovations might shift usage toward specific features that become new expectations.

I've watched SaaS companies struggle with this during economic downturns: Customers don't cancel entirely, but they shift usage patterns toward features that justify cost rather than exploratory usage. This changes both retention forecasts and expansion predictions in ways that simple trend analysis misses.

Addressable market size can change rapidly based on regulatory changes, economic conditions, or technology adoption patterns. Demand planning should consider scenarios where markets expand or contract beyond your current customer base.

Cryptocurrency adoption created scenarios where financial services markets expanded dramatically to include customers who previously had no banking relationships. Companies that only forecast existing market growth missed the market expansion opportunity entirely.

Supply Planning: Flexible Fulfillment Across Scenarios

Supply planning scenarios should explore how fulfillment capabilities and service levels might need to adapt under different conditions while maintaining value delivery for different customer segments. Different scenarios might require different approaches to service-level differentiation based on resource constraints, competitive pressure, or customer value evolution. Economic pressure might increase the importance of efficiency while growth scenarios might emphasize premium service capability.

Here's a concrete example: During COVID, supply chain disruptions created scenarios where companies couldn't maintain standard service levels for all customers. Those that had scenario planning for constrained resources could quickly prioritize Value Partners for available inventory. Those without clear prioritization frameworks made ad-hoc decisions that sometimes allocated scarce resources to low-value customers while disappointing high-value relationships.

Flexibility capabilities often provide value across multiple scenarios by enabling rapid adaptation to changing conditions. Organizations that invest in adaptable supply capabilities—modular systems, flexible workforce arrangements, diverse supplier relationships—can respond more effectively to scenario changes than those optimized for specific conditions.

Cost structure scenarios should consider how different conditions might require different approaches to maintain value delivery across customer segments while preserving profitability. Variable cost structures might provide advantages during uncertain periods by enabling rapid scaling down. Fixed cost investments might generate superior returns during growth scenarios by creating economies of scale.

Financial Planning: Valuing Options and Flexibility

Financial planning scenarios should explore how different conditions might affect customer lifetime value, segment profitability, and investment returns while maintaining financial discipline across multiple possible futures.

Customer lifetime value (CLV) calculations depend on assumptions about retention rates, expansion patterns, and cost structures that might change significantly under different scenarios. Economic uncertainty might reduce expansion rates while increasing retention focus (customers become more conservative but also more loyal to proven solutions). This shifts CLV calculations and investment priorities even though topline revenue forecasts might look similar.

Different scenarios might also change the relative value of different customer segments. Small business customers might become more valuable during economic uncertainty if their lower acquisition costs and faster decision-making provide advantages. Enterprise customers might become more attractive during growth periods when their higher expansion potential generates superior returns.

Investment prioritization across scenarios requires evaluating which investments provide value regardless of which future materializes. Customer acquisition investments might provide better returns during growth scenarios when markets are expanding. Retention and efficiency investments might generate superior returns during contraction periods when maintaining existing relationships matters more than adding new ones.

Capability development investments should be evaluated across multiple scenarios to identify investments that provide value in multiple futures. Technology investments that enhance both efficiency and customer experience might provide value across more scenarios than investments optimizing for specific conditions.

The financial challenge is that scenario planning often reveals that "safe" investments generating returns across all scenarios don't exist. You're forced to make judgment calls about which scenarios to prepare for most heavily, knowing you might be wrong. The goal isn't eliminating this uncertainty. It's making these trade-offs explicit and intentional rather than implicit and accidental.

Executive Review: Making Scenario-Informed Strategic Decisions

Executive review integration ensures scenario planning influences strategic decision-making and organizational preparation rather than remaining analytical exercises that don't affect operational planning. Scenario planning should generate strategic options that can be activated quickly if specific scenarios begin materializing. These options might include partnership opportunities, acquisition targets, capability development accelerations, or market expansion initiatives requiring advance preparation.

Microsoft's acquisition strategy demonstrates option development: They continuously evaluate potential acquisitions that could enhance their capabilities if specific market scenarios develop. When LinkedIn became available, they'd already done scenario planning about the value of professional network data for their enterprise strategy. They could move quickly because the option was already developed.

Effective scenario integration requires identifying specific indicators that suggest scenarios are beginning to materialize and preparing response plans that can be implemented quickly. These triggers might include customer satisfaction changes, competitive moves, economic indicators, or technology adoption patterns.

The triggers need to be specific enough to prompt action but not so hair-trigger that you're constantly responding to noise. Customer satisfaction declines of 5% might just be normal variation, but declines of 15% probably indicate meaningful scenario development requiring response.

Making Scenarios Actually Work: Workshops and Collaboration

This Section's Executive Takeaway

High-quality scenarios emerge from collective intelligence, not isolated analysis. Leaders must create the conditions for cross-functional dialogue, challenge, and synthesis so that different perspectives on customers, markets, technology, and operations shape a shared view of future risks and opportunities. Scenario planning becomes a strategic capability only when it is organizational, not departmental.

For Implementation Teams

This section goes deeper into how to design and facilitate cross-functional scenario workshops, integrate diverse functional insights, and build collaborative processes that translate alternative futures into aligned response strategies and coordinated action.

I've seen too many scenario-planning exercises produce beautiful documentation that sits in shared drives while the organization makes decisions as if the scenarios never existed. Effective scenario development requires cross-functional perspectives, bringing different expertise and viewpoints to the planning process. Marketing, sales, product development, operations, and finance teams often have different insights about how scenarios might develop and what responses would be most effective.

Different Functions See Different Futures

Sales teams have direct customer interaction insights. They hear the early signals of changing priorities and concerns. Product teams understand technology trends and development constraints that might enable or prevent certain scenarios. Operations teams understand capability limitations and cost implications that affect feasibility of scenario responses.

Customer-facing teams often provide insights about early warning indicators, suggesting scenarios are beginning to materialize. Your customer success team might notice satisfaction trends months before they show up in formal metrics. Your sales team might hear competitive positioning changes before they're officially announced.

Cross-functional workshops should systematically gather these different perspectives while building consensus around scenario likelihood and response priorities. The goal is comprehensive scenario development considering all relevant factors, not just the perspectives of whichever function dominates the planning process.

I've watched scenario planning fail when it's driven primarily by finance (scenarios become too conservative) or primarily by product (scenarios become too technology-focused). The scenarios that actually help are ones that integrate all these perspectives into realistic possibilities.

Collaborative Scenario Development

Effective scenario development benefits from collaborative processes engaging multiple perspectives in scenario design rather than just scenario evaluation. Different functions might identify scenario possibilities others wouldn't consider based on their specific expertise and market exposure.

The workshops should include structured brainstorming about scenario possibilities, not just "what could happen" but "what would we do if it did?" This grounds scenarios in actionable response planning rather than abstract speculation.

Systematic evaluation of scenario likelihood and impact helps prioritize where to invest preparation resources. Not all scenarios warrant equal preparation. Some are low-probability but high-impact, suggesting modest preparation that could be rapidly scaled. Others are high-probability but lower-impact, suggesting routine operational integration rather than special planning.

Collaborative development of response strategies leveraging different functional capabilities ensures that when scenarios materialize, you have coordinated responses rather than functional silos working at cross-purposes.

Customer value protection during scenarios often requires coordination across multiple functions simultaneously. Product development might need to accelerate specific capabilities while marketing adjusts messaging and sales adapts pricing strategies. If these responses aren't coordinated, you might confuse customers or waste resources duplicating effort.

Turning Scenarios Into Action:
Triggers and Responses

This Section's Executive Takeaway

Scenarios only matter if the organization can recognize when one is unfolding and respond faster than competitors. Leaders must insist on clear early-warning indicators, predefined decision thresholds, and prepared response options so that uncertainty leads to decisive action rather than paralysis or debate under pressure.

For Implementation Teams

This section describes how to design practical early-warning systems, define trigger thresholds, link them to pre-agreed response playbooks, and integrate monitoring and activation into existing planning, performance, and governance routines.

The most sophisticated scenarios are useless if you can't recognize when they're starting to happen or don't know what to do when they do. Let's look into this.

Building Early Warning Systems

Leading indicators should provide advance warning of scenario development while being specific enough to trigger appropriate responses. Customer satisfaction trends might indicate relationship quality scenarios developing. Competitive pricing changes might suggest margin pressure scenarios emerging.

Technology adoption patterns often provide leading indicators of customer value evolution and competitive disruption. If you see early adopters rapidly embracing a new approach, you have time to prepare before mainstream customers start demanding it. If you wait until mainstream customers are already demanding it, you're too late.

Social media sentiment might indicate reputation scenarios brewing before they explode into full crises. Economic indicators suggest financial pressure scenarios before they fully materialize in customer behavior.

The indicators should be quantifiable and monitorable through existing systems rather than requiring special data collection that might not be sustainable. If monitoring your indicators requires heroic effort, it won't happen consistently. Integration with regular reporting systems ensures indicator monitoring becomes part of routine planning processes rather than special effort.

Netflix monitors content engagement patterns, subscriber growth trends, and competitive content announcements as leading indicators of scenarios affecting their content strategy and customer retention approaches. They don't wait for massive subscriber losses to realize a scenario is developing. They see the leading indicators and adjust proactively.

Setting Triggers That Actually Trigger Action

Effective trigger systems require specific thresholds that initiate response plans rather than just general monitoring that might not prompt action. "Customer satisfaction is declining" is too vague. "Customer satisfaction has declined 10% over two consecutive months" is specific enough to trigger a predetermined response.

Threshold setting should balance sensitivity with stability to prevent overreaction to normal variations while ensuring rapid response to significant changes. Statistical approaches can help identify when changes exceed normal variation and suggest meaningful scenario development rather than just noise.

Response triggers should be tied to specific action plans rather than just alerting systems that require additional decision-making during potentially stressful periods. When the trigger hits, everyone knows what happens next because the response was planned in advance.

This doesn't mean responses are automatic—executive judgment still matters—but it means the playbook exists and can be executed quickly rather than being designed under pressure after the scenario is already developing.

Learning from What Actually Happens

Scenario planning effectiveness improves through organizational learning that refines scenario development, indicator accuracy, and response strategy effectiveness based on actual experience.

Regular assessment of scenario accuracy helps improve future scenario development. Scenarios that consistently prove accurate suggest effective planning processes worth reinforcing. Scenarios that repeatedly miss the mark indicate systematic biases or missing factors needing correction.

But here's the tricky part: Sometimes your scenarios don't materialize because your preparation prevented them. If you scenario-plan for customer churn and implement retention initiatives that work, the churn scenario doesn't happen. That doesn't mean the scenario was wrong. It means your response worked.

Response strategy evaluation should assess not just outcome achievement but also resource efficiency, timing accuracy, and coordination effectiveness across functions. Successful outcomes achieved through inefficient resource usage indicate strategy improvement opportunities. Well-executed strategies producing poor outcomes suggest scenario development problems, as in: Maybe you prepared for the wrong thing.

Cross-functional coordination effectiveness often determines response strategy success more than individual functional excellence. Marketing campaigns that successfully communicate value but aren't supported by adequate sales capability development might generate interest without conversion. Product development responses that create competitive advantages might fail to achieve market impact without coordinated go-to-market strategy.

The evaluation should consider both intended and unintended consequences of response strategies. Customer protection strategies that successfully prevent churn might inadvertently reduce profitability if implemented too broadly. Growth acceleration strategies that successfully increase revenue might strain operational capabilities if scaling wasn't adequately planned.

The Real Value of Scenario Planning

The reality is that scenario planning won't make you a psychic. You will still be surprised. Markets will still do unexpected things. Competitors will still make moves you didn't anticipate. The value of scenario planning isn't perfect prediction. It's organizational agility and response capability.

Organizations that practice scenario planning develop muscles for recognizing change, adapting quickly, and coordinating responses across functions. When unexpected scenarios emerge, they have frameworks for rapid assessment and response deployment that organizations without scenario-planning discipline don't have.

They've practiced asking "what would we do if ...?" enough times that doing it for real during actual scenario development feels familiar rather than overwhelming. They've built the cross-functional relationships and communication patterns that enable coordinated responses under pressure. They've identified which capabilities provide value across multiple scenarios and invested in building flexibility that lets them adapt rather than optimizing for specific conditions that might not materialize.

Perhaps most importantly, scenario planning creates organizational comfort with uncertainty. Instead of treating unexpected developments as failures of planning, teams recognize them as inherent aspects of operating in complex environments. This mindset shift enables faster adaptation because energy goes into responding rather than analyzing what went wrong with predictions.

The Integration Challenge

Integrating dynamic scenario planning into Value-Centric IBP substantially increases planning complexity. You're asking teams that may already struggle with basic monthly planning cycles to consider multiple possible futures, develop response strategies for each, monitor indicators, and maintain readiness for rapid adaptation.

This is a lot.

For organizations still mastering fundamental IBP discipline—getting the right people to meetings consistently, making clear decisions, executing those decisions effectively—adding comprehensive scenario planning might be overwhelming.

Start simpler if you need to. Pick two or three critical scenarios most likely to affect your business. Develop basic response plans. Identify a few key indicators. Build the discipline of scenario thinking before trying to implement the full framework.

The goal is building capability progressively, not implementing perfect processes immediately. Organizations that try to go from basic planning to sophisticated scenario integration in one leap often fail at both. Those that build gradually, starting with simple scenarios and expanding as capabilities develop, create sustainable practices that actually influence decisions.

Moving Forward

Dynamic scenario planning transforms Value-Centric IBP from "here's what we think will happen" to "here are the futures we're preparing for and how we'll succeed in each one." It integrates customer value dynamics, competitive positioning, and capability development into planning that embraces uncertainty while maintaining strategic focus. Product management considers how customer needs might evolve. Demand planning recognizes that customer behavior might change in discontinuous ways. Supply planning builds flexibility enabling adaptation. Financial planning values options and agility alongside efficiency.

The tools and frameworks emphasize customer value dynamics and competitive positioning rather than just operational and financial variables. They recognize that customer value isn't static and that preparing for multiple value evolution scenarios matters more than predicting a single future accurately.

For organizations implementing Value-Centric IBP, dynamic scenario planning represents the evolution from prediction-based approaches to adaptation-based approaches. Customer value creation requires anticipating and responding to changing customer needs, competitive dynamics, and market conditions that static planning cannot address effectively.

Organizations implementing effective dynamic scenario planning position themselves to thrive in uncertain and rapidly changing markets while maintaining the customer value focus that drives sustainable competitive advantage. Because in the end, you can't predict the future. But you can prepare for multiple versions of it. And that preparation—the agility, the response capabilities, the organizational muscles for adaptation—might be more valuable than any prediction could ever be.

Preparing for multiple futures only matters if the organization is capable of acting on them. Scenarios, options, and early-warning systems are necessary, but they are not sufficient on their own. Agility, customer focus, and value-centric decision making ultimately live in people, behaviors, and leadership, not in models or plans. That brings us to the final step of the journey: turning frameworks into practice and intention into sustained action.

CHAPTER 15

The Beginning

*The journey of a thousand miles
begins with a single step.*
—Lao Tzu

An End and a Beginning

I'm both happy and sad to write this last chapter.

Happy because we've covered so much ground together, from understanding what customer value really means to building integrated planning systems that align entire organizations around value creation. If you've made it this far, you've invested significant time and thought into transforming how you think about business strategy and planning.

Sad because our conversation is ending, at least in this format. There's so much more to explore, so many nuances to discuss, so many contexts and challenges that we couldn't possibly cover in a single book.

But here's what I hope: that this end of the book is a new beginning for you as a reader.

I hope you enjoyed reading it. More importantly, I hope it made a difference, not just in how you think about planning, but in what you do on Monday morning when you walk into your office or log into your first meeting.

What We've Learned

Let me recap the journey we've taken together, not as a summary of chapters, but as a progression of insights that build on each other.

We started with a fundamental truth: The customer is the business. Not the product, not the technology, not the organizational chart. Everything flows from understanding and serving customer needs in ways that create sustainable competitive advantage.

We learned that value is multidimensional: It's not just functional benefits or economic savings. It's emotional resonance, social identity, future security, and the synergies that make integrated solutions more valuable than their component parts. Understanding these dimensions transforms how you think about product development, marketing, and customer relationships.

We discovered that value exists in dynamic systems: The Three Cs—Customer, Corporation, Competition—constantly interact and evolve. What creates value today may become table stakes tomorrow. Static strategies fail; dynamic planning succeeds.

We explored how to compete differently: The ten systematic approaches to value innovation showed us that breakthrough success comes from redefining the game rather than just playing it better. Value dimension reconstruction, journey redefinition, and ecosystem creation aren't just tactics, they're fundamental ways of thinking about competitive strategy.

We learned to measure what matters: Customer value and business value aren't opposing forces. They're interconnected dimensions that create four distinct strategic quadrants. Value Partners, Margin Diluters, Retention Risks, and Value Destroyers each require fundamentally different strategies and capabilities.

We discovered the power of customer migration: Not all customers are created equal, and honest portfolio optimization means helping some customers find better solutions elsewhere while systematically developing others toward Value Partner status. This requires courage and discipline that most organizations lack.

We built frameworks for capability identification: Sustainable competitive advantage comes from systematic capability development aligned with customer needs and competitive dynamics. Building moats takes time, so you must choose carefully where to invest.

We recognized the criticality of culture: The most sophisticated processes fail without organizational cultures that genuinely prioritize customer value creation. Culture isn't what's written on walls. It's what people do when no one is watching.

We explored Value-Centric IBP: Traditional planning optimizes internal coordination. Value-Centric IBP aligns every function—product, demand, supply, finance—around customer value delivery and competitive capability building. It transforms planning from reactive coordination into proactive advantage creation.

We learned how to evolve existing IT infrastructure and leverage AI: You don't need to rip out your legacy systems to implement Value-Centric IBP. We explored practical approaches for integrating customer value data into existing planning systems, using AI to uncover patterns humans miss, and automating routine analysis so planners can focus on strategic decisions. Technology doesn't replace human judgment. It amplifies it, enabling organizations to scale customer understanding and response capabilities in ways that weren't possible even five years ago.

We understood ecosystem competition: Today's battles aren't just company versus company; they're value chain versus value chain. Success requires orchestrating capabilities across organizational boundaries while maintaining competitive differentiation.

We integrated dynamic scenario planning: The future is uncertain, but organizations that prepare for multiple possible futures build agility and response capabilities that enable success regardless of which scenario materializes.

And finally, **we learned that building customer-centric cultures and planning systems requires patience, persistence, and genuine commitment** to transformation that touches every aspect of how organizations operate.

Implementation: Where the Slides End and Reality Begins

The reality is that no book has ever transformed an organization. Books can spark ideas, provide frameworks, and point out better paths, but they don't do the work.

Change happens because people do.

You will. More accurately, you and the people around you—the teams you lead, the colleagues you inspire, and the culture you shape day by day—will drive the transformation. This book can serve as a guide, a set of tools, and perhaps a companion for the journey, but the real engine of change is you. Without your effort, it's just ink on paper. With your effort, it can become the blueprint for lasting impact.

The frameworks in this book are tools. Tools don't build things by themselves. They require skilled hands, sustained effort, and the courage to persist when implementation gets difficult, which it will.

You'll face resistance. People who've optimized for internal metrics their entire careers won't immediately embrace customer value as the primary organizing principle. Functions that have operated independently won't naturally collaborate around integrated value delivery. Short-term financial pressures will constantly tempt you to abandon long-term capability investments.

This is normal. This is expected. This is where most transformations fail, not because the frameworks are wrong, but because organizations lose commitment when the work gets hard.

The question isn't whether you'll face these challenges. The question is whether you'll persist through them.

What Success Looks Like

Success doesn't happen overnight. It unfolds gradually as your organization builds new capabilities and develops new reflexes. You'll know you're making progress when:

Conversations change. Meetings that once focused exclusively on internal metrics start including systematic discussion of customer value delivery and competitive positioning. "Will this improve forecast accuracy?" expands to "Will this enhance customer outcomes?"

Decisions improve. Resource allocation choices that once optimized functional efficiency start balancing customer value creation with operational excellence. Trade-offs become explicit rather than implicit.

Coordination strengthens. Functions that once planned independently start naturally collaborating around customer value delivery. Cross-functional tensions decrease as shared customer focus creates common purpose.

Planning evolves. Monthly planning cycles that once felt like administrative burdens start generating insights that influence strategic decisions. The line between operational planning and strategic planning blurs as they become integrated parts of the same value-creation system.

Technology enables rather than constrains. Your existing systems start serving customer value objectives rather than just tracking operational metrics. AI surfaces insights that change planning conversations. Data flows more freely across functional boundaries. Technology investments are evaluated based on their contribution to customer value delivery rather than just efficiency gains.

Capabilities compound. Investments in customer understanding, data analytics, scenario planning, and value delivery capabilities start reinforcing each other, creating competitive advantages that become increasingly difficult for competitors to replicate.

Results follow. Customer satisfaction improves. Retention strengthens. Expansion accelerates. Premium pricing becomes sustainable. Market share grows not through price competition but through superior value delivery.

Most importantly, **your organization develops a sense of purpose beyond profit**. People understand that they're not just hitting numbers. They're creating value that makes customers' lives or businesses better. This sense of purpose becomes a source of engagement, innovation, and resilience that spreadsheets can never capture.

The Spark That Ignites a Fire

I hope this book serves as a spark that ignites a fire of value-centric revolution, not just in your organization, but across organizations, industries, and markets. Because here's what I believe: The world doesn't need more companies optimizing for short-term profits while destroying long-term value. It needs more organizations genuinely committed to creating value for customers, employees, communities, and shareholders simultaneously.

The Bain research we discussed in Chapter 2 proved what many of us have intuitively known: Companies that excel at stakeholder value creation, particularly customer value, generate superior financial returns. This isn't a trade-off between doing good and doing well. It's a recognition that sustainable financial success flows from genuine value creation.

But transformation doesn't happen in isolation. It requires communities of practice where leaders share experiences, frameworks evolve through practical application, and collective learning accelerates individual progress.

I hope this book starts conversations in your organization, in your industry, in communities of leaders wrestling with similar challenges. I hope it creates networks of collaboration where practitioners share what works, what doesn't, and how frameworks adapt to different contexts.

The philosophy of Value-Centric IBP will continue evolving long after this book is published. New technologies will enable capabilities we can't yet imagine. Competitive dynamics will create challenges requiring new approaches. Customer expectations will evolve in ways that demand fresh thinking.

This evolution should be collaborative rather than individual. The frameworks in this book represent decades of experience from countless practitioners across multiple industries. They should continue evolving through similar collective wisdom. If these ideas resonate with you, challenge you, or spark questions about how Value-Centric IBP could apply in your own organization, I welcome the conversation and would be glad to exchange perspectives with you.

So share your experiences. Question the frameworks. Adapt them to your context. Teach others what you learn. Build on what works and improve what doesn't. That's how philosophies evolve from individual insights into collective wisdom that transforms industries and creates lasting impact.

A Personal Note

I am privileged to have the opportunity to share my thoughts and experiences with you. Thank you for listening.

Writing this book has been a journey of reflection on everything I've learned throughout my career: the successes and failures, the brilliant colleagues and challenging clients, the frameworks that worked and those that didn't, the transformations that succeeded and those that struggled.

But more importantly, thank you for considering these ideas seriously enough to invest your time reading them. In our attention-scarce world, that investment is the greatest compliment any author can receive.

I don't expect you to agree with everything in this book. I hope some parts challenged your thinking or even frustrated you with their departure from conventional wisdom. That tension between established practice and new approaches is where innovation happens.

What I do hope is that you found frameworks, insights, or perspectives that help you lead more effectively, plan more strategically, and create more value for your customers, your organization, and yourself.

Your Journey Begins

The real work starts now.

Not reading about Value-Centric IBP, but implementing it. Not understanding the frameworks intellectually, but applying them practically. Not admiring the philosophy abstractly, but living it concretely in daily decisions.

Start small if you need to. Pick one framework from this book and apply it to one challenge in your organization. Build momentum through small wins before attempting comprehensive transformation.

Or start big if your situation demands it. Some organizations need radical transformation rather than incremental improvement. If you're facing existential competitive threats or fundamental market disruptions, waiting for gradual change may not be an option.

Either way, start.

Start measuring customer value systematically. Start segmenting based on value potential rather than just demographics. Start aligning your planning processes around customer outcomes. Start building capabilities that create sustainable competitive advantages. Start having different conversations in planning meetings.

Start transforming your organization from one that optimizes internal metrics into one that creates customer value so compelling that business success follows naturally.

The Choice Remains Yours

We began Chapter 1 with a choice: Continue optimizing around internal metrics while hoping customers will appreciate your efforts, or transform your business around what customers actually value. That choice hasn't changed. Reading this book doesn't make the decision for you. But I hope it equipped you to make that choice more confidently, understand its implications more clearly, and implement it more effectively.

The companies mastering value-centric planning are building stronger customer relationships, more sustainable competitive advantages, and more resilient business models. They're not just surviving in complex and competitive markets. They're thriving.

The companies avoiding this transformation are finding themselves trapped in spirals of price competition, feature proliferation, and customer indifference. They work harder and harder to achieve results that become more and more elusive. Which future you choose for your organization depends entirely on what you do next.

Final Thoughts

Business strategy books often end with rousing calls to action or predictions about future trends. I'm not going to do that.

Instead, I'll end with simple recognition of reality: Transforming organizations is hard work. It requires sustained commitment, genuine courage, and persistent effort over years, not months.

There will be setbacks. There will be resistance. There will be moments when reverting to familiar approaches feels easier than pushing forward with transformation. In those moments, remember why this matters.

Remember that customer value creation isn't just a business strategy. It's the fundamental purpose of business itself. Companies exist because they create value for customers in ways that justify what they charge.

Remember that employees want purpose beyond profits. Organizations that genuinely focus on customer value creation engage people more deeply than those that only optimize shareholder returns.

Remember that sustainable competitive advantages come from creating value customers can't easily find elsewhere. The moats you build through superior value delivery compound over time, creating advantages that become increasingly difficult to replicate.

And remember that the choice is yours. Nobody can force value-centric transformation on your organization. It only happens when leaders choose to make it happen and persist through the inevitable challenges.

So as we close this book and you begin your journey, I leave you with the same thought we started with:

The customer doesn't just buy your product. They're writing your business plan.

The only question is whether you will read it.

Thank you for allowing me to be part of your journey.

Now go create some value.

ACKNOWLEDGMENTS

This book would not have been possible without the support, insight, and encouragement of many exceptional people. I am deeply grateful to the colleagues, mentors, and friends who generously offered their time to review chapters, challenge my thinking, and strengthen the clarity and impact of the ideas presented here.

My sincere thanks to Greg Smith, Matt Elenjickal, Razat Gaurav, Nikhil Sagar, Sanjiv Sidhu, Benjamin Gordon, Charles Liu, Amjad Hussain, Ariel Palones, Alex Rotenberg, Igor Rikalo, Kelly Thomas, Mark Blackwell, Nancy Pile, Matt Smalley, Sanjay Bonde, Molham Aref, Luis Solana, Tom Lubotsky, Jonathan Shenkman, Brian Veronesi, and Sue Adelman for their thoughtful reviews, constructive feedback, and meaningful conversations. Each of you helped shape this work in ways that go far beyond individual comments. Your experience, candor, and perspective made this a better and more useful book.

To the many executives, practitioners, and teams across industries who shared their real-world challenges and insights, your stories added depth and relevance that theory alone could never provide.

To the editors, reviewers, and early readers who pushed me to refine the narrative and deepen the analysis, thank you for your honesty, rigor, and dedication. Your input elevated this work far beyond its initial drafts.

And to my family—Judith, Alex, and Jonathan—thank you for your patience, love, and unwavering belief throughout this journey. Every page carries your imprint.

ABOUT THE AUTHOR

Dov Shenkman, former Vice President of Global Supply Chain at **Medtronic**, is the CEO and founding member of **Atid Group**. With more than three decades of executive experience spanning healthcare, retail, automotive, and industrial markets, Dov is recognized for orchestrating large-scale, end-to-end supply-chain transformations. At Medtronic, he led a multiyear overhaul of global planning, logistics, inventory, and fulfillment networks—boosting resilience, agility, and efficiency for one of the world's largest medical-technology companies.

Before Medtronic, Dov served as Group Vice President of Supply Chain Operations at **Walgreens Boots Alliance**, where he modernized planning, distribution and last-mile capabilities across a 10,000-store network. Earlier in his career he held senior roles at **General Motors, OfficeMax, Federal-Mogul, EDS/AT Kearney, and i2 Technologies**, spearheading multi-billion-dollar logistics and operational-turnaround programs on five continents and cumulatively delivering billions of dollars in working capital optimization and hundreds of millions of dollars in top and bottom-line benefits.

Shenkman also contributes to the broader supply chain and operations community through advisory positions. He serves on Bain Advisor Network and the advisory boards of several organizations, including **Cambridge Capital**, **FourKites, Algo, CB4, RelationalAI, 1TCC, Emerix and Amphorica**, and held a leadership position on the **Business Advisory Council at Northwestern University's Transportation Center.** Dov also served on the **United States Department of Commerce –Advisory Committee on Supply Chain Competitiveness** during two administrations.

Throughout his career, Shenkman has been recognized for his innovative and resourceful leadership, particularly in developing and executing turnaround strategies that yield high-impact results in manufacturing, retail, service, and distribution-oriented businesses with a global focus. He was recently recognized as one of the **Top 10 Most Influential People in Supply Chain (2023)** for his impact on operational innovation in healthcare and beyond.

Dov can be contacted at dov@atidgrp.com

REFERENCES

Chapter 1

Anderson, James C., and James A. Narus. 1998. "Business Marketing: Understand What Customers Value." *Harvard Business Review* 76, no. 6: 53–65.

Bain & Company. 2022. "The B2B Elements of Value." Accessed [insert date]. https://www.bain.com/insights/the-b2b-elements-of-value/.

Christensen, Clayton M., Taddy Hall, Karen Dillon, and David S. Duncan. 2016. *Competing Against Luck: The Story of Innovation and Customer Choice*. New York: Harper Business.

Drucker, Peter F. 1954. *The Practice of Management*. New York: Harper & Row.

Hamel, Gary, and C. K. Prahalad. 1994. *Competing for the Future*. Boston: Harvard Business School Press.

Kaplan, Robert S., and David P. Norton. 1996. *The Balanced Scorecard: Translating Strategy into Action*. Boston: Harvard Business School Press.

Kim, W. Chan, and Renée Mauborgne. 2015. *Blue Ocean Strategy: How to Create Uncontested Market Space and Make the Competition Irrelevant*. Expanded ed. Boston: Harvard Business Review Press.

Kotler, Philip, and Kevin Lane Keller. 2016. *Marketing Management*. 15th ed. Boston: Pearson.

Levitt, Theodore. 1960. "Marketing Myopia." *Harvard Business Review* 38, no. 4: 45–56.

McKinsey & Company. 2020. "How B2B Decision Makers Are Responding to the Coronavirus Crisis." Accessed [insert date]. https://www.mckinsey.com/business-functions/growth-marketing-and-sales/our-insights/how-b2b-decision-makers-are-responding-to-the-coronavirus-crisis.

Nagle, Thomas T., John E. Hogan, and Joseph Zale. 2016. *The Strategy and Tactics of Pricing: A Guide to Growing More Profitably.* 6th ed. New York: Routledge.

Porter, Michael E. 1996. "What Is Strategy?" *Harvard Business Review* 74, no. 6: 61–78.

Reichheld, Frederick F. 2003. "The One Number You Need to Grow." *Harvard Business Review* 81, no. 12: 46–54.

Senge, Peter M. 1990. *The Fifth Discipline: The Art and Practice of the Learning Organization.* New York: Doubleday.

Welch, Jack, and Suzy Welch. 2005. *Winning.* New York: Harper Business.

Chapter 2

Airbnb, Inc. *Form S-1 Registration Statement.* Washington, DC: U.S. Securities and Exchange Commission, 2020. https://www.sec.gov/Archives/edgar/data/1559720/000119312520303821/d87104ds1.htm.

Apple Inc. *Apple Annual Report 2022.* Cupertino, CA: Apple Investor Relations, 2022. https://investor.apple.com.

Bezos, Jeff. *Amazon Shareholder Letters, 1997–2021.* Seattle: Amazon.com, Inc. https://www.aboutamazon.com/news/company-news/amazon-shareholder-letters.

Christensen, Clayton M., Taddy Hall, Karen Dillon, and David S. Duncan. *Competing Against Luck: The Story of Innovation and Customer Choice.* New York: Harper Business, 2016.

Drucker, Peter F. *The Practice of Management.* New York: Harper & Row, 1954.

First, Zachary. "Financial or Stakeholder Value? For Shareholders, Both Are Best." Bain & Company, July 2024. https://www.bain.com/insights/financial-or-stakeholder-value-for-shareholders-both-are-best-snap-chart/.

FourKites. *Company Overview and Case Studies.* Chicago: FourKites, 2023. https://www.fourkites.com.

Inter IKEA Group. *IKEA Sustainability and Business Strategy Report.* Leiden, Netherlands: Inter IKEA Group, 2021. https://www.ikea.com.

Owner.com. *The Future of Restaurant Direct Ordering.* Palo Alto, CA: Owner.com, 2023. https://www.owner.com.

Reichheld, Frederick F. "The One Number You Need to Grow." *Harvard Business Review* 81, no. 12 (2003): 46–54.

Chapter 3

Airbnb, Inc. *Form S-1 Registration Statement.* Washington, DC: U.S. Securities and Exchange Commission, 2020. https://www.sec.gov/Archives/edgar/data/1559720/000119312520303821/d87104ds1.htm.

Almquist, Eric, John Senior, and Nicolas Bloch. "The Elements of Value." *Harvard Business Review* 94, no. 9 (2016): 46–53.

Almquist, Eric, Jamie Cleghorn, and Lori Sherer. "The B2B Elements of Value." *Harvard Business Review* 96, no. 3 (2018): 72–81.

Anderson, James C., James A. Narus, and Wouter van Rossum. "Customer Value Propositions in Business Markets." *Harvard Business Review* 84, no. 3 (2006): 90–99.

Apple Inc. *Apple Annual Report 2022*. Cupertino, CA: Apple Investor Relations, 2022. https://investor.apple.com.

Balenciaga. *Balenciaga × Crocs Collaboration*. Paris: Balenciaga, 2021. https://www.balenciaga.com.

Bezos, Jeff. *Amazon Shareholder Letters, 1997–2021*. Seattle: Amazon.com, Inc. https://www.aboutamazon.com/news/company-news/amazon-shareholder-letters.

Buffett, Warren E. *Berkshire Hathaway Annual Shareholder Letter*. Omaha, NE: Berkshire Hathaway Inc., 2008. https://www.berkshirehathaway.com/letters/2008ltr.pdf.

Christensen, Clayton M., Taddy Hall, Karen Dillon, and David S. Duncan. *Competing Against Luck: The Story of Innovation and Customer Choice*. New York: Harper Business, 2016.

CrowdStrike Holdings, Inc. *Annual Report 2023*. Austin, TX: CrowdStrike, 2023. https://ir.crowdstrike.com.

Dollar Shave Club. "Our Blades Are F**ing Great." Video. YouTube, 2012. https://www.youtube.com/watch?v=ZUG9qYTJMsI.

Drucker, Peter F. *The Practice of Management*. New York: Harper & Row, 1954.

First, Zachary. "Financial or Stakeholder Value? For Shareholders, Both Are Best." Bain & Company, July 2024. https://www.bain.com/insights/financial-or-stakeholder-value-for-shareholders-both-are-best-snap-chart/.

Inter IKEA Group. *IKEA Sustainability and Business Strategy Report.* Leiden, Netherlands: Inter IKEA Group, 2021. https://www.ikea.com.

Kotler, Philip, and Kevin Lane Keller. *Marketing Management.* 15th ed. Boston: Pearson, 2016.

Nike, Inc. *Just Do It Campaign.* Portland, OR: Wieden + Kennedy, 1988. https://about.nike.com.

Patagonia, Inc. *Don't Buy This Jacket Campaign.* Ventura, CA: Patagonia, 2011. https://www.patagonia.com.

Reichheld, Frederick F. "The One Number You Need to Grow." *Harvard Business Review* 81, no. 12 (2003): 46–54.

Salesforce.com, Inc. *Annual Report 2022.* San Francisco: Salesforce, 2022. https://investor.salesforce.com.

Smith, J. B., and Mark Colgate. "Customer Value Creation: A Practical Framework." *Journal of Marketing Theory and Practice* 15, no. 1 (2007): 7–23.

Snowflake Inc. *Form S-1 Registration Statement.* Washington, DC: U.S. Securities and Exchange Commission, 2020. https://www.sec.gov/Archives/edgar/data/1640147/000119312520242051/d791907ds1.htm.

Southwest Airlines Co. *Southwest Airlines 2019 Annual Report.* Dallas, TX: Southwest Airlines, 2019. https://www.southwest.com.

Stanley. *Quencher Tumbler Press Release.* Seattle: Stanley PMI, 2023. https://www.stanley1913.com.

Supreme. *VF Corporation Acquires Supreme for $2.1 Billion.* Greensboro, NC: VF Corporation, 2020. https://www.vfc.com.

UiPath, Inc. *Form S-1 Registration Statement*. Washington, DC: U.S. Securities and Exchange Commission, 2021. https://www.sec.gov/Archives/edgar/data/1734722/000162828021006853/uipath-s1.htm.

Zeithaml, Valarie A. "Consumer Perceptions of Price, Quality, and Value: A Means-End Model and Synthesis of Evidence." *Journal of Marketing* 52, no. 3 (1988): 2–22.

Chapter 4

Airbnb, Inc. *Form S-1 Registration Statement*. Washington, DC: U.S. Securities and Exchange Commission, 2020. https://www.sec.gov/Archives/edgar/data/1559720/000119312520303821/d87104ds1.htm.

Anderson, James C., James A. Narus, and Wouter van Rossum. "Customer Value Propositions in Business Markets." *Harvard Business Review* 84, no. 3 (2006): 90–99.

Bain & Company. "Financial or Stakeholder Value? For Shareholders, Both Are Best." July 2024. https://www.bain.com/insights/financial-or-stakeholder-value-for-shareholders-both-are-best-snap-chart/.

Christensen, Clayton M., Michael E. Raynor, and Rory McDonald. "What Is Disruptive Innovation?" *Harvard Business Review* 93, no. 12 (2015): 44–53.

Kim, W. Chan, and Renée Mauborgne. *Blue Ocean Strategy: How to Create Uncontested Market Space and Make the Competition Irrelevant.* Expanded ed. Boston: Harvard Business Review Press, 2015.

Kotler, Philip, and Kevin Lane Keller. *Marketing Management.* 15th ed. Boston: Pearson, 2016.

McKinsey & Company. "How B2B Decision Makers Are Responding to the Coronavirus Crisis." 2020.

https://www.mckinsey.com/business-functions/growth-marketing-and-sales/our-insights/how-b2b-decision-makers-are-responding-to-the-coronavirus-crisis.

Porter, Michael E. "What Is Strategy?" *Harvard Business Review* 74, no. 6 (1996): 61–78.

Sun Tzu. *The Art of War.* Translated by Samuel B. Griffith. Oxford: Oxford University Press, 2015. Originally published ca. 5th century BCE.

Tesla, Inc. *Tesla 2022 Impact Report.* Austin, TX: Tesla, 2022. https://www.tesla.com/impact.

Westerman, George, Didier Bonnet, and Andrew McAfee. *Leading Digital: Turning Technology into Business Transformation.* Boston: Harvard Business Review Press, 2014.

Yuan, Eric. "A Message to Our Users." *Zoom Video Communications Blog,* 2020. https://blog.zoom.us.

Chapter 5

Adner, Ron. "Ecosystem as Structure: An Actionable Construct for Strategy." *Journal of Management* 43, no. 1 (2017): 39–58.

Airbnb, Inc. *Form S-1 Registration Statement.* Washington, DC: U.S. Securities and Exchange Commission, 2020. https://www.sec.gov/Archives/edgar/data/1559720/000119312520303821/d87104ds1.htm.

Amazon.com, Inc. *Amazon 2022 Annual Report.* Seattle: Amazon.com, Inc., 2022. https://www.aboutamazon.com.

Anderson, James C., James A. Narus, and Wouter van Rossum. "Customer Value Propositions in Business Markets." *Harvard Business Review* 84, no. 3 (2006): 90–99.

Apple Inc. *Apple Annual Report 2022*. Cupertino, CA: Apple Investor Relations, 2022.

Christensen, Clayton M., Michael E. Raynor, and Rory McDonald. "What Is Disruptive Innovation?" *Harvard Business Review* 93, no. 12 (2015): 44–53.

Dollar Shave Club. "Our Blades Are F**ing Great." Video. YouTube, 2012. https://www.youtube.com/watch?v=ZUG9qYTJMsI.

Gawer, Annabelle, and Michael A. Cusumano. "Industry Platforms and Ecosystem Innovation." *Journal of Product Innovation Management* 31, no. 3 (2014): 417–433.

Kim, W. Chan, and Renée Mauborgne. *Blue Ocean Strategy: How to Create Uncontested Market Space and Make the Competition Irrelevant.* Expanded ed. Boston: Harvard Business Review Press, 2015.

McAfee, Andrew, Erik Brynjolfsson, Thomas H. Davenport, D. J. Patil, and Dominic Barton. "Big Data: The Management Revolution." *Harvard Business Review* 90, no. 10 (2012): 60–68.

Netflix, Inc. *Netflix 2021 Annual Report.* Los Gatos, CA: Netflix, Inc., 2021. https://ir.netflix.net.

Pine, B. Joseph, and James H. Gilmore. *The Experience Economy.* Boston: Harvard Business School Press, 1999.

Porter, Michael E. "What Is Strategy?" *Harvard Business Review* 74, no. 6 (1996): 61–78.

Rolls-Royce Holdings plc. *Power by the Hour: Celebrating 50 Years.* London: Rolls-Royce Holdings plc, 2019. https://www.rolls-royce.com.

Salesforce.com, Inc. *Annual Report 2022.* San Francisco: Salesforce, 2022. https://investor.salesforce.com.

Shopify Inc. *Shopify 2021 Annual Report.* Ottawa: Shopify Inc., 2021. https://investors.shopify.com.

Spotify Technology S.A. *Form F-1 Registration Statement.* Washington, DC: U.S. Securities and Exchange Commission, 2018. https://www.sec.gov/Archives/edgar/data/1639920/000119312518064008/d494294df1.htm.

Starbucks Corporation. *Starbucks Company Timeline.* Seattle: Starbucks Corporation, 2019. https://stories.starbucks.com.

Stripe, Inc. *Stripe Press and Company Overview.* San Francisco: Stripe, Inc., 2023. https://stripe.com.

Sun Tzu. *The Art of War.* Translated by Samuel B. Griffith. Oxford: Oxford University Press, 2015. Originally published ca. 5th century BCE.

Tesla, Inc. *Tesla 2022 Impact Report.* Austin, TX: Tesla, Inc., 2022. https://www.tesla.com/impact.

Warby Parker Inc. *Form S-1 Registration Statement.* Washington, DC: U.S. Securities and Exchange Commission, 2021. https://www.sec.gov/Archives/edgar/data/1504776/000119312521259191/d152327ds1.htm.

Zappos.com. *Our Philosophy on Customer Service.* Las Vegas: Zappos.com, 2009. https://www.zappos.com.

Zoom Video Communications, Inc. "Zoom Announces Fourth Quarter and Fiscal Year 2020 Results." San Jose, CA: Zoom Video Communications, Inc., 2020. https://investors.zoom.us.

Chapter 6

Adamson, Brent, Matthew Dixon, and Nicholas Toman. "The End of Solution Sales." *Harvard Business Review* 90, nos. 7–8 (2012): 60–68.

Almquist, Eric, John Senior, and Nicolas Bloch. "The Elements of Value." *Harvard Business Review* 94, no. 9 (2016): 46–53.

Breiman, Leo. "Random Forests." *Machine Learning* 45, no. 1 (2001): 5–32.

Cameron, W. Bruce. *Informal Sociology: A Casual Introduction to Sociological Thinking.* New York: Random House, 1963.

Christensen, Clayton M., Taddy Hall, Karen Dillon, and David S. Duncan. *Competing Against Luck: The Story of Innovation and Customer Choice.* New York: Harper Business, 2016.

Dixon, Matthew, Karen Freeman, and Nicholas Toman. "Stop Trying to Delight Your Customers." *Harvard Business Review* 88, nos. 7–8 (2010): 116–122.

Fader, Peter S. *Customer Centricity: Focus on the Right Customers for Strategic Advantage.* Philadelphia: Wharton Digital Press, 2012.

Gupta, Sunil, and Donald R. Lehmann. *Managing Customers as Investments: The Strategic Value of Customers in the Long Run.* Upper Saddle River, NJ: Wharton School Publishing, 2005.

Hair, Joseph F., William C. Black, Barry J. Babin, and Rolph E. Anderson. *Multivariate Data Analysis.* 8th ed. Andover, UK: Cengage, 2019.

Jain, Anil K., and Richard C. Dubes. *Algorithms for Clustering Data.* Englewood Cliffs, NJ: Prentice Hall, 1988.

Kaufman, Leonard, and Peter J. Rousseeuw. *Finding Groups in Data: An Introduction to Cluster Analysis.* Hoboken, NJ: Wiley, 1990.

Kline, Rex B. *Principles and Practice of Structural Equation Modeling.* 4th ed. New York: Guilford Press, 2016.

Kotler, Philip, and Kevin Lane Keller. *Marketing Management.* 15th ed. Boston: Pearson, 2016.

Lemon, Katherine N., and Peter C. Verhoef. "Understanding Customer Experience Throughout the Customer Journey." *Journal of Marketing* 80, no. 6 (2016): 69–96.

Louviere, Jordan J., David A. Hensher, and Joffre D. Swait. *Stated Choice Methods: Analysis and Applications.* Cambridge: Cambridge University Press, 2000.

Parasuraman, A., Valarie A. Zeithaml, and Leonard L. Berry. "SERVQUAL: A Multiple-Item Scale for Measuring Consumer Perceptions of Service Quality." *Journal of Retailing* 64, no. 1 (1988): 12–40.

———. "Reassessment of Expectations as a Comparison Standard in Measuring Service Quality." *Journal of Marketing* 58, no. 1 (1994): 111–124.

Payne, Adrian, and Pennie Frow. "A Strategic Framework for Customer Relationship Management." *Journal of Marketing* 69, no. 4 (2005): 167–176.

Reichheld, Frederick F. "The One Number You Need to Grow." *Harvard Business Review* 81, no. 12 (2003): 46–54.

Rust, Roland T., Valarie A. Zeithaml, and Katherine N. Lemon. *Driving Customer Equity: How Customer Lifetime Value Is Reshaping Corporate Strategy.* New York: Free Press, 2000.

Smith, J. B., and Mark Colgate. "Customer Value Creation: A Practical Framework." *Journal of Marketing Theory and Practice* 15, no. 1 (2007): 7–23.

Ulwick, Anthony W. *What Customers Want: Using Outcome-Driven Innovation to Create Breakthrough Products and Services.* New York: McGraw-Hill, 2005.

Wedel, Michel, and Wagner A. Kamakura. *Market Segmentation: Conceptual and Methodological Foundations.* 2nd ed. Boston: Kluwer, 2000.

Zeithaml, Valarie A. "Consumer Perceptions of Price, Quality, and Value: A Means-End Model and Synthesis of Evidence." *Journal of Marketing* 52, no. 3 (1988): 2–22.

Chapter 7

Almquist, Eric, John Senior, and Nicolas Bloch. "The Elements of Value." *Harvard Business Review* 94, no. 9 (2016): 46–53.

Amazon.com, Inc. "Amazon.com Announces Third Quarter 2018 Results." Press release and earnings materials. Seattle: Amazon Investor Relations, 2018.

Brynjolfsson, Erik, and Andrew McAfee. *The Second Machine Age: Work, Progress, and Prosperity in a Time of Brilliant Technologies.* New York: W. W. Norton, 2014.

Buffett, Warren E. *Berkshire Hathaway Inc. Annual Report: Letter to Shareholders.* Omaha, NE: Berkshire Hathaway Inc., 2007.

Collis, David J., and Michael G. Rukstad. "Can You Say What Your Strategy Is?" *Harvard Business Review* 86, no. 4 (2008): 82–90.

Davenport, Thomas H., and Jeanne G. Harris. *Competing on Analytics: The New Science of Winning.* Updated ed. Boston: Harvard Business Review Press, 2017.

Drucker, Peter F. *The Practice of Management.* New York: Harper & Row, 1954.

Edmondson, Amy C. *The Fearless Organization: Creating Psychological Safety in the Workplace for Learning, Innovation, and Growth*. Hoboken, NJ: Wiley, 2018.

Farris, Paul W., Neil T. Bendle, Phillip E. Pfeifer, and David J. Reibstein. *Marketing Metrics: The Definitive Guide to Measuring Marketing Performance*. 2nd ed. Upper Saddle River, NJ: Pearson FT Press, 2010.

Gale, Bradley T. *Managing Customer Value: Creating Quality and Service That Customers Can See*. New York: Free Press, 1994.

Garvin, David A. "Building a Learning Organization." *Harvard Business Review* 71, no. 4 (1993): 78–91.

Gupta, Sunil, and Donald R. Lehmann. *Managing Customers as Investments: The Strategic Value of Customers in the Long Run*. Upper Saddle River, NJ: Wharton School Publishing, 2005.

Harrington, H. James. *Business Process Improvement: The Breakthrough Strategy for Total Quality, Productivity, and Competitiveness*. New York: McGraw-Hill, 1991.

Haskel, Jonathan, and Stian Westlake. *Capitalism without Capital: The Rise of the Intangible Economy*. Princeton, NJ: Princeton University Press, 2018.

Hubbard, Douglas W. *How to Measure Anything: Finding the Value of Intangibles in Business*. 3rd ed. Hoboken, NJ: Wiley, 2014.

Kaplan, Robert S., and David P. Norton. "The Balanced Scorecard— Measures That Drive Performance." *Harvard Business Review* 70, no. 1 (1992): 71–79.

Kaplan, Robert S., and David P. Norton. *Strategy Maps: Converting Intangible Assets into Tangible Outcomes*. Boston: Harvard Business School Press, 2004.

Lev, Baruch, and Feng Gu. *The End of Accounting and the Path Forward for Investors and Managers.* Hoboken, NJ: Wiley, 2016.

Marr, Bernard. *Key Performance Indicators: The 75+ Measures Every Manager Needs to Know.* Harlow, UK: Pearson FT Press, 2015.

McGrath, Rita Gunther. *The End of Competitive Advantage: How to Keep Your Strategy Moving as Fast as Your Business.* Boston: Harvard Business Review Press, 2013.

Porter, Michael E. *Competitive Advantage: Creating and Sustaining Superior Performance.* New York: Free Press, 1985.

Provost, Foster, and Tom Fawcett. *Data Science for Business: What You Need to Know about Data Mining and Data-Analytic Thinking.* Sebastopol, CA: O'Reilly Media, 2013.

Reichheld, Frederick F. "The One Number You Need to Grow." *Harvard Business Review* 81, no. 12 (2003): 46–54.

Senge, Peter M. *The Fifth Discipline: The Art and Practice of the Learning Organization.* New York: Doubleday, 1990.

Uber Technologies Inc. *Form S-1 Registration Statement.* Washington, DC: U.S. Securities and Exchange Commission, 2019.

Wamba, Samuel Fosso, Shahriar Akter, Andrew Edwards, Geoffrey Chopin, and Denis Gnanzou. "How 'Big Data' Can Make Big Impact: Findings from a Systematic Review and a Longitudinal Case Study." *International Journal of Production Economics* 165 (2015): 234–246.

Chapter 8

Anderson, Brian. *Best Buy Co. Investor Presentation: Customer-Centricity Strategy.* Richfield, MN: Best Buy Co., 2004.

Bendle, Neil T., Paul W. Farris, Phillip E. Pfeifer, and David J. Reibstein. *Marketing Metrics: The Manager's Guide to Measuring Marketing Performance.* 3rd ed. Boston: Pearson, 2020.

Blair, Tony. *A Journey: My Political Life*. New York: Alfred A. Knopf, 2010.

Bretthauer, Kurt M., and Murray J. Côté. "Managing Customer Contact Systems: A Portfolio-Based Approach." *European Journal of Operational Research* 108, no. 2 (1998): 211–225.

Brynjolfsson, Erik, Yu (Jeffrey) Hu, and Mohammad S. Rahman. "Competing in the Age of Omnichannel Retailing." *MIT Sloan Management Review* 54, no. 4 (2013): 23–29.

Cao, Lanlan, and Li Li. "The Impact of Cross-Channel Integration on Customer Retention." *Journal of Retailing and Consumer Services* 27 (2015): 90–101.

Christensen, Clayton M., Taddy Hall, Karen Dillon, and David S. Duncan. *Competing Against Luck: The Story of Innovation and Customer Choice*. New York: Harper Business, 2016.

Davenport, Thomas H., and Jeanne G. Harris. *Competing on Analytics: The New Science of Winning*. Updated ed. Boston: Harvard Business Review Press, 2017.

Fader, Peter S., and Bruce G. S. Hardie. *Customer-Base Management: Mathematical and Behavioral Models*. Philadelphia: Wharton Digital Press, 2013.

Fader, Peter S. *Customer Centricity: Focus on the Right Customers for Strategic Advantage*. Revised ed. Philadelphia: Wharton School Press, 2020.

Grewal, Dhruv, Anne L. Roggeveen, and Jens Nordfält. "The Future of Retailing." *Journal of Retailing* 93, no. 2 (2017): 168–181.

Hall, Kevin G. "Sprint Cuts Customers for Complaining Too Much." *Washington Post*, July 6, 2007.

Harvard Business Review Editors. "Sprint Nextel's Decision to Fire Customers." *Harvard Business Review* Digital Articles, 2007.

HubSpot. *HubSpot Customer Success and Academy Impact Report.* Cambridge, MA: HubSpot Research, 2019.

Kumar, V., and Werner Reinartz. "Creating Enduring Customer Value." *Journal of Marketing* 80, no. 6 (2016): 36–68.

Lemon, Katherine N., and Peter C. Verhoef. "Understanding Customer Experience Throughout the Customer Journey." *Journal of Marketing* 80, no. 6 (2016): 69–96.

McCarthy, Daniel, Peter Fader, and Bruce Hardie. "Valuing Subscription-Based Businesses Using Customer Lifetime Value Models." *Journal of Marketing* 81, no. 1 (2017): 17–35.

Reinartz, Werner J., and V. Kumar. "The Mismanagement of Customer Loyalty." *Harvard Business Review* 80, no. 7 (2002): 86–94.

Salesforce. "Salesforce.com Announces AppExchange, the World's First On-Demand Application Marketplace." Press release. San Francisco: Salesforce Investor Relations, 2005.

Salesforce. *Annual Reports and Form 10-K Filings.* San Francisco: Salesforce Investor Relations, 2008–2020.

Sheth, Jagdish N., Rajendra S. Sisodia, and Arun Sharma. "The Antecedents and Consequences of Customer-Centric Marketing." *Journal of the Academy of Marketing Science* 28, no. 1 (2000): 55–66.

Sprint Nextel Corp. *Customer Service Operations Review.* Internal report, publicly referenced in 2007 media coverage.

Urban, Glen L. *Don't Just Relate—Advocate: A Blueprint for Profit in the Era of Customer Power.* Upper Saddle River, NJ: Wharton School Publishing, 2005.

Verhoef, Peter C., P. K. Kannan, and J. Jeffrey Inman. "From Multi-Channel Retailing to Omni-Channel: Introduction to the Special Issue." *Journal of Retailing* 91, no. 2 (2015): 174–181.

Winer, Russell S., and Ravi Dhar. *Marketing Management.* 4th ed. Boston: Pearson, 2016.

Chapter 9

Alphabet Inc. *Form 10-K Annual Report.* Washington, DC: U.S. Securities and Exchange Commission, 2023.

Amazon.com, Inc. *Form 10-K Annual Report.* Washington, DC: U.S. Securities and Exchange Commission, 2023.

Apple Inc. *Form 10-K Annual Report.* Washington, DC: U.S. Securities and Exchange Commission, 2023.

Barney, Jay. "Firm Resources and Sustained Competitive Advantage." *Journal of Management* 17, no. 1 (1991): 99–120.

Buffett, Warren E. *Berkshire Hathaway Inc. Annual Report: Letter to Shareholders.* Omaha, NE: Berkshire Hathaway Inc., 2007.

Eisenhardt, Kathleen M., and Jeffrey A. Martin. "Dynamic Capabilities: What Are They?" *Strategic Management Journal* 21, nos. 10–11 (2000): 1105–1121.

Hsieh, Tony. *Delivering Happiness: A Path to Profits, Passion, and Purpose.* New York: Business Plus, 2010.

Kniberg, Henrik, and Anders Ivarsson. *Scaling Agile @ Spotify with Tribes, Squads, Chapters & Guilds.* Stockholm: Spotify, 2012.

Knott, Anne Marie. "The Fallacy of Resource-Based Strategy." *Harvard Business Review* 93, no. 4 (2015): 76–81.

Liker, Jeffrey K. *The Toyota Way: 14 Management Principles from the World's Greatest Manufacturer.* New York: McGraw-Hill, 2004.

Medtronic plc. *Annual Report and Form 10-K.* Washington, DC: U.S. Securities and Exchange Commission, 2023.

Netflix, Inc. *Annual Report on Form 10-K.* Washington, DC: U.S. Securities and Exchange Commission, 2023.

Ohno, Taiichi. *Toyota Production System: Beyond Large-Scale Production.* Portland, OR: Productivity Press, 1988.

Porter, Michael E. *Competitive Advantage: Creating and Sustaining Superior Performance.* New York: Free Press, 1985.

Porter, Michael E. "What Is Strategy?" *Harvard Business Review* 74, no. 6 (1996): 61–78.

Prahalad, C. K., and Gary Hamel. "The Core Competence of the Corporation." *Harvard Business Review* 68, no. 3 (1990): 79–91.

Teece, David J., Giovanni Pisano, and Amy Shuen. "Dynamic Capabilities and Strategic Management." *Strategic Management Journal* 18, no. 7 (1997): 509–533.

Ulrich, Dave, and Norm Smallwood. "Capitalizing on Capabilities." *Harvard Business Review* 82, no. 6 (2004): 119–127.

Womack, James P., Daniel T. Jones, and Daniel Roos. *The Machine That Changed the World.* New York: Rawson Associates, 1990.

Chapter 10

Amazon.com, Inc. *Form 10-K Annual Report.* Washington, DC: U.S. Securities and Exchange Commission, 2023.

Anthony, Scott D., Clark Gilbert, and Mark W. Johnson. *Dual Transformation: How to Reposition Today's Business While Creating the Future.* Boston: Harvard Business Review Press, 2017.

Bower, Joseph L., and Clayton M. Christensen. "Disruptive Technologies: Catching the Wave." *Harvard Business Review* 73, no. 1 (1995): 43–53.

Chase, Richard B., F. Robert Jacobs, and Nicholas J. Aquilano. *Operations Management for Competitive Advantage*. New York: McGraw–Hill, 2017.

Christopher, Martin. *Logistics & Supply Chain Management*. Harlow, UK: Pearson, 2016.

Digital McKinsey. *The Digital Effect: How Digital Transformation Is Reshaping Industries*. New York: McKinsey & Company, 2017.

Eisenhower, Dwight D. *Mandate for Change: 1953–1956*. New York: Doubleday, 1963.

Fisher, Marshall L. "What Is the Right Supply Chain for Your Product?" *Harvard Business Review* 75, no. 2 (1997): 105–116.

Hammer, Michael, and James Champy. *Reengineering the Corporation: A Manifesto for Business Revolution*. New York: Harper Business, 1993.

Hax, Arnoldo C., and Nicolás S. Majluf. *The Strategy Concept and Process: A Pragmatic Approach*. Englewood Cliffs, NJ: Prentice Hall, 1991.

Lapide, Larry. "Sales and Operations Planning after 50 Years." *Journal of Business Forecasting* 24, no. 3 (2005): 10–12.

Lapide, Larry. "The Evolution of S&OP." *Journal of Business Forecasting* 28, no. 4 (2009): 4–12.

McGrath, Rita Gunther. *The End of Competitive Advantage*. Boston: Harvard Business Review Press, 2013.

Netflix, Inc. *Annual Report on Form 10-K*. Washington, DC: U.S. Securities and Exchange Commission, 2023.

Oliver Wight. *Manufacturing Resource Planning (MRP II): Unlocking America's Productivity Potential*. New York: Oliver Wight Publications, 1980.

Oliver Wight International. *Integrated Business Planning: A Guide to Successful Implementation*. Atlanta: Oliver Wight Americas, 2016.

Prahalad, C. K., and Venkat Ramaswamy. *The Future of Competition: Co-Creating Unique Value with Customers*. Boston: Harvard Business School Press, 2004.

Reeves, Martin, Simon Levin, and Daichi Ueda. "The Biology of Corporate Survival." *Harvard Business Review* 98, no. 5 (2020): 72–81.

Reinartz, Werner J., and V. Kumar. "The Mismanagement of Customer Loyalty." *Harvard Business Review* 80, no. 7 (2002): 86–94.

Senge, Peter M. *The Fifth Discipline: The Art and Practice of the Learning Organization*. New York: Doubleday, 1990.

Snow, Charles C., Øystein D. Fjeldstad, Christopher Lettl, and Raymond E. Miles. "The Networked Business Model." *Organizational Dynamics* 40, no. 2 (2011): 99–108.

Treacy, Michael, and Fred Wiersema. *The Discipline of Market Leaders: Choose Your Customers, Narrow Your Focus, Dominate Your Market*. Reading, MA: Addison-Wesley, 1995.

Wight, Thomas E. *The Oliver Wight Class A Standard for Business Excellence*. Hoboken, NJ: Wiley, 1999.

Womack, James P., and Daniel T. Jones. *Lean Thinking: Banish Waste and Create Wealth in Your Corporation*. New York: Simon & Schuster, 1996.

Chapter 11

Amabile, Teresa M., and Steven J. Kramer. *The Progress Principle: Using Small Wins to Ignite Joy, Engagement, and Creativity at Work*. Boston: Harvard Business Review Press, 2011.

Benioff, Marc, and Carlye Adler. *Behind the Cloud: The Untold Story of How Salesforce.com Went from Idea to Billion-Dollar Company*. San Francisco: Jossey-Bass, 2009.

Brown, Tim. *Change by Design: How Design Thinking Transforms Organizations and Inspires Innovation*. New York: HarperBusiness, 2009.

Christensen, Clayton M., and Michael E. Raynor. *The Innovator's Solution: Creating and Sustaining Successful Growth*. Boston: Harvard Business Review Press, 2013.

Deal, Terrence E., and Allan A. Kennedy. *Corporate Cultures: The Rites and Rituals of Corporate Life*. New York: Perseus Books, 2000.

Denison, Daniel R. *Corporate Culture and Organizational Effectiveness*. New York: Wiley, 1990.

Drucker, Peter F. *Management: Tasks, Responsibilities, Practices*. New York: Harper & Row, 1973.

Gallup. *State of the American Workplace*. Washington, DC: Gallup Press, 2017.

Hamel, Gary, and Michele Zanini. *Humanocracy: Creating Organizations as Amazing as the People Inside Them*. Boston: Harvard Business Review Press, 2020.

Heskett, James L., W. Earl Sasser Jr., and Leonard A. Schlesinger. *The Service Profit Chain: How Leading Companies Link Profit and Growth to Loyalty, Satisfaction, and Value*. New York: Free Press, 1997.

HubSpot. *The HubSpot Culture Code*. Version 2024. Cambridge, MA: HubSpot Research, 2024.

Katzenbach, Jon R., Ilona Steffen, and Caroline Kronley. "Cultural Change That Sticks." *Harvard Business Review* 90, nos. 7–8 (2012): 110–117.

Katzenbach, Jon R., and Douglas K. Smith. *The Wisdom of Teams: Creating the High-Performance Organization*. Boston: Harvard Business School Press, 1993.

Kim, W. Chan, and Renée Mauborgne. *Blue Ocean Shift: Beyond Competing*. New York: Hachette Books, 2017.

Kirkpatrick, David. *The Facebook Effect: The Inside Story of the Company That Is Connecting the World*. New York: Simon & Schuster, 2010.

Lencioni, Patrick. *The Five Dysfunctions of a Team*. San Francisco: Jossey-Bass, 2002.

Lencioni, Patrick. *The Advantage: Why Organizational Health Trumps Everything Else in Business*. San Francisco: Jossey-Bass, 2012.

Luthans, Fred, and Bruce J. Avolio. "Authentic Leadership: A Positive Developmental Approach." *Leadership Quarterly* 14, no. 3 (2003): 241–261.

Meyer, Christopher, and Andre Schwager. "Understanding Customer Experience." *Harvard Business Review* 85, no. 2 (2007): 116–126.

Netflix, Inc. *Netflix Culture Memo: Freedom & Responsibility*. Los Gatos, CA: Netflix, Inc., 2020.

O'Reilly, Charles A., and Michael L. Tushman. *Lead and Disrupt: How to Solve the Innovator's Dilemma*. Stanford, CA: Stanford Business Books, 2016.

Peters, Thomas J., and Robert H. Waterman Jr. *In Search of Excellence: Lessons from America's Best-Run Companies*. New York: Harper & Row, 1982.

Reichheld, Frederick F. "The One Number You Need to Grow." *Harvard Business Review* 81, no. 12 (2003): 46–54.

Reichheld, Frederick F., and Rob Markey. *Winning on Purpose: The Unbeatable Strategy of Loving Customers*. Boston: Harvard Business Review Press, 2021.

Schein, Edgar H. *Organizational Culture and Leadership*. 4th ed. San Francisco: Jossey-Bass, 2010.

Seligman, Martin E. P. *Flourish: A Visionary New Understanding of Happiness and Well-Being*. New York: Free Press, 2011.

Southwest Airlines. *Southwest Culture & Values Report*. Dallas, TX: Southwest Airlines Corporate Communications, 2023.

Spotify Technology S.A. *Spotify Engineering Culture*. Parts 1 and 2. Stockholm: Spotify Labs, 2014.

Stone, Brad, and Shayla Love Frier. *Amazon Unbound: Jeff Bezos and the Invention of a Global Empire*. New York: Simon & Schuster, 2020.

Ton, Zeynep. *The Good Jobs Strategy: How the Smartest Companies Invest in Employees to Lower Costs and Boost Profits*. Boston: Houghton Mifflin Harcourt, 2014.

Zappos Insights. *Zappos Culture Book*. Las Vegas: Zappos.com LLC, 2019.

Chapter 12

Skinner, B. F. *Beyond Freedom and Dignity*. New York: Knopf, 1971.

Drucker, Peter F. *The Effective Executive: The Definitive Guide to Getting the Right Things Done*. New York: Harper & Row, 1967.

Westerman, George, Didier Bonnet, and Andrew McAfee. *Leading Digital: Turning Technology into Business Transformation*. Boston: Harvard Business Review Press, 2014.

Fitzgerald, Michael, Nina Kruschwitz, Didier Bonnet, and Michael Welch. "Embracing Digital Technology: A New Strategic Imperative." *MIT Sloan Management Review* 55, no. 2 (2013): 1–12.

Kane, Gerald C., Doug Palmer, Anh Nguyen Phillips, David Kiron, and Natasha Buckley. "Strategy, Not Technology, Drives Digital Transformation." *MIT Sloan Management Review* and *Deloitte University Press*, 2015.

Kane, Gerald C., Doug Palmer, Anh Nguyen Phillips, David Kiron, and Natasha Buckley. "Aligning the Organization for Its Digital Future." *MIT Sloan Management Review* and *Deloitte*, 2016.

McAfee, Andrew, and Erik Brynjolfsson. *Machine, Platform, Crowd: Harnessing Our Digital Future*. New York: W. W. Norton, 2017.

Davenport, Thomas H., and Rajeev Ronanki. "Artificial Intelligence for the Real World." *Harvard Business Review* 96, no. 1 (2018): 108–116.

Standish Group. *CHAOS 2020: Beyond Infinity*. West Yarmouth, MA: Standish Group International, 2020.

Gartner. *Why So Many High-Potential IT Projects Fail to Deliver*. Research report. Stamford, CT: Gartner, Inc., 2020.

Fitzgerald, Michael, Nina Kruschwitz, Didier Bonnet, and Michael Welch. "Digital Transformation Is Not About Technology." *Harvard Business Review* 92, no. 11 (2014).

McKinsey Digital. *Unlocking Success in Digital Transformations*. New York: McKinsey & Company, 2018.

McKinsey Digital. *The Keys to Success in Digital Transformations*. New York: McKinsey & Company, 2019.

Bain & Company. *Beyond the Technology: Capturing the Full Value of Digital Transformation*. Bain Insights. Boston: Bain & Company, 2020.

Bughin, Jacques, Thomas Catlin, Martin Hirt, and Paul Willmott. "Why Digital Strategies Fail." *McKinsey Quarterly*, January 2018.

LaBerge, Laura, Chris O'Toole, Jeremy Schneider, and Kate Smaje. "How COVID-19 Has Pushed Companies over the Technology Tipping Point—and Transformed Business Forever." New York: McKinsey & Company, 2020.

Kalsotra, Shubham, et al. "Knowledge Graphs: Fundamentals, Techniques, and Applications." *Communications of the ACM* 64, no. 12 (2021): 96–104.

RelationalAI. *Knowledge Graphs and the Future of Decision Intelligence.* White paper. Berkeley, CA: RelationalAI, 2023.

Kinaxis. *RapidResponse: Concurrent Planning for End-to-End Supply Chain Visibility.* Product overview. Ottawa: Kinaxis, 2022.

o9 Solutions. *The o9 Digital Brain: Integrated Business Planning Platform.* Solution brief. Dallas: o9 Solutions, 2022.

Blue Yonder. *Luminate Platform: AI-Driven Supply Chain Planning and Execution.* Technical white paper. Scottsdale, AZ: Blue Yonder, 2021.

McKinsey & Company. "The Keys to Organizational Agility." *McKinsey Quarterly*, December 2015.

Chapter 13

Adner, Ron. *The Wide Lens: What Successful Innovators See That Others Miss.* New York: Portfolio/Penguin, 2012.

Adner, Ron. "Ecosystem as Structure: An Actionable Construct for Strategy." *Journal of Management* 43, no. 1 (2017): 39–58.

Amazon, Inc. *Annual Report (Form 10-K).* Washington, DC: U.S. Securities and Exchange Commission, 2023.

Apple Inc. *Annual Report (Form 10-K).* Washington, DC: U.S. Securities and Exchange Commission, 2023.

Bain & Company. *Ecosystem Services: The Next Frontier for Competitive Advantage.* Bain Insights. Boston: Bain & Company, 2021.

Baldwin, Carliss Y., and Kim B. Clark. *Design Rules, Volume 1: The Power of Modularity.* Cambridge, MA: MIT Press, 2000.

Bharadwaj, Anandhi, Omar A. El Sawy, Paul A. Pavlou, and N. Venkatraman. "Digital Business Strategy: Toward a Next Generation of Insights." *MIS Quarterly* 37, no. 2 (2013): 471–482.

Boston Consulting Group (BCG). *The Rise of Business Ecosystems: How Partners Create and Capture Value Together.* Boston: BCG, 2020.

Christopher, Martin. *Logistics & Supply Chain Management.* 5th ed. Harlow, UK: Pearson, 2016.

Cusumano, Michael A., Annabelle Gawer, and David B. Yoffie. *The Business of Platforms: Strategy in the Age of Digital Competition, Innovation, and Power.* New York: Harper Business, 2019.

Eisenmann, Thomas, Geoffrey Parker, and Marshall W. Van Alstyne. "Strategies for Two-Sided Markets." *Harvard Business Review* 84, no. 10 (2006): 92–101.

Gawer, Annabelle, and Michael A. Cusumano. "Industry Platforms and Ecosystem Innovation." *Journal of Product Innovation Management* 31, no. 3 (2014): 417–433.

Hagel, John III, John Seely Brown, and Lang Davison. *The Power of Pull: How Small Moves, Smartly Made, Can Set Big Things in Motion.* New York: Basic Books, 2010.

Iansiti, Marco, and Roy Levien. *The Keystone Advantage: What the New Dynamics of Business Ecosystems Mean for Strategy, Innovation, and Sustainability.* Boston: Harvard Business School Press, 2004.

Jacobides, Michael G., Carmelo Cennamo, and Annabelle Gawer. "Towards a Theory of Ecosystems." *Strategic Management Journal* 39, no. 8 (2018): 2255–2276.

Ketchen, David J., Jr., and Christopher W. Craighead. "Research at the Intersection of Supply Chain Management and Strategic Management." *Journal of Supply Chain Management* 56, no. 1 (2020): 3–16.

McKinsey & Company. *Ecosystem 2.0: Climbing the S-Curve to Maximum Advantage.* McKinsey Digital Insight. New York: McKinsey & Company, 2019.

McKinsey & Company. *How Do Companies Create Value in Digital Ecosystems?* New York: McKinsey & Company, 2020.

Moore, James F. "Predators and Prey: A New Ecology of Competition." *Harvard Business Review* 71, no. 3 (1993): 75–86.

Moore, James F. *The Death of Competition: Leadership and Strategy in the Age of Business Ecosystems.* New York: HarperCollins, 1996.

Parker, Geoffrey G., Marshall W. Van Alstyne, and Sangeet Paul Choudary. *Platform Revolution: How Networked Markets Are Transforming the Economy.* New York: W. W. Norton, 2016.

Porter, Michael E. *Competitive Advantage: Creating and Sustaining Superior Performance.* New York: Free Press, 1985.

Porter, Michael E., and James E. Heppelmann. "How Smart, Connected Products Are Transforming Competition." *Harvard Business Review* 92, no. 11 (2014): 64–88.

Simchi-Levi, David. *Operations Rules: Delivering Customer Value Through Flexible Operations.* Cambridge, MA: MIT Press, 2010.

Sodhi, ManMohan S., and Christopher S. Tang. "Supply Chain Management for Extreme Conditions: Managing Multi-Tier Risk." *Manufacturing & Service Operations Management* 23, no. 3 (2021): 656–666.

Van Alstyne, Marshall W., Geoffrey G. Parker, and Sangeet Paul Choudary. "Pipelines, Platforms, and the New Rules of Strategy." *Harvard Business Review* 94, no. 4 (2016): 54–62.

Chapter 14

Chermack, Thomas J. *Scenario Planning in Organizations: How to Create, Use, and Assess Scenarios*. San Francisco: Berrett-Koehler Publishers, 2011.

Drucker, Peter F. *Management Challenges for the 21st Century*. New York: HarperBusiness, 1999.

Edelman, Benjamin G., and Damien Geradin. "Efficiencies and Regulatory Shortcuts: How Uber and Airbnb Achieve Success." *Harvard Business School Working Paper / University of Chicago Coase-Sandor Institute Working Paper*, 2015.

Fishman, Charles. "Patagonia's 'Don't Buy This Jacket' Campaign." *Fast Company / Harvard Business Review* online case discussion. Boston: Harvard Business School Publishing, 2012.

Kahane, Adam. *Transformative Scenario Planning: Working Together to Change the Future*. San Francisco: Berrett-Koehler Publishers, 2012.

Rigby, Darrell, and Sarah Täger. "The 'Amazon Effect': How Online Leaders Are Reshaping Customer Expectations." *Bain & Company Insight*, 2021.

Schoemaker, Paul J. H. "Scenario Planning: A Tool for Strategic Thinking." *Sloan Management Review* 36, no. 2 (1995): 25–40.

Schwartz, Peter. *The Art of the Long View: Planning for the Future in an Uncertain World*. New York: Doubleday, 1991.

Strifor Research. "The Evolution of Netflix: From DVD Rental to Global Streaming Giant." *Strifor Blog*, 2024.

Teece, David J., Giovanni Pisano, and Amy Shuen. "Dynamic Capabilities and Strategic Management." *Strategic Management Journal* 18, no. 7 (1997): 509–533.

Varum, Celeste A., and Carla Melo. "Directions in Scenario Planning Literature – A Review of the Past Decades." *Futures* 42, no. 4 (2010): 355–369.

van der Heijden, Kees. *Scenarios: The Art of Strategic Conversation*. 2nd ed. Chichester, UK: John Wiley & Sons, 2005.

Wack, Pierre. "Scenarios: Uncharted Waters Ahead" and "Scenarios: Shooting the Rapids." *Harvard Business Review* 63, nos. 5–6 (1985).

Chapter 15

Bain & Company. *The Firm of the Future*. Boston: Bain & Company, 2017.

Bain & Company. "Putting Stakeholders First Pays Off." *Bain & Company Brief*, 2020.

Barton, Dominic, Dennis Carey, and Ram Charan. *Talent Wins: The New Playbook for Putting People First*. Boston: Harvard Business Review Press, 2018.

Collins, Jim. *Good to Great: Why Some Companies Make the Leap… and Others Don't*. New York: HarperBusiness, 2001.

Drucker, Peter F. *The Practice of Management*. New York: Harper & Row, 1954.

Drucker, Peter F. "The Theory of the Business." *Harvard Business Review* 72, no. 5 (1994): 95–104.

Freeman, R. Edward, Kirsten E. Martin, and Bidhan L. Parmar. *The Power of And: Responsible Business Without Trade-Offs*. New York: Columbia Business School Publishing, 2020.

Gale, Bradley T. *Managing Customer Value: Creating Quality and Service That Customers Can See*. New York: Free Press, 1994.

Heifetz, Ronald A., and Marty Linsky. *Leadership on the Line: Staying Alive Through the Dangers of Leading*. Boston: Harvard Business School Press, 2002.

Henderson, Rebecca, and Eric Van den Steen. "Why Do Firms Have 'Purpose'? The Firm's Role as a Carrier of Identity and Reputation." *American Economic Review* 105, no. 5 (2015): 326–330.

Iansiti, Marco, and Karim R. Lakhani. *Competing in the Age of AI: Strategy and Leadership When Algorithms and Networks Run the World*. Boston: Harvard Business Review Press, 2020.

Kaplan, Robert S., and David P. Norton. "The Balanced Scorecard— Measures That Drive Performance." *Harvard Business Review* 70, no. 1 (1992): 71–79.

Kim, W. Chan, and Renée Mauborgne. *Blue Ocean Strategy: How to Create Uncontested Market Space and Make the Competition Irrelevant*. Boston: Harvard Business Review Press, 2005.

Kotter, John P. *Leading Change*. Boston: Harvard Business School Press, 1996.

Lao Tzu. *Tao Te Ching*. Translated by D. C. Lau. London: Penguin Classics, 1963.

Levitt, Theodore. "Marketing Myopia." *Harvard Business Review* 38, no. 4 (1960): 45–56.

McKinsey Digital. "Unlocking Success in Digital Transformations." New York: McKinsey & Company, 2018.

McKinsey Digital. "The Keys to Success in Digital Transformations." New York: McKinsey & Company, 2019.

Porter, Michael E. *Competitive Strategy: Techniques for Analyzing Industries and Competitors*. New York: Free Press, 1980.

Reichheld, Frederick F., and W. Earl Sasser Jr. "Zero Defections: Quality Comes to Services." *Harvard Business Review* 68, no. 5 (1990): 105–111.

Senge, Peter M. *The Fifth Discipline: The Art and Practice of the Learning Organization*. New York: Doubleday, 1990.

Treacy, Michael, and Fred Wiersema. *The Discipline of Market Leaders: Choose Your Customers, Narrow Your Focus, Dominate Your Market*. New York: Basic Books, 1995.

Zook, Chris, and James Allen. *The Founder's Mentality: How to Overcome the Predictable Crises of Growth*. Boston: Harvard Business Review Press, 2016.